Making Millions

FOR

DUMMIES®

Making Millions FOR DUMMIES®

by Robert Doyen and Meg Schneider

Wiley Publishing, Inc.

Making Millions For Dummies®

Published by
Wiley Publishing, Inc.
111 River St.
Hoboken, NJ 07030-5774
www.wiley.com

For general information on our other products and services, please contact our Customer Care Department within the U.S. at 877-762-2974, outside the U.S. at 317-572-3993, or fax 317-572-4002.

For technical support, please visit www.wiley.com/techsupport.

Wiley also publishes its books in a variety of electronic formats. Some content that appears in print may not be available in electronic books.

Library of Congress Control Number: 2008940662

ISBN: 978-0-470-27674-7

Manufactured in the United States of America

10 9 8 7 6 5 4 3 2 1

About the Authors

Robert Doyen: Robert Doyen earned his bachelor's degree in business administration and accounting from Drake University in the 1960s and went to work for Bankers Life (now Principal Financial Group) as a pension administrator. A few years later, he took over and expanded the family farm, supplementing his agriculture operations with income from his own tax preparation and small-business accounting service.

As part of his self-education in money management and investing over the past four decades, Doyen became an Enrolled Agent with the Internal Revenue Service and a Registered Representative with the Securities and Exchange Commission. Because he is no longer active in either of those roles, he is free of the restrictions that generally bar active agents and representatives from sharing their knowledge and expertise.

He still owns the expanded family farm in North Central Iowa, but, because he established and realized his financial goals, he was able to retire from active farming in 2004. In 2007, he closed his tax and accounting business, and he now splits his time between Iowa and Arizona, while actively managing a diverse seven-figure investment portfolio.

Meg Schneider: Meg Schneider is an award-winning writer with more than two decades of experience in television, radio, and print journalism and public relations. Meg has authored or coauthored several books, including *The Good-for-You Marriage* (Adams Media) and *COPD For Dummies* (Wiley). Her other book credits include two books for writers and one on New York State history.

Her journalism honors include awards from the Iowa Associated Press Managing Editors, Women in Communications, the Maryland-Delaware-D.C. Press Association, Gannett, the New York State Associated Press, and the William Randolph Hearst Foundation.

A native of Iowa, Meg now lives in upstate New York with two cats and an obsessively balanced checkbook.

Dedication

Robert dedicates this book to his wife, Barbara, without whose encouragement he never would've gotten involved in publishing. He also wouldn't have gotten involved in the selection of fabric, tableware, bedding, color-coordinated towels, or appliances, nor would he have planted so many trees or gotten to know so many delivery people by their first names. She keeps his life exciting, and he's never bored (except in a fabric store).

Meg dedicates this book to Dick and Jan Schneider, who exhibited patience of biblical proportions during her "odyssey years," when she was figuring out (at an agonizingly slow pace) how to manage her own finances.

Authors' Acknowledgments

The authors offer their thanks to the following people:

Our editors, Tracy Boggier and Elizabeth Kuball, two of our very favorite people to work with.

Our agent, Barb Doyen, for her insight, knowledge, and encouragement.

Mark Dixon, for helping Meg walk the fine line between dedication to one's craft and irreversible madness.

Mike Elliott, our technical editor, for keeping us on track.

Doug Carson, Cliff Isaacson, Aaron Larson, Joe Vella, and Lance Vella, for sharing their stories and expertise.

Publisher's Acknowledgments

We're proud of this book; please send us your comments through our Dummies online registration form located at www.dummies.com/register/.

Some of the people who helped bring this book to market include the following:

Acquisitions, Editorial, and Media Development

Project Editor: Elizabeth Kuball

Acquisitions Editor: Tracy Boggier

Copy Editor: Elizabeth Kuball

Assistant Editor: Erin Calligan Mooney

Editorial Program Coordinator: Joe Niesen

Technical Editor: Michael J. Elliott

Senior Editorial Manager: Jennifer Ehrlich

Editorial Supervisor and Reprint Editor: Carmen Krikorian

Editorial Assistants: Jennette ElNaggar, David Lutton

Cover Photos: © Steve McAlister

Cartoons: Rich Tennant (www.the5thwave.com)

Composition Services

Project Coordinator: Erin Smith

Layout and Graphics: Reuben W. Davis, Nikki Gately, Christine Williams

Proofreaders: Dwight Ramsey, Kathy Simpson, Amanda Steiner

Indexer: Joan Griffitts

Publishing and Editorial for Consumer Dummies

Diane Graves Steele, Vice President and Publisher, Consumer Dummies

Joyce Pepple, Acquisitions Director, Consumer Dummies

Kristin Ferguson-Wagstaffe, Product Development Director, Consumer Dummies

Ensley Eikenburg, Associate Publisher, Travel

Kelly Regan, Editorial Director, Travel

Publishing for Technology Dummies

Andy Cummings, Vice President and Publisher, Dummies Technology/General User

Composition Services

Gerry Fahey, Vice President of Production Services

Debbie Stailey, Director of Composition Services

Contents at a Glance

Table of Contents

Introduction

*A*s this chapter is being written, in mid-2008, the real estate market is largely in the dumps, the stock market is having a hard time hanging onto any gains it makes, credit for both businesses and consumers is drying up, and gas and food prices are straining more and more budgets every day. We may be in a recession; then again, we may be just stuck in an ill-defined "economic slowdown" — not a great place to be, but not as scary as the R word. Either way, money is tight, and it'll probably be a while before the markets loosen up again.

So where do we get off writing *Making Millions For Dummies* now, against this shaky economic landscape?

The answer is that we know something every millionaire knows: If you wait for conditions to be perfect before you start on your plan for financial independence, you'll spend your life with a lot of dreams but, most likely, very little cash.

In truth, there's no better time to take charge of your own financial health than when the economy acts like it's out to break your legs. You can't will the stock market to rise or gas prices to fall, but you can control your spending, get creative with your budget, and come up with a plan that will help insulate you from the twitches, spasms, and convulsions that are so common a feature of globalization.

About This Book

Our main objective with this book is to show you that you do, in fact, have control over your financial future. Sure, the stock market, interest rates, and the overall economy play a role in how quickly and how safely you achieve your goals. But too many people rely too heavily on these outside forces for their own financial stability. We want to show you how you can run your own finances, making adjustments as required when economic conditions — or your goals — change. The nice thing about being in charge is that, instead of having to roll with the economy's punches, you can look for the signs that telegraph those punches and revise your own strategy accordingly.

Another objective, which is only slightly less important, is to show you the simple, everyday steps you can take to achieve this control and, thus, your financial goals. Contrary to conventional wisdom, one person's financial success does not require another's financial failure; there's plenty of room for everyone to be financially secure. When you understand that you do indeed control your own purse strings, you have so much fun exerting that control that you don't have time to feel envious of anybody else's financial situation.

Finally, this book is *not* just for the already-wealthy, or even just for the middle-class earners who max out their retirement contributions every year and have thousands stashed in their children's college accounts. This book is also for people who may be struggling financially, who aren't sure how to grasp that control over their finances so they can pursue their dreams. No matter where you are moneywise today, this book offers tips and resources and information that will help you start out on your own path to making millions.

Conventions Used in This Book

For the sake of consistency and readability, we use the following conventions throughout the text:

- Terms we're using for the first time are in *italics*. Plain-English explanations or definitions of these terms are nearby, often in parentheses.

- When we give you steps to follow in a particular order, we number the steps and put the action part of each step in **bold.**

- Web addresses are in monofont. *Note:* When this book was printed, some Web addresses may have needed to break across two lines of text. If that happened, rest assured that we haven't put in any extra characters (such as hyphens) to indicate the break. So, when using one of these Web addresses, just type in exactly what you see in this book, as though the line break doesn't exist.

One last thing: We're writing this book as a team, but when one of us has something to say, we use our first names — for example, "When Meg's husband died . . ." or "Bob recommends. . . ."

What You're Not to Read

As with all *For Dummies* books, this one is structured so you can skip over the parts that don't interest you or apply to your situation. But even in the chapters you do read, there are some things you can skip if you want. Anything labeled with a Technical Stuff icon, for example, is safe to ignore. These are snippets of information that some readers may enjoy, but you won't lose anything by not reading them. (For more on icons, turn to the "Icons Used in This Book" section, later.)

In some chapters, you may come across *sidebars,* shaded boxes of text. We present this information for the curious reader, but our feelings won't be hurt — and you won't be missing out on any vital information — if you decide to skip them.

Foolish Assumptions

In putting together the information we present in this book, we've made some assumptions about you, the reader. We assume that you:

✔ Want financial security, even if you don't want or expect to amass millions

✔ Want to understand how you can take control of your financial situation today so you can meet your goals for the future

✔ Want practical advice that you can use immediately, even if you don't have a lot of extra money (or even any) to devote right now to your financial security plan

✔ Are ready to examine your own relationship with money and figure out ways to cultivate more productive money attitudes and habits

✔ Aren't interested in get-rich-quick schemes, plans that sound too good to be true, illegal activities, or anything that forces you to take risks you're not ready for

✔ Are interested in knowing how others have achieved their financial dreams, so you can take away from these experts those insights that apply to you

✔ Want a comprehensive resource that demystifies the world of finance and brings it down to ground level — without making you feel like a dummy

How This Book Is Organized

We split the information in this book into five parts to help you find the information you want quickly and easily. Here's an overview.

Part 1: Getting Your Finances in Order

As Yogi Berra once said, if you don't know where you're going, you'll end up somewhere else. We start with the basics in this part. First, we look at money personalities, because different personalities have different relationships with and attitudes toward handling finances. Then we devote a chapter to setting goals and figuring out what you can do today to reach goals that are a year, five years, ten years, and longer away.

Money consistently ranks among the top three problem areas for couples, so we also discuss ways you and your spouse or partner can resolve your money differences and come up with a plan that suits each of you and still lets you achieve the goals you've set together.

Part II: Strategies for Building Wealth

This part focuses on the things you can do immediately to improve your finances, no matter how poor they may be at the moment. These are the things millionaires do regularly, even after they've made their fortunes. But, more important, they're the basic things you have to do if you're serious about long-term financial security.

Here, we show you how living below your means lays the groundwork for all your financial-security goals, and we give you solid, practical advice for adjusting your lifestyle so you're following this golden rule.

Because debt is such a problem for so many Americans, we discuss the difference between good debt — the kind that helps you build wealth — and bad debt — the kind that drains your wallet without building any value for you. We also offer tips on getting rid of your bad debt and protecting your credit-worthiness by handling your debt responsibly.

If you believe the statistics, saving doesn't come naturally to Americans, at least not in the 21st century. Yet getting into the saving habit is a vital component of your overall financial health. We show you how to start a savings plan and stick with it, even if you've got only a few dollars to work with.

Finally, because most people rely on third parties — employers — for a regular paycheck, we show you how to get the most out of the various benefits your job provides.

Part III: Paths Paved with Gold

Making millions is a goal, and there are lots of ways to achieve any given goal. In this part, we cover the most common ways people build wealth, as well as some less common methods.

Lots of folks build wealth working for themselves in their own business. Others invent gadgets that take consumers by storm. Still other invest in the stock market or real estate to make their fortunes. Then there are those lucky few — a very few — who win the lottery or beat the house at blackjack, and others who get their wealth the old-fashioned way: by inheriting it.

This part provides an overview of each of these wealth-building methods, including the pitfalls and poor practices that can sabotage your dreams of financial independence.

Part IV: Managing Your Wealth

You've heard stories again and again of people who have made (or, often, won) vast fortunes, only to see their newly drilled financial well dry up in an alarmingly short time. Making your millions is only the first part of the equation; keeping your wealth is the second, and arguably more critical, part.

In this part, we look at elements that go into managing — and keeping — your wealth after you've amassed it. We discuss the various professionals who can help you manage your money and how they can hurt you if you don't know what to look for. We look at your options as your priorities change from acquiring wealth to maintaining it and using it to enhance your lifestyle. We talk about taxes and how to minimize your tax liability — legally, of course.

We also cover planning — both for the unexpected and for the inevitable — and the roles insurance and estate planning play in your overall financial picture. And we discuss how to stay on top of your finances so you don't have to start all over again sometime down the road.

Part V: The Part of Tens

We love The Part of Tens, because it's a chance to share our favorite information and advice in snack-size nuggets — and in a simple format that makes those nuggets easy to digest.

Here, we give you ten of the most common traits millionaires exhibit. We also share our ten favorite ways to free up your own money, and our ten favorite ways for making that free money work for you. And we end by telling you ten ways you can tell you're a millionaire.

Icons Used in This Book

Throughout the book, you'll find icons in the margins that alert you to specific kinds of information. Here's what each of the icons means:

This is practical information that you can use right away to make managing your finances easier. It may include a Web site to visit, a suggestion for keeping your goals visible, or even a couple of financial options to check out.

This icon indicates information that we want to reinforce and that you may want to file away for future reference.

This little bomb tips you off to potential problems or murky financial waters you should be aware of.

Building and keeping wealth is part knowledge, part discipline, and part attitude. This icon alerts you to the things wealthy people know, the ways in which they stay on track to meet their goals, and the attitudes they have about handling their money.

Finances can be complicated. We do our best to break down complex financial terms and ideas into everyday language, but sometimes we just can't avoid going into the technical details. We mark those sections with this icon. You can safely skip anything marked with this icon if you want — or you can read it and gather all kinds of information to impress your friends with.

Where to Go from Here

For Dummies books are structured so you can either start at the beginning and go straight through to the end or jump around among the chapters or sections that interest you most right now.

If you've got a stash of money you want to put in the stock market, go to Chapter 13 for advice on developing an investment philosophy and picking stocks that will help you meet your goals. Chapter 16 offers a discussion of investing for growth versus investing for income, as well as information on determining your risk tolerance, which may change over time.

If you're more interested in the options real estate offers, check out Chapter 14. If your path to wealth lies in starting your own business, go to Chapter 9. If you're concerned about whether you have enough (or too much) insurance, head to Chapter 18. For information on estate planning, turn to Chapter 19.

Even if you've been working on building your financial security for a while, you may find useful reminders in the chapters on money personality (Chapter 2), setting goals (Chapter 3), and working out finances with your partner (Chapter 4).

Part I
Getting Your Finances in Order

The 5th Wave   By Rich Tennant

"I just don't know where the money's going."

In this part . . .

You could be like many people and leave your fiscal health to chance, figuring it will all somehow work out fine. But if you're serious about making millions, you have to take charge of your money, and that means budgeting, setting goals, and devising a plan to build your wealth. You also need to understand your own emotional relationship with money, and, if you're married or mingling finances with a significant other, you need to know how to pull together to reach the goals you've set.

In this part, we take you through each of the building blocks you must assemble as a foundation for your financial future. We show you how your feelings about money can sabotage your financial goals, and how to overcome those issues. We show you how to create a budget you can live — and save — with. And we show you how to talk to your partner about money and reach reasonable compromises that will allow both of you to feel more comfortable with your finances.

Chapter 1

Gathering the Building Blocks

* *

In This Chapter

▶ Knowing the truth about money: wanting it, getting it, and having it

▶ Assessing your attitude toward money

▶ Identifying your destination and mapping your route

▶ Holding onto your wealth when you get it

▶ Thinking like a rich person

* *

There's an old axiom in finance: If you suddenly made rich people poor and poor people rich, and then fast-forwarded ten years, those who originally were poor would be poor again, and those who originally were rich would be rich again. Why? Because poor people spend their money, and rich people keep theirs.

That's the "secret" to building wealth. Simple, isn't it? But if it's so simple, why isn't everybody rich?

Ah, that's where it gets more complex. For many people, money — and the handling of it — is tied to a cornucopia of conflicting emotions and desires. In the most basic terms, we want to have our cake and eat it, too.

Rich people have figured out how to do that. They have homes, cars, their particular "toys," all the things they want to buy with their money. But they also have money, because they make conscious decisions about how much cake they want to eat and how much they want to have. So their homes and cars may not be what you'd expect a millionaire to buy, and their toys may seem modest in comparison to their net worth. This is because they've developed the attitude and discipline that allow them to pick and choose what they spend their money on, instead of throwing their money at the newest, biggest, or most expensive thing they see.

This book is *not* about how to spend your money. It's about how to keep it so you can build your own financial security, and how to develop the attitude and discipline you need to do it. It doesn't matter whether you're dead broke right now or whether you've got a healthy savings account or investment portfolio. No matter where you are in your financial journey, there are steps you can take to improve your situation and be on your way to making millions.

Shattering Money Myths

"The conventional view," the famous economist John Kenneth Galbraith wrote, "serves to protect us from the painful job of thinking." When it comes to money, following conventional wisdom also can serve to keep you trapped in a feast-or-famine financial cycle. To break that cycle, first you have to break your faith in several conventional myths about building wealth:

- **You don't have to accept your "lot in life."** The way things are is not necessarily the way things must be. The first step to changing your life in any area — not just financially — is formulating the desire for something different. Only when you have the desire can you figure out how to make it happen.

- **Wanting money doesn't make you selfish, materialistic, or evil.** Money gives you the means to lead the kind of life you want: fulfilling, interesting, secure, and independent. Being financially rich gives you choices so you can live a more rewarding life.

- **Having wealth doesn't mean someone else has to be poor.** Economics, whether personal or global, isn't like a math problem where something added to one side has to be subtracted from the other. You don't have to take anything away from anybody else to build your wealth. (Of course, this also means that rich people haven't taken anything away from *you* to build *their* wealth, so there's no reason to resent people who have more money than you do.)

- **Becoming rich doesn't require dishonesty.** Certainly, there are some people who have made their fortunes through fraud or other dishonest means (Enron, anyone?), but those people usually are more interested in shortcuts to wealth than in truly understanding and managing their money. You can live your values and still create your own financial security.

- **You don't have to have a lot of money to make more money.** Small sums can add up to big dividends if you properly use the money you do have. The poverty mentality thinks, "There's such a tiny bit of cake; I might as well eat it." The rich mentality thinks, "I would rather have this tiny bit of cake than eat it and have none."

✔ **You don't have to be lucky to create your own financial security.** Some things in this life are outside your control, and you'll doubtless encounter unexpected setbacks on your road to wealth — a car or home repair or a medical emergency that delays your savings or investing goal, for example. But you can overcome even bad luck by using your desire and self-discipline to direct the things you can control.

✔ **Making money is not a race.** Competition certainly fuels some people's desire to build wealth, and sometimes these competitors are tempted to do things they shouldn't for the sake of a bigger payoff. But if you stay focused on your own goals and ignore what the other guy is doing (except to the extent that you can learn from it), competition is no longer a factor.

✔ **You don't have to give up anything to become wealthy.** Financial security is a choice, not a sacrifice. There will be trade-offs, of course; you may not buy or do something today so you can buy or do something else later. But that, too, is a choice. You're deciding what's most important to you, so whatever you don't buy or do today isn't really a sacrifice — it's just something that isn't as important to you.

Wealth doesn't come quickly or without effort. It requires a combination of thinking about what you want and doing the things that will get you there. Thinking without acting is just another way of dreaming. Thinking plus acting equals achieving.

Understanding Your Relationship with Money

Everyone has her own way of relating to money. To some people, money represents power — not just in the political sense, but in terms of independence or security. To others, money is a tool that lets you improve your life — by paying for education or training, for example. Still others think of money primarily as a scorecard — a way to measure their success and self-worth.

Nearly everyone has some negative reactions to money-related topics and situations. Those who go on to make millions minimize those negative reactions. How? By understanding the root cause of such negativity and retraining themselves to think and act positively.

There are two key steps to understanding where your own negative thoughts come from and training yourself to minimize their impact. First is to ask yourself how you think about money. Second is to focus on positive thoughts and seek out ways to change negative ones.

Asking yourself how you think about money

How do you feel when you hear that someone has become a millionaire? When you read of someone winning a huge jackpot in the lottery, for example, or look at the enormous bonuses some Wall Street brokers get? If you say to yourself, "Good for him," and then go about your business, you've probably got a pretty healthy relationship with money.

But if you seethe with envy or resentment, assume the money was obtained through unfair advantages, or think having all that money isn't good for a person, your own thoughts and feelings may be getting in the way of achieving your financial goals.

This isn't some wishy-washy, think-it-and-it-will-come-true mumbo jumbo. Research has shown that people who are generally positive in their mental outlook live longer and are healthier than people whose outlook is generally negative. Likewise, people who have positive attitudes about money *and their ability to achieve financial security* tend to be wealthier than those who see themselves as victims of bad luck, the machinations of other people, or the universe at large.

Of course, your beliefs and attitudes about money are more complex than just these issues. You have a whole money personality — a set of traits, beliefs, and common behaviors that constitutes your "default" mode for handling money. We discuss money personalities in Chapter 2. For now, the important thing is to start examining how you relate to money. Here are some other questions to help you begin:

✔ Do you think of yourself as unlucky when it comes to your finances?

✔ Do you think there's a limited amount of wealth in the world?

✔ Do you think you're morally superior to the ultra-wealthy?

✔ Do you feel guilty when you think about wanting money?

✔ Do you think you'll never be rich?

A "yes" to any of these questions shows that you're ceding your own wealth-building power to outside forces. If you rely on luck for your financial security, chances are, you'll spend the rest of your life chasing pipe dreams, like winning the lottery or staking your little all on your favorite number at the roulette wheel. If you view wealth as a finite pie, you're automatically competing with everyone else for your slice of it. If you think there's something inherently bad or immoral about having money, you'll find yourself fighting between wanting wealth and wanting to be a good person. If you feel guilty about wanting money, your guilt will prevent you from getting it. And if you believe you'll never be rich, guess what? You'll never be rich.

Changing your thinking

It takes some practice to convert negative thoughts into positive ones, partly because many negative thoughts seem so natural that you barely recognize them as negative. "I can't afford it" is a good example of a veiled negative. On the surface, this sounds like a financially responsible attitude; you shouldn't spend money on stuff you can't afford, right?

But *can't* is really a denial: You want something, and the answer from your wallet is, "No." And then you feel deprived, and maybe even a little depressed. And if you watch someone else buying the thing your wallet said you can't have, you feel envious and resentful. If these feelings are powerful enough, you may even end up buying the thing anyway, regardless of what it means for your current financial situation or your wealth-building plans.

Millionaires don't think that they can't afford something. Instead, millionaires figure out *how* they can afford something they want. This is part of the continual goal-setting that wealthy people do (see Chapter 3 for more on goals).

If you think millionaires have nothing to be envious about, remember that wealth is relative. If you've got a couple million but you're hanging out with people who have tens of millions, they're probably going to spend money on things that are out of your reach — at least for the time being.

Here are some other common negative thoughts and their positive counterparts:

Negative	Positive
I don't make enough money.	How can I make more money?
I want *x*.	How much is *x* worth to me?
Others have more than I do.	If others can do it, so can I.
I want what they have.	What do I want for myself?
Times are tough.	What opportunities are there?
I need someone to help me.	I want to learn to do this myself.
I'm dependent on my job.	How can I rely less on my paycheck?
I can't catch a break.	What can I do to help myself?
Making money is too risky.	How can I minimize the risk?
I can't do what I want to do.	How can I do what I want to do?

Notice that most of the positive items are questions. There's a good reason for that: Questions take you out of the powerless pity-me mode and get you thinking about things from a different angle.

Whenever you catch yourself thinking or saying negative things, rephrase the thought as a question. You may be surprised at how quickly your mood lifts, and how much more empowered you feel, especially as you get more adept at this technique.

Making a Plan

Even if you're living paycheck to paycheck, you can figure out a plan to change your situation. It won't necessarily be easy, and you won't see progress overnight. But just writing down a plan can open your mind to possibilities and choices that are harder to see when you're focused on getting by until the next payday.

There are three main elements to any financial plan (see Chapter 3 for more information):

- **Visualizing your future:** Imagining what your life can be five or ten years from now provides powerful inspiration to look for ways you can make your vision a reality. And keeping that vision in mind motivates you to do today the things that will get you closer to your goal.

- **Managing debt:** Some debt is good; it builds value for you. Other debt is onerous; it makes you overpay for the things you have. (See Chapter 6 for more on good debt and bad debt.) Managing debt means getting rid of the onerous kind and taking steps to ensure you don't have to rely on it in the future.

- **Starting a savings plan:** Even if all you can manage is $5 a week to start with, the important thing is to start. Without savings, you're more likely to fall back on harmful debt when something unexpected comes up. And, without savings, you can't take advantage of other opportunities to grow your money, like investing in the stock market, starting your own business, or buying real estate.

Why did we put visualizing at the top of the list? Because, without that, managing your debt and starting on your savings don't take on their proper importance. Only when you decide where you want to be in the future can you take full charge of the financial decisions you make today.

Lots of things that are beyond your control can affect your finances. A useful and successful plan focuses on the things you can do to improve your situation, regardless of what's happening on Wall Street or Main Street.

Choosing Your Path to Wealth

Your financial plan gives you your destination. Now you just have to figure out how to get there.

There are nearly as many ways to create wealth as there are people thinking about how to do it. You can invest in the stock market or in real estate. You can invent a new way to play music, read the written word, or send television signals through the air. You can peddle your expertise in a specialized area, provide a service that no one else provides, or build the next international fast-food franchise. You can win money, marry money, or inherit money (although these things fall outside the "millionaire mindset" of taking control of your own financial future, because they all rely to at least some extent on outside forces to come true).

Whichever path you choose, keep these things in mind to improve your likelihood of success:

- **Will it make you enough money?** You can't put your financial plan into operation if you don't make enough money to cover your basic expenses *and* have some left over for your long-term goals.

- **Is it something you enjoy?** You're more likely to stick with something you like doing, and therefore you're more likely to stick with your financial plan. Engineers can make a lot of money, but if you hate math, it's probably not the right path for you. Besides, the world already has enough people who hate their jobs, self-employed or otherwise.

- **Is it something you have a talent for?** You might dream of making it big as a musician when you're playing "Guitar Hero" in your living room, but if you don't know an A chord from an anthill, that's probably just a fantasy. Figure out what you're good at and then look for opportunities where you can put your natural talent to work.

- **Is it something you have the skills for?** If you don't know anything about accounting except that the figures are supposed to balance, you probably don't want to set up your own accounting business. You can always learn, of course, but your learning curve will affect the timetable for your financial plan.

Pursuing money for its own sake is neither enriching nor rewarding. The happiest millionaires are those who combine work they truly enjoy with the financial goals they've set for themselves. They have a powerful desire for a fuller, better, more abundant life, and money is only part of the riches they seek.

Staying There When You Get There

What image do you have of being rich? Does it mean being able to buy whatever you want, whenever you want it? Does it mean acquiring a certain sum and then not thinking about money any more?

Both these ideas of wealth are common for poor people. Rich people may have the financial wherewithal to buy whatever they want whenever they want it, but they seldom do. For one thing, when you get in the habit of assigning your own value and priorities to the trappings of wealth, you never really get out of it. For another, rich people don't get that way by spending their money on every fleeting desire.

And we're going to let you in on a little secret about money: No one *ever* reaches a point where he doesn't have to think about it. If you don't have enough to meet your basic needs, you have to think about how to make more or how to trim your needs to match the money you have. When you have enough to cover your basic needs, you have to think about what you want to do with whatever is left over — whether you want the instant gratification that comes from spending it right away, or whether you want to save it or invest it for the future. When you have money to save or invest, you have to think about how you want to save or invest it. And when you have millions, you have to think about the best use of that money, now and for your future goals.

Wealth is like a perpetual-motion machine: It's always moving. Sometimes it goes forward, sometimes back, but it never stands still. How many times do you hear that the stock market was "flat" during a day's trading? Not often; it gains some or loses some nearly every day. Your money is the same. The only difference is how much or how little it moves every day.

Okay, you say, that makes sense if you're investing in the stock market. But what if I just took my money and stuffed it under my mattress? It would stand still then. No, it wouldn't. It would lose value, thanks to that insidious economic ogre called inflation. Even when the economy is good, inflation devalues your cash — not as deeply as it does during sluggish economic periods, but it still lowers your purchasing power.

 Even a low inflation rate devalues your dollar. A 2 percent annual inflation rate means that what your dollar could buy a year ago will cost you $1.02 today. Money in your mattress won't buy as much a year from now as it will today, so its value actually is going backward.

Inflation and the overall economy dictate how much harder your money has to work to grow in real value, and that means you continually have to think about the best choices you can make with your money, no matter how big your net worth is.

Things Wealthy People Know

You may think that rich people have some secret store of knowledge that enables them to accumulate wealth and that, without this secret knowledge, there's no way you can realize your financial dreams. The truth is, there are things wealthy people know — but there's no secret about it. Most of it is common sense, and a lot of it lies in your way of thinking.

Here are some of the things wealthy people know — things you need to know so you can start making your millions:

- **Your financial security is in your hands.** Wealthy people take charge of their finances; they don't entrust it to anyone else, because they know that their financial security isn't as important to anyone else. They listen to advice and ideas from others, but they never give anyone else the power to make decisions for them.

- **Knowledge is power.** Wealthy people educate themselves about their investment options. They learn how money works and how to make more money. They study, ask questions, and investigate. And if they don't understand something, they wait to act on it until they do understand it.

- **Your money should work for you.** Wealthy people think of money as a resource to be cultivated — that is, if you plant your money in the right place under the right conditions, it will yield more money. Certainly some of it is to be spent, but some of it serves as "seed" for future gains.

- **Being broke is temporary.** This is why you read of people who've made fortunes, lost them, and made new ones. Wealthy people know they have the desire and the skills to overcome financial challenges, so they don't fall into the bad habit of thinking things will never get better.

- **Risk can be managed.** To make your money work for you, you have to take some risk. But wealthy people aren't put off by risk; instead, they learn what needs to be done to keep risk as low as possible. When you have knowledge in your corner, you have the power to accurately assess risk and decide whether you want to take it.

✔ **Money should be talked about.** Taboos against discussing money only add to the false veil of secrecy drawn over building wealth. You can't learn how money works, or how to make it work for you, if you aren't even willing to talk about it.

✔ **Positive thinking leads to positive actions, yielding positive results.** Your attitude influences what you do, and what you do influences what you get. Wealthy people know that a positive attitude opens their eyes to possibilities they wouldn't consider if they had a negative attitude. Possibilities lead wealthy people to investigate, to learn as much as they can, and then to take action. And their actions lead them to their goals.

Take whatever steps you can take today on your wealth-building road, even if they're small ones. The old Chinese proverb applies to reaching your financial goals as well as to any other challenge: "A journey of a thousand miles begins with a single step."

Chapter 2

Understanding Your Money Personality

*M*ost people know that different personalities use money differently. But surprisingly few people can identify their *own* money personality or why they use money the way they do. For one thing, the average person isn't trained to discuss money — in fact, most people were raised to believe it's not nice to talk about it. For another, money is inextricably linked with your emotions — your sense of self-worth; your feelings of being loved and lovable; your ideas of fairness and justice; and your ability to comfort yourself when you feel sad, angry, or depressed. Talking about money isn't easy because of the social taboos, and being honest with yourself about money isn't easy because people are so good at disguising their emotions about money.

Unfortunately, it's just about impossible to change your financial situation if you don't understand why you handle your finances the way you do. In this chapter, we consult with an expert in personality traits to help you identify the traits of each of the five money personalities. Then we give you tips on how to tweak your own money personality so you can be more effective in handling your finances.

We also tell you how to determine how far you're willing to go in pursuit of your financial goals and how you feel about the possibility of losing money when you're trying to make more.

Finally, we give you some simple exercises to help you get started on your new financial path — exercises focused on changing how you feel about money so you can then change how you use it.

Figuring Out How You Feel about Money

Different personalities have different relationships with money. Cliff Isaacson, a counselor who has spent 30 years examining the role personality plays in life's various challenges, says there are five distinct "money personalities," each with its own set of attitudes and challenges.

The planner

According to Isaacson, planners loathe chaos, and they manage their money to create order. "This person has a need for organization, and that applies to money, too," he says. "Planners may be the best at handling their finances, because they always know where their money is coming from and where it's going."

Planners may write out their budgets, or they may keep their budgets in their heads. However, problems can arise when unexpected expenses disrupt the carefully organized budget. "For discretionary items, the planner most often will say, 'It's not in the budget,' and that's the end of it," Isaacson says. "But if something unplanned comes up, like car or house repairs that have to be taken care of right away, the planner will get frustrated because he isn't organized to deal with it."

The good news: That frustration lasts only until the planner reorganizes the finances to accommodate the unexpected change. As soon as the budget is back in order, the planner is emotionally fine, according to Isaacson.

Planners don't deprive themselves of just-for-fun money, but they are less likely than other money personalities to indulge in spur-of-the-moment purchases. According to Isaacson, planners also:

- ✔ **Are more likely to build wealth over time, because they are more likely to come up with a financial plan and stick with it**
- ✔ **See money as a tool to help them enhance their lifestyle, rather than an end in itself**
- ✔ **Can be overwhelmed by sudden wealth, like an inheritance or winning the lottery, at least until they can "organize" it**
- ✔ **Don't usually feel guilty about their wealth, because they attribute their own financial security to their organization and money-management habits**
- ✔ **Don't understand people who don't have the same need to organize and manage their finances**

The spender

Spenders are the polar opposites of planners, Isaacson says. Although the planner knows what he wants and plans for it, the spender tends to follow the crowd without ever asking herself what she wants. "Spenders don't know what they want, so they're more likely to make impulse purchases," Isaacson says. "They rely heavily on other people's opinions. Subconsciously they think, 'If these people have this, it must be good, and if it's good, I should have it or want it, too.'"

Spenders are the most likely to fall into the proverbial trap of keeping up with the Joneses, regardless of what it may mean for their own financial well-being. Spenders also are more likely to dream about future financial success but less likely to take any steps today to reach their dreams. "These personalities are accustomed to waiting for good things to happen, so they spend a lot of energy daydreaming instead of taking practical action to create what they dream of," Isaacson says.

Other traits of this money personality:

- **Because they place so much value on the opinions of others, spenders are more likely to thoroughly research investment options.** In fact, Isaacson says these personalities often delay making decisions because they "can't stop researching."

- **They can be persuaded to make poor financial decisions in order to get another person's approval.** "Because they don't really know what they want, spenders seek approval and agreement from others," Isaacson says. "This trait can make them easy targets for shady financial schemes."

- **They often feel guilty about having money; it can be a real struggle for them to believe they deserve financial security.**

- **Even if they come up with a financial plan, they may have a hard time sticking with it, especially if others disapprove.** "Spenders don't want others to think poorly of them, and they tend to listen to others' opinions rather than their own internal voices," Isaacson says.

- **Their desire for approval can lead them to spend far beyond their means, even if the things they buy don't really matter to them.**

The needster

Isaacson says needsters are less likely to spend money on themselves because "making yourself feel good isn't a good enough reason." Instead, when it comes to purchases for themselves, needsters demand an element of necessity before they'll pull out their wallets. "Wanting a new pair of shoes isn't enough. Needsters have to *need* new shoes to justify the spending," Isaacson says.

But this doesn't mean needsters are necessarily good at saving money. If a needster doesn't spend on himself, he'll spend on his spouse and his children. And needsters often dislike confrontation, which means others can manipulate them into spending more than they want to or should. "If you don't like tension or unpleasantness or tantrums from your children, you're tempted to do whatever it takes to avoid those things," Isaacson says. "So you end up buying the $100 designer jeans for your teenager instead of the $15 store-brand jeans."

The needster's own attitudes also can lead to overspending. More than other money personalities, the needster tends to want only the very best. Saving money until you can afford the best feels good, but saving money by buying a midgrade item instead of the best doesn't feel good.

Isaacson says needsters also exhibit these traits:

- **They tend to be successful in their careers because they're detail-oriented and usually very loyal employees.** However, they can stall in their professional development if they're put in charge of people, because needsters tend not to be very good people-managers.

- **Money and the lifestyle it can buy can be powerful motivators for needsters; they have a driving need for perfection, and that need extends to their financial and social position.** Of the five money personalities, needsters are the most likely to chase status symbols for their own sake. "The spender wants status symbols because other people have them," Isaacson says. "The needster wants them so other people know they're achieving financial perfection."

- **Needsters may have trouble enjoying their wealth once they achieve it.** It's hard to break out of the "This isn't necessary" mindset and buy something just for the fun of it.

- **Needsters also may have trouble keeping their wealth growing after they've reached their preset "need" level.** This is good in the sense that needsters seldom get greedy, but it can be bad when it prevents them from planning for not-so-good financial times.

- **Needsters tend to be fairly cautious in their wealth-building strategies because they do have a talent for spotting ways in which things can go wrong.** Overall, this caution serves them pretty well, but it also can delay their financial goals unnecessarily if taken to the extreme.

The Lord (or Lady) Bountiful

The lords and ladies bountiful among us want everybody to be happy, and if that means they have to give away every last penny, they will. Like the grasshopper in the fable, this money personality lives for the moment and figures the future will take care of itself. "They take a lot of financial risks that other money personalities don't understand and would never consider," Isaacson says. "And when those risks work out in their favor, they start believing they have the Midas touch, that everything they touch will turn to gold."

Not surprisingly, lords and ladies bountiful aren't the best savers in the world. They're the most likely to experience feast-or-famine financial cycles, because, when they have money, they like to use it to shower themselves and their loved ones with the things it can buy. When they don't have money, they may go into debt to buy the things they want; the lack of money can set up an obsession/compulsion dynamic where "I can't have it" and "I want it" play tug of war, and, Isaacson says, "'I want it' often wins."

Other traits of the Lord or Lady Bountiful, according to Isaacson:

- ✔ **Although they get a great deal of pleasure from "providing" for others, they do have their breaking points.** Being financially responsible for everyone else's happiness takes a great deal of emotional strength, and when the Lord Bountiful gets tired, he's likely to burst out with resentment, a feeling of being used, and a fear that, if he stops "providing," he won't be loved.

- ✔ **Fear is a stimulant to people with this money personality, which is why risky investments appeal to them.** They often use phrases like "No problem," "It'll work out," and "No pain, no gain." If their risks pay off, it justifies taking more risks. If they risk and lose, though, they're not any less likely to take risks in the future, because the thrill is in the risk itself — not the outcome.

- ✔ **Lords and ladies bountiful aren't inherently good at planning for the future; they're much more interested in short-term gains than in long-term goals.** It can be difficult for them to stick to a savings plan, and they can chafe considerably at the idea of putting off major (or even minor) purchases.

- ✔ **They'll work like crazy to get the money they need for either basic living expenses or whatever has captured their fancy.** Isaacson knows one man who worked three jobs — between 18 and 20 hours a day — so he would have money for his siblings and parents. "It took his wife a long time to convince him that he didn't have to take financial responsibility for his brothers and sisters, who were all adults. Fortunately, he finally 'got' that working so much was cheating him and his wife of the time they needed together."

> ✔ **When they buy things for themselves, lords and ladies bountiful will enjoy their purchase for a short time and then look around for the next thing they want.** "They get bored easily. For them, *wanting* is actually more fun than *having*, but many of them don't realize that the wanting is what they really enjoy," Isaacson says. The result: This money personality tends to end up with a house (and a garage, and maybe a storage unit) full of unused, unwanted stuff.

The hoarder

If you've ever read or seen one of the movie versions of Charles Dickens's *A Christmas Carol*, you know exactly how the hoarder feels about money (think Ebenezer Scrooge). Other money personalities look at money as a tool, a way to achieve their goals and desires. The hoarder sees the accumulation of money as an end in itself. Hoarders don't enjoy money for what it can do; they derive their enjoyment from collecting it.

Isaacson says the hoarding personality stems from a childhood in which the hoarder wasn't able or permitted to keep anything of her own. "Hoarders grew up in a world where anybody could take anything from them at any time," Isaacson says. "So, as adults, they tend to be very possessive of their things, their money, even the people around them."

Hoarders also tend to be hiders, Isaacson says. They hide money, even from their spouses, and they may live like paupers to prevent others from knowing about their collection of money. "I know one miser who lives in a house that should be condemned," Isaacson says. "He has a big collection of valuable artwork that he keeps in a storage closet; he doesn't even enjoy displaying it. He's worth millions, but he lives as though he's penniless."

Hoarders often exhibit these traits, according to Isaacson:

> ✔ **They're the most likely to complain that they can't afford something or about the cost of living in general.** This is part of the hiding technique they use to protect their possessions, Isaacson says. "They present this 'poor' image to the world so others won't guess their secret."

> ✔ **Spending money, even on necessities, causes real distress — in extreme cases, even actual physical pain.** "The possession instinct is very strong, and it can be hard for a hoarder to voluntarily give away anything, even money in exchange for something else," Isaacson says.

> ✔ **Hoarders may be envious of how other people spend their money.** To them, it's not fair that others use their money to buy things when the hoarder feels compelled to stash her cash.

- ✔ **Hoarders tend to be suspicious of everyone, even their spouses and other loved ones, because, deep down, they're afraid these people will take away what the hoarder has amassed.** They also may choose to leave their fortunes to charity rather than to their families; Isaacson knows of one man who left millions to the Salvation Army, cutting his children out of his will completely.

- ✔ **Hoarders are the least likely of all the money personalities to take the investing plunge, because that requires some level of trust (as well as the "giving away" of money).** They're more likely to keep their money under the proverbial mattress because growth involves risk, and hoarders are extremely averse to risk.

Changing How You Feel about Money

Changing your attitude toward money — and the feelings involved in how you handle your money — may sound akin to asking you to change your whole personality. But your feelings about money are just one tiny part of your overall personality, and your personality is like computer code: It can be tweaked to operate more effectively.

Isaacson offers the following tweaks for each money personality.

For the planner: Focusing on flexibility

The frustration that planners feel over unexpected expenses comes from not having a plan to deal with them, Isaacson says. Building a little wiggle room into the budget can defuse that frustration.

"A budget is Plan A, and it can be followed as long as things work out the way the planner expects them to. Without a Plan B, though, the planner may spend a lot of energy worrying about how she'll cope if things don't work out the way she thinks they will," Isaacson says.

No matter what your money personality is, you benefit from having an emergency fund, of course. For the planner personality, that emergency fund is more than just a financial cushion; it's insurance against the unexpected and a simple way to ease the frustration that so often accompanies life's unpredicted rough spots.

If you make alternate plans for your emergency fund, you may find yourself just as frustrated if you end up having to use it for unplanned expenses. If you start thinking you could use that money for a new car, for example, and instead a tree falls on your house and you have to replace the roof, you're right back where you started, frustrationwise. You're better off emotionally if you determine a set level for your emergency fund — call it your plan for the unplanned — and use any extra money to fund your other plans.

For the spender: Discovering yourself

Because the spender doesn't really know what he wants, Isaacson recommends starting with writing out a wish list. "It's okay if the wish list consists of things other people have; in fact, that's very common. But the act of writing them down helps the spender focus on what he thinks he wants," Isaacson says.

After you've finished your list, put the items in order of importance. This may take more thought, because you'll have to think about why you want the things on your list. If you have trouble with this part, try writing down the pros and cons of each item.

"Often when spenders really start focusing on the things they think they want, they discover that a lot of those things really aren't very important to them at all," Isaacson says. "It also helps to refer to the list often, so the spender doesn't fall back into the habit of following the crowd."

After you have your list prioritized, keep it on the refrigerator or your bathroom mirror — somewhere where you'll see it often and can use it to remind yourself of what you really want and why.

For the needster: Unlocking emotions

This flies in the face of what every financial advisor out there tells you about spending: We get in trouble, the experts argue, when we spend with our feelings instead of with our logic.

But the problem for the needster is the opposite, Isaacson says. "They're following a rule that says you should only spend money on what you need. So they disconnect from their emotions when they deal with money, because the rules say you're not supposed to feel anything when you're spending."

Handling money solely from a rational standpoint is impossible, Isaacson says. Research has shown that our emotions get involved in purchasing decisions long before the rational parts of our brains start tackling them, and trying to deny that is like, in the old biblical phrase, trying to get the leopard to change his spots.

"Of course money should be used for the things you need," Isaacson says. "But it also can be used to enhance your enjoyment of life. Focusing on what you need and ignoring what you want is a very narrow and unfulfilling way of handling money."

Needsters, like spenders, can benefit from writing down the things they want and why. There's a different rule for this exercise, though: You can't write down anything you need, only things you *want*. If you have trouble getting started, ask yourself this: If you knew you always would have everything you needed, and you could buy anything you wanted on top of that, what would you choose? Another way to do this is to envision yourself winning the lottery and write down how you would enjoy the money — again, not the things you need, but the things you *want*.

For Lord (or Lady) Bountiful: Compromising

Because lords and ladies bountiful like taking risks, but risks can seriously frighten the spouses and other loved ones of this money personality, Isaacson recommends a middle-ground course. "Take those risks with a smaller investment, and put the rest of the money in safer places. You can still enjoy the thrill of the riskier investment, but you don't put your entire financial security in jeopardy," he says.

Remember, too, that for every risky investment that turns out well, you're likely to experience two or more investments that turn out badly. People who really have the Midas touch — like Warren Buffett, for example — don't actually take a lot of risks. Instead, they do careful research, and when they decide to invest, it's because their research has shown them the investment isn't as risky as it looks on the surface.

Figuring out how much of your money to risk can be tricky, because your impulse is always to play big. Before you decide to jump in, ask yourself this: "If I lose all of my investment, am I okay with that?" If the answer is no, reduce the amount you plan to risk until you can honestly say you'll feel okay if you lose it all.

For the hoarder: Growing up

Hoarders collect money — and often hide it — because they're afraid someone will take it away from them. In the process, though, they cheat themselves of the opportunity to enjoy the things money can do to enhance their lives. The key, Isaacson says, is for hoarders to remember that they're adults now.

"You're not a child anymore, helpless to prevent other people from taking away your things," Isaacson says. "It may be hard to believe, but you're grown up now, and you can decide how you want to use your money without worrying that someone will come and take it away from you."

Isaacson doesn't recommend drastic steps for hoarders, like plunging into risky investments. Instead, he says hoarders first must learn to get comfortable with spending on the things they need and want. "Learning that money can actually work for you to make your life better is a one-step-at-a-time process for the hoarder," Isaacson says. "Start with something small, and make it something that you really enjoy — the gear you need to pursue a hobby, or a new suit, or a pretty piece of jewelry. Something that will make you smile and feel good about having it."

If you can't bring yourself to part with much of your money to enhance your lifestyle, try starting out in increments of 5 percent, 2 percent, or even 1 percent of the money you've accumulated.

We're not advocating spending *all* of your money. We do advocate steps that help you achieve a healthy balance between saving and spending — a balance that gives you financial security while still allowing you to enjoy the ways in which spending money can improve your quality of life.

Knowing What You Won't Do for Money

Part of understanding your money personality is knowing where your boundaries are in terms of making money. In the 1980s, for example, many people (and pension funds) pulled their investments from companies that did business in South Africa because they didn't approve of apartheid. In the 21st century, many people and companies are facing the same moral choices about investing in companies that do business in China and some South American countries because of human rights abuses there.

The advantage of knowing what you won't do for money is that it gives you power over your financial choices, and that, in turn, takes away a lot of the resentment you may feel toward people who have more wealth than you do. Maybe you don't believe in gambling, for example; in that case, you probably don't want to invest in casino companies. But because this is a choice you've made, based on what's more important to you, there's no reason to resent other people who make their money buying shares of casino companies.

You're less likely to stick to your financial plan if you don't feel good about how you're achieving your goals. It's okay that some things are more important to you than money.

Living your values

Choosing your investment options is one way to live your values. This also applies to how you conduct yourself in your job or business. Face it, there are some people in any profession who will do virtually anything to get ahead. But if the price of a promotion or a raise or a new sale is feeling like you've sold your soul, it's not worth it.

Values are inherently personal, and you're the only one who knows where your particular line in the sand is when it comes to making money. Most people will never come up against that line, but it can be useful to imagine the circumstances that could place you in a money-versus-values dilemma. Try this formula: If you could get $5,000 in exchange for doing X, what would you do? X represents any activity that challenges your personal values. For example, if you could get $5,000 by lying to a customer, what would you do? What if the lie involves something relatively minor? Does that change your answer?

Thinking about these "what if" scenarios can help you stay attuned to your own moral compass when it comes to making financial decisions. You're less likely to regret passing up opportunities that don't fit your values, and you're less likely to make financial choices that you'll feel bad about later on.

Understanding trade-offs

Everything in life involves a trade-off of some kind. When you moved out on your own for the first time, you had more independence than ever, but you also had more responsibility than before. Delaying marriage and having a family of your own gives you time to build your career, travel, or what have you, but it also may make it more difficult later on to find your life mate and make the changes that are inevitable when children enter the picture.

There are trade-offs in your financial life, too. If you're not willing to take much risk in your investments, the trade-off is that your money probably won't earn as much as it could. On the other hand, if you do make risky investments, the trade-off is that you could lose much, most, or even all of your money.

The trick is to use trade-offs to your advantage. In the following sections, we cover two common trade-offs you may face.

Cash versus assets

Farmers, small business owners, and even people who get a late start on saving for retirement often find themselves in a cash-poor/asset-rich situation, where their available cash is plowed into paying down debt, making improvements to the business, or building up savings funds. During this kind of cycle, it's easy to feel poorer than you are because you don't have a lot of disposable income.

The upside of being cash-poor is that, in these circumstances, it's a matter of choice; you've decided it's more important to buy more land, expand your business, or pay down your debt than to have a lot of extra cash in your pocket to blow. And even if you expect to be cash-poor for a fairly long time — five years or even ten years — it's the short-term trade-off of achieving your long-term goals.

You're the only one who can decide which trade-offs are worth it to you. You have to decide whether you can live with the downside of your choices in order to achieve the upside. And you can adjust your goals and trade-offs any way you want to make the mix comfortable for you.

Time versus money

A 2008 survey by the Pew Research Center found that two-thirds of Americans value time more than money. Having "enough free time to do things you want to do" was the top personal priority in the survey, ranked "very important" by 67 percent of the respondents. "Being wealthy" was rated "very important" by only 13 percent — dead last in the list of seven personal priorities. Every other item — professional success, being married, having children, involvement with charities or civic groups, and living a religious life — was ranked "very important" by at least half of those surveyed.

The survey seems to indicate, not surprisingly, that what we want the most is what we don't have. Wealthy people were more likely than poor people to answer that free time was very important to them, and poor people were more likely to say being wealthy was very important to them.

But time and money are trade-offs, too. If you work for someone else, or even for yourself, you exchange your time for income. The more free time you have, the lower your income is likely to be. (After you've amassed your millions, of course, this will no longer be true. But it's all too true while you're working *toward* your millions.)

Neither time nor money will always be the most important to you. Those priorities can change as your life changes; they may even change from day to day or hour to hour. As with other trade-offs, you can avoid feeling guilty or otherwise bad about how you make the exchange between time and money by recognizing which is more important to you at any given point.

Minimizing Your Risk

The first thing financial planners do when they meet with new clients is ask about risk tolerance. Some of them even will give you a quiz to gauge how conservative or aggressive you are when it comes to investing your money. Risk tolerance is a fancy way of describing whether you're more comfortable putting your money where it will earn predictable-but-modest gains (conservative) or going for potentially much higher earnings at the risk of losing some or all of your initial investment (aggressive).

Lots of factors affect your risk tolerance. If you're years away from retirement, you're probably more interested in making your money grow faster, which requires a more aggressive investment strategy. If you're on the brink of retirement, though, and you're counting on the money you already have to keep you in the style you want, you're more interested in protecting that money, so you'll go for a more conservative portfolio. You can assess your risk tolerance without going to a financial planner; there are lots of risk-tolerance calculators on the Internet. The Rutgers New Jersey Agricultural Experiment Station site (`http://njaes.rutgers.edu/money/riskquiz/`) has a useful quiz that asks you a series of questions and rates your risk tolerance according to a point scale. When you finish the quiz, you can see a sample list of investments that are organized by their risk.

After you know what your risk tolerance is, you can focus on minimizing your risk — by educating yourself and cultivating a long-term outlook.

Knowing what you're getting into

Educating yourself is the vital step in minimizing your risk. Multi-billionaire Warren Buffett is widely regarded as an investing genius, but, to hear him tell it, it's really pretty simple: "Never invest in a business you don't understand."

Buffett's success stems in large part from his willingness to educate himself about where he's putting his money. If he doesn't know how a business makes a profit, or if the business model doesn't make sense to him, he passes on it. That's not to say that he's never made a bad investment. But his track record is the mark every other investor in the world shoots for, and he's created that record by following the principle of educating himself about every investment he considers.

Developing a long-term outlook

You can insulate yourself from the daily vagaries of the markets by reminding yourself of your long-term goals. In fact, some experts recommend not even tracking the stock market more than once or twice a quarter. It's really just simple psychology: Declining markets instill fear, which tempts you to sell low, and rising markets instill overconfidence, which tempts you to buy high — and that's a surefire way to lose money.

Buffett's company, Berkshire Hathaway, has perfected the long-term outlook. In fact, the Oracle from Omaha himself is often quoted as saying, "Our favorite holding period is forever." His advice to individual investors: "Only buy something you'd be perfectly happy to hold if the market shut down for ten years." In other words, investing is for the long term, not for quick profits.

The other reason to ignore short-term performance is that, historically, the stock market has always recovered from bad times and soared to new heights. Of course, no one, not even Warren Buffett, can predict what will happen 10, 20, or 50 years from now, but the odds are very good that, even if your investment lost 10 percent of its value today, it would recover that and more over the long run.

Starting Your New Life with Money

When you've identified your money personality and your tolerance for risk, you realize that you really do have choices when it comes to your finances. And that's liberating, because now you're in charge of your financial well-being.

Change won't happen overnight, of course. The way you feel about and deal with money is a habit, just like any other, and Isaacson says it takes at least three weeks to replace any old habit with a new one. After the three weeks are up, it's not uncommon to suffer a relapse into the old habit you're trying to break — whether it's a question of watching your diet, exercising regularly, quitting smoking, or dealing with your finances in a new way.

Relapses are normal, so don't beat yourself up if you backslide now and then. Instead, recognize those times for what they are — temporary slips — and start over.

For the first few weeks of your new life with money, do these things regularly — every day, or every other day — to instill your new and better habits:

- ✔ **Read your list of goals.** Your list will remind you what you're working toward.

- ✔ **Write down what you spent today, how you felt about it when you made the purchase, and how you feel about it now.** This helps you identify areas where you're inclined to be impulsive and whether you tend to regret your impulses.

- ✔ **Write down your money successes.** This can be anything from opening your first savings account to resisting an impulse purchase that you knew you'd regret later. Keeping track of these small triumphs reinforces the behavior you're trying to instill in yourself, and it provides a record of your progress.

- ✔ **Practice the tips for your money personality (see "Changing How You Feel about Money," earlier in this chapter).** If you're like most people, you'll feel awkward at first when you try Isaacson's recommendations. But it will get easier the more you practice, and, soon, you'll have a new set of money habits that feel just as comfortable as your old ones.

Chapter 3

Setting Your Financial Goals

The Roman philosopher Seneca said that "Luck is what happens when preparation meets opportunity." Wealthy people never trust their financial security to chance; they set goals and come up with plans to meet those goals. And because they do this, they're prepared to take advantage of opportunities that present themselves.

Sounds like work, doesn't it? Well, we won't lie to you: It *is* work. That's why get-rich-quick schemes don't pan out for those who fall for them. They work only for the people who propagate them — the ones who are willing to do the work to separate other people from their money. If you want to achieve your financial goals, you have to put forth some effort. It's not always easy — sometimes it's downright difficult. It requires discipline and attitude and a willingness to spend some energy thinking about what you want and how you can get it.

Difficult, yes, but not impossible. And, like any other skill, the more you practice identifying and pursuing your goals, the easier it will get. In this chapter, we show you how to get started developing these skills — first by identifying exactly what your goals are and then by sorting them into categories so you know which ones are immediate and which ones are long-term goals. After you've got your goals categorized, you can figure out your action plan for each one, and we show you how to identify the steps you can take today and how to prepare for the steps you'll be able to take later on. Finally, we show you how to stick to your plan after you've got it figured out.

You see, we have a goal with this chapter, too: We want you to know how to be prepared to take advantage of the opportunities that will come your way, so that, someday, people will marvel at your "luck."

Identifying What's Important to You

The first step in setting your goals is deciding what you want — not what other people want for you, or even what others want for themselves, but what *you* want for *yourself.* Deciding on your goals can be tough — many people aren't used to listening to their own internal voices; instead, they rely on other people's advice and experience to guide them toward what they think they *should* want.

But if you follow the crowd on the main road, you may miss out on byways that you would find much more interesting and fulfilling.

Goals can be broadly classified as personal, professional, or financial. Sometimes they'll mesh beautifully: Your goal to earn your MBA, for example, may help you achieve your goal of landing a job with more responsibility and better pay. The MBA itself is a personal goal that dovetails with your professional goal of moving up in your career and your financial goal of earning more money.

Sometimes, though, your goals will clash, and you'll have to decide which goal takes priority. Pursuing your MBA may interfere with your goal of writing your novel, for example; you won't have the time or the mental energy to do both. Writing your novel, on the other hand, may mean delaying or dropping your goal of getting a better-paying job.

There are two tricks to figuring out what you really want. The first is to name the things you think you want, and the second is to think about what, if anything, you're willing to give up to get those things. Here are some examples to help you get started thinking about what you want and how important it is to you:

- **Buying a house:** Are you willing to trade the freedom of being able to pick up and move someplace else when an opportunity arises? How will you feel about being responsible for maintenance and repairs?

- **Starting a family:** Will you have to make trade-offs in your career? If so, are you okay with that? How will having children affect your time, money, and energy? What kind of sacrifices will you have to make, and are you willing to make them?

✔ **Pursuing your "dream" job:** Maybe you want to be an actor, a writer, a singer, a painter, or a dancer. You'll probably have to work at some sort of job that pays the bills but still leaves you time to pursue your dreams. But you probably won't get rich at your supporting job, and you may even be broke. Are you willing to do that? For how long? How will you decide when you've had enough?

✔ **Advancing in your career:** Will that promotion mean you have to travel more? Will you be expected to work longer hours — evenings, weekends, holidays? Which is more important to you — time or money?

It may seem strange to read about setting personal and professional goals in a book about building wealth. But, despite what you may think, millionaires don't believe money is everything, or the only thing. They take a holistic approach to setting goals: They consider not just their financial well-being, but their spiritual fulfillment and quality of life, too.

After you've identified what you want, the next step is figuring out the time frame for each of your goals. Some will be immediate. Some will take a few years to achieve. And some will be long-range goals — the things you want for your future, like when and how you want to retire.

Figuring out a time frame for your goals helps you identify the steps you can take now to reach both your immediate and your longer-term goals. It's part of the preparation you do so you can turn opportunity into luck.

It may seem counterintuitive, but we recommend thinking about your mid-range goals first, then your long-term goals, and finally your immediate goals. Why? Because, for most people, it's much easier to visualize what they'd like their lives to look like five years from now than to think decades into the future, or even to decide what they want right this minute. Five years is far enough away to allow your imagination to explore possibilities and near enough to provide some motivation for figuring out an action plan.

After you've thought about your life five years from now, it's natural to think even farther ahead. And we leave immediate goals for last because, for many people, today's circumstances may be such that they just don't see any way to make changes. But by the time you've thought about your five-year and long-term goals, you're mentally and emotionally ready to consider the options that are available to you today.

What you want in the next five years

Many people are more comfortable thinking beyond the immediate future, because sometimes their current situation feels too confining to think about today's goals. There's nothing wrong with that. In fact, sometimes it's easier to think backward, starting with your longer-term goals and backtracking to see what you can do now to get you closer to those goals.

Think about where you want to be five years from now personally. Do you want to be raising your family? Buying a house or remodeling your current house? Selling your house and buying an RV? Restoring a '57 Chevy and taking road trips all summer? Do you want to learn how to cook, or play the piano, or speak Ukrainian?

What are your professional goals for the next five years? Do you want to finish college or get an advanced degree that will help you advance in your career? Do you want to change careers? Open your own business?

And what do you want your finances to look like in five years? Do you want to be completely out of debt except for your mortgage? Have an extra $100,000 in your retirement fund? Be able to help your children with college expenses or your parents with their expenses? Be able to buy a vacation home or take a special trip to celebrate a special anniversary or birthday?

If you have trouble thinking five years ahead, try thinking about where you were five years ago first — how old you were then; what you were doing in terms of work, education, and family life; and where you thought you'd be by now. Then think about how old you'll be five years from now and what you'd like to be able to say to yourself about what you've done between now and then.

Don't despair if your current situation falls short of where you thought you'd be by now. Instead, look on it as motivation to take your goals seriously this time around.

What you want for the future

Long-term goals are those that will take you several years — maybe even decades — to achieve. This is where plans for retirement come in, as well as things like financing college for your kids. Think in terms of the kind of lifestyle you want in the distant future. Do you want to have a winter home in Arizona when you retire or a summer home in Minnesota, for example? Do you want to go on a 'round-the-world cruise? Volunteer for your local adult literacy program? Work part-time? Take up a hobby you don't have time (or money) for now?

The best thing about wealth is neither amassing a fortune nor having it. The best thing is the choices wealth gives you. Millionaires don't think solely in terms of their balance sheets. They think in terms of what they want to do, and they use money as a tool to help them reach those goals.

Goals are fluid. They may change direction over time for any number of reasons — not least of which may be changes in your own desires and attitudes. Unexpected obstacles and detours can mess up the time frame for achieving your goals, too.

What you want now

Sometimes goal-setting seems pointless because the things you want are big things — things that can't be accomplished today, tomorrow, next week, or next month. And in a consumer-driven, instant-gratification society like ours, it's frustrating to think that you have to wait to get what you really want.

But long-term goals almost always have an element of immediacy to them — something you can do right away — and those elements constitute what you want now.

Say you want to buy a house. That goal actually encompasses a couple other goals. You want to have enough money saved up so you can get a mortgage to buy a house; that's a goal in itself. Those two goals are tied to another goal: having a savings account where you can stash the money you want to save for your down payment so you can buy a house. That's what your immediate goal is: setting up a savings account for the down payment on a house. And when you have the account set up, your next goal is to start funding it.

Another example: You want to pay off your credit cards. Depending on how much debt you're carrying, that could easily be a long-term goal. But it includes short-term goals, too. For example, if you want to get rid of the debt you already have, you don't want to add to it. So the immediate element of that goal is to stop using your credit cards.

Whatever your long-term goals are, there are portions that really are immediate goals. For buying a house, what you want now is to have a special savings account for your down payment. For paying off your credit cards, what you want now is to stop using your credit cards for purchases. If you want to go back to college, your immediate goal is to find out the details that can help you plan for that goal — how much it will cost, financing options, how many classes you can take each term, how long it will take you to earn your degree, and so on.

If you have trouble identifying your immediate goals, trying starting with this one: You want to be in charge of your financial well-being. We know you have this goal because, otherwise, you wouldn't be reading this book, right? The next step is to figure out what you can do right away to take charge — trim expenses, pay down debt, open an investment account, and so on.

What you can do today may seem miniscule in comparison with your long-term goals, so you may feel tempted to skip doing anything. But your immediate goals will help you reach your intermediate goals, which in turn will help you reach your long-term goals. So what you're doing today is laying the groundwork for what you want to do 5, 10, or 20 years from now.

Putting Your Goals in Writing

You've heard this advice from every financial planner and money guru out there: Write down your financial goals. "What's the point?", you're asking yourself. "Is there something magic about putting my desires in writing?"

Well, no — and yes. The premise of books like *The Secret,* by Rhonda Byrne, is that you can harness the energy of the universe to attract the things you want in life — money, a soul mate, your ideal job, even your dream house. Science scoffs at the idea, but there is anecdotal evidence that writing "magical" lists can at least assist you in achieving your heart's desire.

We take a more practical view. Writing down your desires may not give you any special power over the forces of the universe, but it does help you focus your own energy on what you really want. That may well be enough to redirect you so you're more open to opportunities that bring you closer to your goals. And, since the whole process *after* writing down your goals often seems to take place in the mystical twilight between conscious thought and subconscious self-instruction, it's not surprising that the end results seem to have a magical quality about them.

Don't confuse wishes with goals. You're probably not going to win the lottery, you're probably not going to find 1,000 original shares of Coca-Cola in your attic, and you're probably not going to be adopted by Bill Gates. But you can get yourself out of debt, make wise investments, and lay the foundation for your financial security.

"Wait a minute," you may be thinking. "I wrote down once that I wanted to lose weight (or make more money, or become an opera singer), and it never happened." That's because there's a trick to writing effective goals. Many people identify their general goals and then wait for the "magic" to kick in. But you have to drill a little deeper to unleash the magic in yourself. Start with the general — but then take the next step and make your goals specific.

Starting with the general

General goals provide a starting point for figuring out what you want. Losing weight, learning a foreign language, continuing your education, becoming financially fit — all these are broad, general goals. Even things like buying a house, starting your investment portfolio, saving for retirement, traveling, and writing a book of poetry are general goals.

So this is your first step in writing effective goals for yourself: Make a list of your general goals — all of them. Don't worry about organizing them or putting similar or related goals together — right now, your goal is to identify as many of your goals as you can. You may think of new goals to add later, and you may decide later on that some of the goals you wrote down the first time aren't really all that important to you.

You can do this on your home computer, but we recommend using pad and pen or pencil. There's a different kind of connection between your thinking and physically writing down your thoughts, a different sense of ownership when you set your goals down in your own handwriting. This is especially true when you look at your list again after a lapse of a few weeks or months.

Making your goals SMART

After you've identified your general goals, you can take the next step: making them SMART. SMART is an acronym for the characteristics of effective goals. There are several variations; for our purposes, SMART stands for specific, measurable, action-based, realistic, and timed.

Specific

Think of your general goal as a big block of marble. You can't move it all at once, so you need to break it down into smaller, manageable blocks. For example, if one of your general goals is to become debt free, break that down among the kinds of debt you have. The specific elements of that general goal may be paying off your credit cards, or paying off your car loan, personal loans, and student loans.

You can do this for all your goals. Say you want to buy a house. What kind of house do you want? How many bedrooms do you need? Do you want to live near your job, or would you rather live in the country? Your general goal is to buy a house, but when you make that goal specific, you've identified that you want to buy a four-bedroom ranch within 15 miles of your job in a well-respected school district.

Specific goals quantify your general goals. They tell you in detail the "what" of your goals — an essential step to help you stay focused on doing the things that really matter to you.

Measurable

If you can't tell whether you're making progress toward your goal, you're less likely to stick with your plan. Break your specific goal into smaller segments you can measure so you stay motivated.

Losing 20 pounds is a specific goal. But it's difficult to stick to an exercise or eating regimen if you can't measure incremental progress toward that goal. On the other hand, if you lose 2 pounds a week, you can see you're making progress, and that gives you confidence and inspiration to continue.

It's the same with financial goals. If your goal is to pay off your credit cards, you can measure your progress by watching the balance decrease every month. So part of your goal is to drop your credit card balance by, say, $200 every month until it's paid off. Just as with losing weight, seeing your financial progress helps you stay motivated to complete your plan.

Measurable increments give you small successes to build on, increasing the odds that you'll stick with your plan and ultimately reach the goals you set for yourself.

Action-based

There are so many things that are outside your control — why add your finances to that list? Your monetary goals should focus on the actions *you* can take, not on the whims of the stock market or the overall economy. Relying on things beyond your control to make your financial dreams come true is a sure recipe for disappointment.

Take a look at the buying-a-house goal. There are lots of elements of buying a house that you can't control: mortgage rates, the state of the market where you want to buy, even the prices that sellers are asking. So focus instead on the things you *can* control: how much you want to have for a down payment, how much you want to spend on a house, and how much work you're willing to put into the house you buy.

This strategy applies to other financial goals, too. You don't have much control over how much of a raise you'll get this year, but you do control how you spend (or save) any extra money in your paycheck. You can't erase the debts you've already incurred, but you can avoid adding to your debt load, and you can take steps to pay down your debt.

Directing your financial goals toward things you can do gives you confidence, even when outside forces seem to be working against you.

Realistic

We believe that your reach should exceed your grasp, but we don't believe in setting yourself up for failure. Set your goals somewhere between "I could do this right now" and "Never gonna happen."

What does that mean, exactly? Your goals should be a stretch for you — something you'll have to put some time and energy into. Goals that are too easy don't give you the same sense of accomplishment when you finally reach them. It's like running 5k races for years and never once trying to finish a 10k. You already know you can do the 5k, but if you never try a 10k, you won't know just how far you can go.

On the other hand, running 5k races well doesn't mean you're ready for the Ironman Triathlon, either. That's not to say you won't get there someday, but it may take a lot more time and effort than you're willing to put in.

There are all kinds of reasons why you may never become the world's richest person. Maybe the profession you love doesn't pay the big bucks; maybe you've got a lot of calls on your purse that force you to be more modest in your goals. Maybe, as much as you'd like to retire to the Mexican Riviera and spend your days deep-sea fishing, it just isn't a practical option for you.

There are other ways of being unrealistic, too. We ran across one financial advice column that urged readers to limit their total debt — mortgage, car, credit cards, student loans, personal loans, everything you can classify as a debt — to just 36 percent of your total income. That may be possible after you've made your millions, but for most households, that's a ridiculously low figure — especially because a third or more of most people's income is devoted solely to their housing costs. A much more realistic goal, at least when you're starting out on your road to making millions, is to put aside 10 percent of your annual income for savings and wealth-building investments (not including retirement-fund contributions).

Your goals should be bigger than what you can do in your current situation; the sense of striving for something is a basic human instinct that itself adds value to life. But goals that are *too* big can easily tip into the abyss of unfulfilled wishes, leaving you prone to depression and inertia.

Timed

There's nothing inherently wrong with saying "someday," as in, "Someday, I'd like to take a ceramics course" or, "Someday, I want to sail around the world." But — and this is a big *but* — if you're serious about attaining your financial goals, you have to avoid the "someday" trap.

Setting target dates for your goals is a critical element in achieving them. If you have no deadline, you have no motivation to get started on your action steps. You convince yourself that you can start any time — no deadline, no hurry — and chances are good that your goals will get pushed aside in favor of more immediate concerns or, at the very least, delayed so long that achieving them becomes a lot harder (if not virtually impossible).

Set reasonable target dates to achieve your financial goals: paying off your credit cards in six months, for example, or having the down payment for your house by this time next year. Some target dates can be immediate: setting up a high-interest savings account this week, or switching to a lower-cost Internet service provider (ISP) before the end of the month.

Unexpected expenses, a poor economy, loss of a job, health issues — any of these may affect your timeline for reaching your goals. If and when that happens, simply adjust your financial schedule so you have a plan for getting back on track.

Giving yourself deadlines for your financial goals helps you get started on the things you need to do to achieve them. But your target deadlines have to be realistic. Give yourself too long to achieve a goal, and you may put off doing anything at all; put too much time pressure on yourself, and you may be overwhelmed by a sense of futility.

Write your goals in positive terms — things you want to do, rather than things you want to avoid. "Keep the credit cards at home" is a positive statement; "Don't use the credit cards" is a negative one. Positive statements reinforce your sense of control over your own financial destiny.

Keeping your goals in mind

One of the reasons financial advisers (and life coaches and others) recommend writing down your goals is so you remember what they are. Without some sort of reminder, it's awfully easy to just coast along through your life, never achieving the grand dreams you've seen only in your mind's eye.

Create a *goal book* — a notebook or three-ring binder where you write down your goals and your SMART plan (see the "Making your goals SMART" section, earlier in this chapter) for achieving them. The advantage of having a goal book is that you can add new goals as they arise — and, instead of saying to yourself, "I can't afford this," you're primed to focus on figuring out how to make your new goal happen.

You also can adapt your goal book so it suits your organizational and planning style, and that will make your goals easier to attain.

Use the chart on the Cheat Sheet in the front of this book to list the main points of your goals, and post it where you'll see it often: on the fridge, on your bathroom mirror, or next to your computer. You can always refer to your goal book for specifics, but it's helpful to have the broad outline of your goals out in the open as a reminder.

Staying on Track

You've thought about your goals. You've figured out the things you can do to bring them to fruition. You have a timetable. Maybe you've even taken some of the first steps.

So how do you keep up the good work?

As the saying goes, "Life is what happens when you're busy making other plans," and you can't insulate yourself from every twist, turn, or setback on your road to financial security. However, you can make it easier to stick to your plan — or to get back on track when life gets in the way.

Try these techniques to help yourself stay on track:

- ✔ **Get rid of your financial clutter.** Shred credit card offers, or, better yet, call 888-567-8688 and have your name removed from the mailing lists that generate unwanted credit offers. You can make the removal permanent, or you can choose to opt out for two years — but then you have to renew your opt out (if you want).

- ✔ **Create a workable budget (see Chapter 6).** You may have to make adjustments for the unexpected, but even then, having a written budget to refer to makes it easier to see which adjustments make the most sense and — just as important — how quickly you'll be able to get back to your plan.

- ✔ **Devise a system for paying bills and keeping records.** Mail organizers are inexpensive and handy for storing bills according to their due dates. Label a file folder for the current year's tax records, and put any relevant receipts in it as soon as possible.

- ✔ **Use technology to help you.** Online banking is easy and usually free; you can make bill payments automatically and usually won't have to pay a fee for that. Plus, you save money on postage, envelopes, and checks.

Chapter 4

Working Out Finances with Your Spouse or Partner

In This Chapter

▶ Knowing each other's business

▶ Figuring out where you differ

▶ Getting your priorities straight

▶ Balancing each other out

*H*andling money consistently ranks at or near the top of conflict areas for couples, partly because it's fairly rare for two people to have exactly the same ideas about managing money and partly because most people aren't very good at talking about money. If you and your significant other have different priorities, different ideas of what you want your lifestyle to be, and different attitudes toward spending and saving, household finances are bound to be a touchy subject.

Even if you aren't married, you and your partner have more than just a romantic relationship: You have an economic partnership. That means you both have a stake in how you manage your money together, and you both should have a say in structuring your finances. Of course, it also means you have to be able to communicate with each other about money — what it means for each of you, what each of you wants to accomplish financially, and even what scares you about your finances.

In this chapter, we provide a blueprint for opening the discussion, figuring out goals together, and crafting a financial plan that works for both of you. For our purposes here, we assume that, even if you aren't married, you and your partner have a committed, long-term relationship in which each of you contributes financially to the household and that you want your financial arrangements to reflect what each of you needs and wants.

Spill Your Guts: Sharing Your Financial Story

If your reaction to the headline above is, "Well, duh," congratulations! You're among those couples who have at least some idea of what your joint financial life looks like. An appalling number of couples don't — about half, according to one study, were off by more than 10 percent in estimating their household's income and by 30 percent in estimating their combined net worth. Another study showed that more than a third of couples in their 40s, 50s, and 60s didn't know when their spouses planned to retire; a third also admitted to lying to their partners about money. And, in yet another survey, four out of five people said they hide purchases from their partners.

Add to that the fact that more people are delaying marriage (meaning they're more likely to bring a greater array of assets — and liabilities — to the relationship), and it's not really surprising that so many people are so clueless about their spouse's finances. (And we haven't even discussed the financial complexities of second marriages.)

How much you know

To see how much you really know about each other's finances, try this experiment: Answer the following questions about your partner, and then ask your partner how accurate (or not) you are. Then trade places, and have your partner answer these questions about you.

- ✔ How much did your partner make last year?
- ✔ What are the balances on your partner's credit cards?
- ✔ What was your partner's last major purchase, and how much did it cost?
- ✔ True or false: Your partner pays alimony, child support, or a court-ordered judgment.
- ✔ What loans, other than your mortgage, are in your partner's name only?
- ✔ How much does your partner have in retirement accounts?
- ✔ If your partner dies, how much life insurance will you receive?

If you both know all the answers, you're way ahead of many couples. If not, consider it a reality check — and an indication that you need to work on your communication about finances.

What you need to know

You can't make good financial decisions if you don't have the raw data to base those decisions on. Here is the absolute *minimum* information you and your partner need to share with each other:

- ✔ **Income sources:** Beyond your base salaries (both gross and take-home), tell each other about any additional compensation you're eligible for, like bonuses, commissions, profit-sharing, or stock options. If one of you has a side business or does freelance work, you also need to know basics about that, such as revenue and net income, even if it's just an estimate.

 Going over your tax returns, whether individual or joint, is an easy way to identify your sources of income and how much you earn.

- ✔ **Retirement accounts:** You can't plan for retirement if you don't know how much each of you is starting out with. Figure out how much each of you has in your 401(k) and IRA accounts and how your accounts are allocated among stocks, bonds, and other options.

- ✔ **Savings, checking, and investment accounts:** It's okay if each of you has your own accounts, but both of you should know about those accounts and have at least a rough idea of how much money is in each one.

 If one of you is especially vulnerable to lawsuits (business owners, doctors, and lawyers can fall into this category), you may want to consult an attorney about the best way to protect your assets. (See Chapter 15 for information on choosing an attorney.) Depending on the state laws where you live, it may make sense to set up a limited liability corporation (LLC) for yourself or your business, or both. Business LLCs generally limit liability to the business assets; your personal assets are protected. Individual LLCs can be structured to limit liability to only one source of income. For more information on LLCs, check out *Limited Liability Companies For Dummies,* by Jennifer Reuting (Wiley).

 Even if you decide to keep some accounts separately, both of you should make a list that includes all your accounts and key information about each one: the name and phone number of the financial institution and the account number. Keep one copy of the list in your files at home, and give another copy to your attorney or put it in a safe-deposit box that both of you have access to.

- ✔ **Credit cards, loans, and other debts or obligations:** This can be tricky, because most people don't like to share information about their debts. But this is a critical piece of your finances, and it isn't fair to let your partner think everything's all beer and skittles when there's a monster of a credit card bill waiting in the mailbox. Disclose to each other both the limits and balances on any credit cards you have. For loans, your partner needs to know how much the monthly payment is and how long you have left to pay on it. Other debts and obligations include things like outstanding medical bills, business loans, alimony or child support, and loans you're repaying to relatives or friends.

✔ **Insurance coverage:** How much life insurance do you and your partner have? Who are the beneficiaries? Are the policies through an employer or individual policies? How about disability insurance? Insurance for a business? How and when are the premiums paid?

When you have all the data together, put it in a filing cabinet at home so you both know where it is and can refer to it when you need to.

Why you need to know

Whether you're married or living together, whether your accounts are joint or separate, your financial well-being is intertwined with your partner's. Even if you're splitting the household expenses right down the middle, chances are, you're enjoying a lifestyle you couldn't afford without your partner's contributions, and vice versa.

There are legal aspects to your financial life together, too. If you're married and you file a joint tax return, you and your spouse are equally responsible for both the accuracy of the return and any taxes due. That means, if your spouse makes a mistake on the return — intentional or not — the feds and the state can come after you for any extra tax payments, interest, penalties, and even criminal liability. Even if you divorce, you can be held responsible for returns you signed.

If you and your partner have loans or credit cards in both your names, either of you can be held solely responsible for repayment.

Unless you sign a waiver, your spouse's 401(k) comes to you if your spouse dies. Your spouse also needs your written consent to withdraw funds or take a loan against a 401(k). If you aren't married, your partner can designate anyone she wants as the beneficiary of her 401(k).

You aren't required to name your spouse as the beneficiary on a life insurance policy or an IRA. You can name your children, your estate, a favorite charity, or your UPS delivery guy as your beneficiary if you like.

If you have joint accounts with survivorship rights, you'll get full ownership of those accounts if your partner dies. But accounts that are only in your partner's name become part of her estate for estate tax purposes, and distribution is dictated by a will or by your state's estate laws if there is no will. The same is true for your home. (See Chapter 19 for a full discussion of estate planning.) Survivorship rights depend on how the account is set up, so ask your financial institution to make sure your accounts are structured the way you want them.

If you're not married, consider having a *living-together agreement* drawn up, and have it notarized for good measure. A living-together agreement is similar to a prenuptial agreement, specifying who owns what, how expenses and assets will be shared, and what happens to your assets if you break up.

Getting the most out of your financial partnership

Sharing information gives you an opportunity to take full advantage of what each of you brings to your financial union. Maybe your employer offers a better health insurance plan; maybe your partner's 401(k) program has a better employer match or a better selection of investments. Compare your benefits and select the ones that will do both of you the greatest good.

Consider maxing out the better of your 401(k) plans first, and then funding the other one. Put in enough to get the full employer match, and, if necessary, use the other spouse's income to compensate for the difference in take-home pay. Then look for ways to start funding the other 401(k).

There may be other, less obvious options to improve your mutual financial standing, too. Maybe you can combine some of your savings to get a better rate on a CD or money market fund. Maybe your spouse's membership in a credit union makes you eligible for benefits you otherwise wouldn't get.

You Like Potato and I Like Potahto: Identifying Your Differences

Everyone thinks and feels differently about money. But people often assume that everybody else thinks and feels the way they do, and those assumptions are responsible for a lot of miscommunication and aggravation.

So how do you get past your assumptions? First, remind yourself that you may not know your partner as well as you think you do when it comes to money. You can learn a lot by observation, but even then, most people are prone to interpret their observations according to their own feelings and values, so be cautious about assigning motivations to the behavior you see. Instead, ask questions, or make statements that invite your partner to agree or disagree. Here are some examples:

- ✔ "You seem frustrated about having to get new brakes for the car."

- ✔ "What are the advantages of buying this now?"

- ✔ "What if we went with a less expensive option?"

- ✔ "I would have a hard time buying (or not buying) this."

- ✔ "Thinking about money makes me nervous."

- ✔ "How do you feel about the money we have now?"

Statements and open-ended questions like these invite discussion without putting either of you on the defensive. Even if you think you know what your partner's money personality is (see Chapter 2), talking about money can give you much greater insight into how each of you deals with (or avoids) money issues.

You don't have to make this a big "money talk." You may have a better discussion — and learn more — by bringing up these topics as the situation warrants. And by talking about money in natural situations, you erase the taboo against discussing money at all.

Differences in your money styles are nothing to be afraid of. You can't create a workable financial plan together if neither of you understands where the other is coming from. Besides, your differences may complement each other, leading to a better-balanced money handling style.

Talking about your expectations

Most people don't think consciously about their relationship with money or what money represents to them. If you ask your partner to describe what money means to him, be prepared for a blank stare and a stammered, "I don't know." But you can get at the answer by talking about your expectations for your financial life together. Money may represent control, or responsibility, or freedom, or security — or all these things and more.

Here are some common areas where couples have different expectations, which can lead to a great deal of strife:

- ✔ **Who's responsible for earning money:** In these days of two-earner households, the idea that you and your partner may have different breadwinner expectations may seem like a throwback to the 1950s. But, although few men these days say it would bother them if their wives earned more than they did, and even fewer say they'd like their wives to not work, serious issues can still arise — especially if there's a big difference in your respective paychecks. In theory, your spouse may agree that you should leave a good-paying but soul-destroying job for one that pays less but gives you more enjoyment. In practice, though, the shift of financial dependence onto your spouse's job can easily spark feelings of fear and resentment.

Don't let the size of your paycheck determine your share of the decision-making when it comes to finances. You're a partnership, and even if one of you contributes more income to the household than the other, each of you should have an equal say in how you handle the household finances.

✔ **Who's responsible for paying the bills:** If one of you is better at balancing the checkbook and making sure the bills get paid on time, it makes sense for that person to handle the bill-paying. But the fact that someone's good at something doesn't necessarily mean she likes doing it or wants the responsibility, especially if the other partner takes a "not my problem" attitude toward the bills. Make sure you both know what bills you have and when they're due. And if your partner is the one in charge of bill-paying, do what you can to help him stay organized and as stress-free as possible.

✔ **How investment decisions are made:** You may feel that, because you know more about investing, you should have the freedom to make investment decisions for you and your spouse. But even if your spouse agrees to defer to your judgment, the two of you may not have the same priorities or risk tolerances. Talk about your goals for your investments and the risks involved in trying to reach those goals, and then find the middle ground that lets you both sleep at night.

✔ **How much discretionary spending each of you can do:** There are some purchases you should never make without consulting your spouse — a car, real estate, or even big-ticket household items like a digital video camera or a new bedroom set, for example. But, unless money is exceptionally tight, you shouldn't have to get each other's permission to treat a friend to lunch or buy a book you've been dying to read. The tricky part is setting a threshold for when you have to talk to your spouse before spending. Some couples budget allowances for each other every pay period, and both partners can do what they like with their allowances. Some have a combination of joint and individual accounts; the money in the joint account is used for bills and spending any extra from that account requires consultation, but the individual accounts are each spouse's own responsibility. Still other couples set a dollar limit, and if you want to spend more than, say, $100, you have to talk it over with your spouse first.

✔ **Philosophies about debt:** For some people, being in debt is a way of life; there will always be car payments and credit card bills, and that's okay in their view. Others think of debt as a dangerous illness; they can't stand to owe anybody for anything, and even having a mortgage makes them feel like their financial health is compromised. Then there are people who see debt as a useful tool for certain basics, like housing, education, and transportation, but who are strongly opposed to going into debt for nonessentials. If you and your spouse have the same philosophy about debt, you probably won't have a lot of arguments, or even spirited discussions, about buying an ATV on the easy-monthly-payment plan or the importance of paying off your credit card balances every month. But if you have different ideas about how to use debt, this will be a significant source of tension, and you'll have to figure out a compromise that doesn't give either of you indigestion.

✔ **Privacy issues:** Your spouse's financial business is your business, and vice versa. But the two of you may have different ideas about sharing the details of your finances with others. Some people love to spread the word about raises, bonuses, and other good money news. Some don't blab to-the-dollar details but brag about big purchases or expensive vacations. If one of you is a bean-spiller, the other one is likely to be not just uncomfortable, but also angry and resentful. Set boundaries on how much information you share and with whom, and respect those boundaries religiously.

✔ **The relative importance of the present and the future:** Some people would rather forgo some luxuries now so they can save more for the future. Others don't see the point of not enjoying what they have now. When couples are on opposite ends of this spectrum, they tend to view the other's attitudes toward and actions with money as a yardstick that measures how much their partner cares about them. The save-for-tomorrow partner interprets the spendthrift's behavior as a sign that the spendthrift doesn't care about her future security, and the spendthrift takes the saver's frugality as an indication that the saver doesn't care about his happiness. Depending on how far apart you are, it may take a lot of effort for each of you to move toward middle ground, and you may have to have more than one discussion to come to a compromise that both of you can live with.

Expectations aside, there are some facts of life you simply can't ignore. You have to have enough money to cover your expenses; if you don't deal with that basic fact, you'll never be able to begin building wealth. If you don't have enough income to meet your expenses, you and your partner either have to cut your expenses or increase your income, or both. And you have to do it together: It doesn't get you any farther ahead if one of you takes on a second job to help pay off debt, for example, and the other keeps adding to your debt load.

Discussing your goals

You and your spouse may have wildly different ideas of what you want your future to look like. Maybe you want to retire in an arts community like Taos, New Mexico; maybe your spouse imagines buying a small acreage and cultivating prize roses in retirement. Maybe you'd like to retire at 50, while your spouse wants to work at least part-time for as long as possible. Maybe one of you wants to go back to college or open a business. Maybe one of you would like to quit your job to focus on raising your family. (See Chapter 3 for more on identifying goals.)

Writing down goals is a good way to clarify your thoughts and remind yourself of what you want to accomplish. Choose a week for each of you to write down what you want to do and what you want to own; then get together at the end of the week and compare lists. (We recommend taking a week to do this because most people find themselves thinking of additions to their lists as a few days pass.)

Couples who are united in their goals have a much easier time building (and keeping) wealth than couples who don't communicate about their goals. Knowing what each of you wants allows you to identify your common goals and understand your individual aspirations, and that alone cements the reasons for building wealth together.

When you compare your lists, keep these two important rules in mind:

- **No criticism is allowed.** The purpose of this exercise is to get you attuned to one another's goals and dreams. Disparaging remarks about your partner's goals only serve to emphasize your differences. Accept your partner's goals as you want your partner to accept yours.

- **Remember that these goals are a starting point.** Don't worry right now about how you'll make it happen. That comes later, as you discuss the commonalities in your lists and identify your priorities as a couple and as individuals.

- **Goals can — and should — change over time.** What you want today may not be what you want five or ten years from now, or even one year from now, so don't take them as lifelong requirements just because you've written them down. You should review your goals periodically — say, once or twice a year, at least — to see if anything in your circumstances or outlook has changed.

When you've shared your lists, put them in a three-ring binder, and add anything you think may be helpful. For example, the Doyens' goal book (which is gold, and which they refer to as their "gold book") includes a collection of inspiring quotes about attitudes toward money, building wealth, and living a full life. You may want to keep a copy of your budget in your goal book, or pictures of your dream house or dream retirement spot — anything that helps keep you focused on what you really want to accomplish.

Go Team! Setting Priorities Together

Once you've identified what each of you wants from your financial life together, you can set about deciding which goals are most important and how to accomplish them. In doing this, you also make a pact with each other to work as a financial team, helping each other work toward your goals, supporting each other when things look less than rosy, and celebrating with each other when you can cross something off your list.

When it comes to finances, two heads really are better than one. Discussing goals and priorities can unleash creativity and generate ideas for lifestyle changes that you may never think of on your own. Be open to your partner's ideas and give them your full consideration.

There's no such thing as throw-away money. Every single purchase, large or small, is important, and having extra cash isn't against the law; there's nothing that says you have to spend it. Small amounts add up over time, whether you're spending them or saving them.

Finding a mutual comfort zone

Some couples are fortunate enough to have the same expectations about and attitudes toward money. But lots of couples really have to work to reconcile their money differences. It's not as simple as spenders versus savers, either: There's the whole messy subconscious jungle of self-worth, power, and love where money attitudes have their roots, too.

To find compromises that will work for each of you, you have to be willing to move toward each other, if only by degrees. If you're a conscientious saver and your spouse likes to spend, for example, the obvious compromise is for you to loosen up a little and your spouse to tighten up a little. If you like to explore riskier investments and your spouse prefers a more conservative portfolio, a possible solution is to devote a small piece of your investment pie to higher-risk options so you can have some fun with it, while keeping the majority of it in safer stocks and bonds so your spouse feels more comfortable.

The key to finding your comfortable compromises is trust. Each of you has to know that the other is concerned about your financial well-being and committed to your financial security. Without that trust, any compromise you reach is bound to fail sooner or later.

If you just can't reach suitable compromises, or you can't stick to the ones you do reach, you may want to consider professional counseling. As we mentioned earlier, money is deeply rooted in emotions and subconscious issues, and sometimes logic isn't enough to override those issues.

Focusing on the positive

In other sections of this book, we discuss the importance of framing your financial goals in a positive light. Negativity shuts down creativity and jeopardizes your resolve to stick to your plan. You and your partner can help each other stay positive, even in the face of setbacks that force you to reorganize your priorities or set a new timeline for your goals.

Here are some suggestions for buoying a positive outlook for each other:

- ✔ **Ban the phrase *can't afford it* from your home.** When you catch each other saying you can't afford something, change it to, "How can we afford it?" or "We choose not to spend our money on this right now."

- ✔ **Be realistic about setbacks.** All kinds of things that are beyond your control can rip your financial plan to shreds. Express your frustration, sure, but then remind each other that these things are temporary. After you've done that, it's easy to start brainstorming about how to get back on track.

- ✔ **Make sure you're both in the loop regarding your finances.** Knowledge is power, and information is the best antidote for baseless concerns. An unexpectedly large electric bill is unlikely to cause panic if you both know there's enough money to cover the extra expense.

- ✔ **Reinforce your shared decision-making power.** Talk about strategies before you implement them, in good times and in bad. Doing it during good times makes it comfortable, and doing it in bad times strengthens your trust in each other.

- ✔ **Be reassuring when the other is pessimistic.** Not all financial problems can be solved with a smile, but a reminder that you're a team and will get through your hard times together can do wonders to restore a sense of hope.

Part II
Strategies for Building Wealth

The 5th Wave   By Rich Tennant

"I think I have a pretty good savings plan. I plan to save 15 percent on a Rolex watch this weekend."

In this part . . .

Despite what you hear from those incessantly upbeat, get-rich-quick infomercials in the wee hours, most people aren't ready to give up the security of a paycheck (and benefits) in exchange for an iffy opportunity in business, real estate, or what have you. That's okay — you can still build wealth as a wage slave, if you know how to take advantage of your current resources.

In this part, we take you through the basics of living below your means so you have money to devote to your financial goals. We discuss ways you can free up your money to do this, by knowing the difference between good and bad debt and avoiding the bad kind. We tell you to save, of course, but we also show you why saving is important and give you easy-to-follow steps to get started on your own savings plan — and stick with it. Finally, we show you how to get the most out of your job, beyond just the paycheck, by taking advantage of other benefits your employer may offer.

Chapter 5

Living below Your Means

In This Chapter

▷ Understanding the factors that lead you to spend more

▷ Identifying and changing your spending habits

▷ Planning for changes in your finances

*M*ost people find it difficult to save money because they're accustomed to living beyond their means — in many cases, far beyond. The mortgage crisis that began making itself felt in 2007 and then created an undertow throughout the rest of the economy in 2008 is a good example of how Americans tend to buy more than they can afford. To be sure, some lenders used shady practices to lure people into mortgages they couldn't pay. But, on the other hand, many borrowers gave into their greed by purchasing more house than their incomes could support.

It doesn't help that we live in a consumer-driven society, either. About two-thirds of the U.S. economy is based on consumer spending for goods and services, and that figure has grown as the cost of many goods and services has dropped. Devices that most Americans take for granted today — refrigerators, washers and dryers, even cars — started out as indulgences of the rich; people with lower incomes couldn't afford them and didn't buy them. But as wages rose and the prices of those goods dropped, more and more people bought refrigerators, washers and dryers, and cars, and now eight out of ten American households have all these things.

A lot of American households these days also have TVs, cellphones, computers, video recorders, digital cameras, MP3 players, CD players, videogame systems — a whole host of high-tech, high-ticket items, often paid for with credit cards, which (no coincidence here) is the easiest way to live beyond your means.

We're not saying you shouldn't buy things, or even that you shouldn't have or use credit cards. We *are* saying that you can't build wealth until you assess your spending habits and overcome the poor ones — the ones that prevent you from saving and investing your money to meet your long-term financial goals. It isn't easy, either. It takes time and dedication, and often continual reminders, to change the way you use your money.

Millionaires, especially the self-made ones, are masters at living below their means. They often drive used cars, live in modest homes, stay at inexpensive hotels, and wear not-the-latest-fashion clothes. Every once in a while, of course, they treat themselves to dinner at a gourmet restaurant or indulge in some form of costly recreation. But, for the most part, they live pretty frugally.

In this chapter, we show you how you may be living beyond your means and offer steps you can take to get control of your spending. We also discuss the ways your "means" can change and give you tips on planning for those potential changes.

Spending Money You Don't Have

Spending money you don't have is the very definition of living beyond your means. As recently as 50 years ago, most people *couldn't* live beyond their means; when the cash was gone, there were no other options.

The proliferation of credit cards changed all that. Not only do credit cards give you access to someone else's money (the bank's), but they also eliminate the pain of spending. Researchers have shown that the brain's pleasure and pain centers both are active when people spend cash: The pleasure centers anticipate good things from the purchase itself, and the pain centers react to parting with cash, putting the brakes on overspending.

But with credit cards and any buy-now-pay-later scheme, the pain centers aren't activated, so there is no natural brake on your spending. Before you know it, you're deeper in debt than you planned, and what you have to show for all that debt may not mean as much to you as it did when you bought it.

Unless you pay your credit card balances in full every month, it costs you money to use them, and this is even more true of personal and home-equity loans. You have to pay back not just what you've borrowed, but the interest too, which can double, triple, or even quadruple the original price of the item you bought with borrowed money.

Wealth-builders don't pay interest unless they absolutely have to — on a mortgage, for instance. Their reasoning is simple: Every dollar you pay in interest on your credit cards or loans is a dollar you can't invest for your own use. You're not losing just that dollar. You're also losing the earnings from that dollar.

So how do you avoid spending money you don't have? The first step is understanding what you're up against — the things that make you overspend. Sometimes it's as simple as your mood: Studies have shown that people tend to spend more when they're feeling down than when they're feeling happy. But most people also have to contend with societal factors — the natural desire for instant gratification and the continual must-have messages of a consumer culture.

The instant gratification factor

Patience may be a virtue, but you wouldn't know it from the ads you see these days. One credit card company's TV spot even uses a theme song with the lyrics, "I want it all, and I want it now." Easy credit, both through credit cards and in-store financing, has more or less stifled the notion of saving for special purchases. Why wait, the ads ask us, when you can have it now and worry about paying for it later?

And people are buying into it, big time. According to CardTrack.com, which covers the credit card industry, Americans racked up more than $2.2 *trillion* on their credit cards in 2007. In the first two months of 2008 alone, Americans added another $10 billion to their credit card balances.

It isn't always the big purchases that get people into trouble; it's the little everyday things, like eating out instead of brown-bagging your lunch, or buying another white blouse when you already have four hanging in your closet, or going to a movie theater instead of renting a DVD. These things aren't really extravagant in themselves, but they can be trouble if they interfere with your goals to build wealth.

How you use your credit cards affects your credit score, called a *FICO score,* and your FICO score affects the interest rates you pay for other types of loans, like mortgages and auto loans. The higher your FICO score, the lower your interest rates. People with the highest FICO scores typically use less than 10 percent of their credit card limits.

These days, you don't even have to get dressed or leave your home to empty your checking account or max out your credit cards, making the allure of instant gratification even more insidious. Short of throwing a shoe through your television set and locking your computer in the attic, how do you resist the voice in your head that keeps repeating, "I want it all, and I want it now"?

First, acknowledge the want. Counselor Cliff Isaacson says denying that you want something actually makes that desire stronger; it sets up a tug-of-war in your brain between "I want it" and "I can't have it." The more you feel you can't have something you want, the stronger your desire to have it. On the other hand, simply saying to yourself, "I want this," cues your brain to start thinking about other aspects of this potential purchase. Now you aren't just feeling that you want something; you're also thinking about it.

And thinking about it is the second step. When you've acknowledged that you want something, you can begin probing the pros and cons of buying it. Here are some questions you can ask yourself:

 ✔ **Why do I want this?** Sometimes the answer is simply that it's cool, or new, or different, and that's okay. Sometimes it's to replace something that's broken or worn out, and sometimes it's something that you've been considering casually for a while.

Don't use "why" to rationalize a purchase. Some reasons are more compelling than others, but there's no such thing as a wrong reason. So be honest with yourself about the real reasons you want a particular thing.

✔ **How will I use this?** Thinking about how an item will fit into your lifestyle can illuminate the item's potential shortcomings. Maybe, on reflection, it's not quite the right color or doesn't have the features you'd really like. And if that's the case, you've just convinced yourself that you don't really want that particular thing after all.

✔ **What's the trade-off?** Very little in this life comes without a trade-off of some kind. Making a purchase now may mean that you have to delay buying something else you really want. It may even mean that you can't pay a bill you need to pay or that money won't be available when you really need it. But even when you have plenty of money, there's always a trade-off in spending it: Money you spend cannot work for you in the same way it does when you don't spend it. Sometimes the trade-off is worth it; sometimes it's not. But you won't know unless you identify what the trade-off is.

According to Isaacson, most people think being rich means they can buy everything they want when they want it, like going on a never-ending lavish shopping spree. But that isn't how millionaires think. Rarely will you hear of a millionaire who buys something just because she can afford it. In fact, most millionaires don't even think in terms of affordability. Instead, they think of purchases this way: "Do I want to spend my money on this?"

Who are you keeping up with again?

It's human nature to compare yourself with your neighbors, co-workers, friends, and family members. It acts as a sort of yardstick to measure your values and your level of professional success and to see how you fit in with the people around you. Unfortunately, it also can be the gateway to financial ruin.

Consumer envy is nothing new. But the fact that it seems to work only one way is interesting. You don't look at your neighbors with the 8-year-old compact car and the smaller house and get jealous over what you think they're saving. No, you look at the neighbor who trades in his luxury car every two years and just added a sunroom and an in-ground pool to his house and envy what he spends. "How does he do it?" you wonder. "He must have a great-paying job."

He probably also has a great deal of debt. And you will, too, if you give in to the idea that you have to keep up with the Joneses.

You're much better off if you try to keep up with the Smiths — the ones who drive the paid-for (albeit older) car and who maintain their home well but don't invest in fripperies they don't need. Even if the Smiths don't have a huge nest egg tucked away somewhere, chances are, they're in better overall financial health than the Joneses simply because they don't have the burden of debt.

According to figures from the Bureau of Labor Statistics, the "household consumption" gap between the richest and poorest Americans isn't nearly as high as the income gap. The average income for the top 20 percent was about $150,000 in 2006, the latest year for which numbers were available at this writing. The average income for the bottom 20 percent was just under $10,000. But while the top-income households spent less than 50 percent of their money on housing, food, clothing, and all the other consumption categories, the low-income households spent almost twice their incomes — an average of more than $18,000.

Changing Your Spending Habits

Most people get hung up financially on their perceptions of their lifestyle — either what they can afford or what they feel they should be able to afford. You see all these images on TV and watch what your neighbors or co-workers are doing, and you think, "If they can do it, I can, too."

Stop. You're about to fall for an illusion that will sabotage every financial goal you have.

What can't you live without?

According to the Pew Research Center, the list of things Americans consider necessities (as opposed to luxuries) has grown considerably in the past ten years — and the list now includes things that weren't even available back in the 1990s, like high-speed Internet service, iPods, cellphones, and flat-screen TVs. More people now consider certain home appliances — washer and dryer, microwave, dishwasher — absolute necessities, and air-conditioning, both at home and in cars, is a can't-live-without-it feature for a good majority of Americans.

The problem with looking at what other people do with their money is that their priorities and values very likely don't mesh with yours. But you can't know for sure unless you know what your priorities and values are. Here are the steps that will help you get a handle on your own wants and needs:

1. **Write down what you want, from the everyday to big things.**

   If you want to be able to eat out three nights a week, write that down. If you want to buy a boat or a new living room set or a big-screen TV, write it down. If you want to take a cruise, piano lessons, or a sabbatical from your job, write it down. Don't make any judgments about whether your desires are sensible or silly; you'll sort that out later. For now, write down everything.

   Put your broader financial goals on this list, too: "I want to have $10,000 in savings," "I want to open an IRA," "I want to pay off the car," or what have you.

2. **Put a price tag next to each item on your list.**

   This will help you identify the things that can fit into your budget now and the things you'll have to make a special effort (that is, save) for.

3. **Prioritize your list.**

   This is where you sort out the things that are most important to you. Maybe eating out three nights a week is how you socialize with your friends; if so, that may be more important to you than a new couch. Remember that these are *your* priorities — not your neighbors', not your parents', not your friends', just *yours.*

4. **Brainstorm options for the most important things on your list.**

   Can any of these things fit into your monthly budget? What things will you have to save for? Just as important is considering ways to get what you want for less. If you really want a new couch, for example, check out auctions, estate sales, and secondhand stores in your area before you head to the retail furniture store; you may be able to get higher quality for quite a bit less money.

5. **Put your list where you can find it easily — and refer to it often.**

   Spending is just like any other habit — it takes time to change it. For the first month, look at your list at least every other day. Doing this keeps you focused on *your* goals and priorities, which helps insulate you from the deleterious magnetism of both instant gratification and consumer envy.

Anticipating Changes in Your Means

Most people are pretty good at anticipating a time when their financial situation will be better — when you'll have your credit cards paid off, when you'll get a raise or a bonus, and so on. But most people tend to forget that their finances can get worse, too, so they don't plan for those times. If you're fortunate, you won't have to deal with anything other than small bumps in your road to making millions. But if you aren't that fortunate, what will you do? Answering that question before you're in the middle of a crisis can remove a lot of stress if and when a crisis does hit.

Losing an income

Even if you're living below your means now, you could be overextended if you or your spouse or partner loses a job or sees a reduction in pay. This happened to Meg and her husband. They bought their home in 2002, when both of them were making good salaries. Eight months later, her husband was laid off, and suddenly they were living way beyond their means, with a mortgage payment and two car payments in addition to their regular living expenses. Unemployment benefits helped, but the benefits were only a fraction of her husband's former salary, and they ended up going through their savings to stay afloat during the nine months it took him to find another job.

There are two good strategies to protect yourself against losing an income, and we recommend using both:

✔ **Build up your rainy-day savings.** Most experts recommend having three to six months' worth of living expenses stashed away in an account that you can access easily in an emergency. Online-only savings accounts typically earn more interest than traditional bank accounts, and, if you keep the ATM card for those accounts in a drawer, you won't be tempted to spend the money until you need it. Even better, you can set them up so they automatically deduct your savings from your regular bank account every month or every pay period.

Don't let the idea of six months of living expenses intimidate you; it's okay to start small and gradually increase the amount you save. Whether it's $25, $50, or $100 a month, whatever you can manage is worth saving.

✔ **If you're part of a two-income household, use only one income as your "means."** When your regular living expenses are covered by one income, you can use the other to build your savings and investments and make special purchases. Then, if you lose an income, you're not in a crisis — and you won't have to dip into your savings to get through the setback.

Dealing with a struggling economy

Until late 2007 and 2008, inflation wasn't a big concern for most people because it was low and wages generally kept pace with it. But as gas and food prices rose in early 2008, suddenly lots of people were finding their budgets sorely strained.

Your normal instinct when the economy isn't so hot is to tighten the belt and cut back on expenses. This works fine for some things and not so great for others. If you can't simply cut back, you may have to get creative to make your money go farther.

Even if the economy isn't hurting your budget, you can save money — and even get more for your money — by following these tips:

✔ **Cut out trips to the convenience store for regular groceries.** You pay — a lot — for the convenience, and you can save a lot by planning ahead and getting your groceries from the grocery store.

✔ **Shop secondhand stores.** You can get some great deals on high-quality used furniture, clothing, and other items without paying anywhere near retail. Plus, secondhand clothes (if you know where to shop) can be retro chic — people will be asking you where you got that great shirt or dress, because you won't be wearing the same clothes as everyone else.

✔ **Route your errands to save gas.** Planning ahead can make the fuel in your tank last longer.

If yours is a two-car household, make sure the one who drives more each day is using the car that gets the higher gas mileage. If you spend $10 less a week to fill up the tank, you're saving $40 a month, which you can apply to other bills — or stash in your rainy-day fund.

✔ **Look for cheaper entertainment options.** Renting a DVD and making popcorn at home is a lot less expensive than going to a movie theater. Visiting garage sales can pass the time and yield treasures at a fraction of the cost of going to the mall. Go to your favorite restaurant once in a while, sure, but look for other, less-expensive eateries to patronize on those nights when you just don't feel like cooking.

You can make your own hamburgers on the grill for a lot less than you'll pay at your local fast-food joint.

Planning for new expenses

Cars, houses, and babies — every one of them is going to cost you more than you expect. That's because they all come with hidden expenses. A new car probably will raise your auto-insurance premium, for example, but few people consider that when they're taking a test drive. Property taxes and insurance premiums on your house can rise with virtually no notice, but when people are figuring out how much they can afford for a mortgage, they rarely think about those expenses. And babies — well, they always cost a lot more than you think they will.

Car expenses

Whether you're buying a new car or a used car, or investing money in your current car to keep it going as long as possible, here are some things you should take into account when you're crunching the numbers:

- **Insurance costs:** New cars generally cost more to insure than older cars, and some models are more costly than others. You can get breaks on the premiums if the car has certain features like antilock brakes, air bags, and antitheft devices. You also can get discounts for taking a defensive driving course, having a good driving record, and insuring your car and home with the same company.

Most states require you to carry liability insurance on your car, but collision insurance may be optional after you've paid off your auto loan. Go to Kelley Blue Book's Web site (www.kbb.com) and look up your car's trade-in value. If it's low and even a minor collision would total your car, consider dropping collision insurance.

Never drop your liability insurance. Even if your state doesn't require it, liability insurance is essential to protect you against costly lawsuits if you have an accident where you're even partially at fault. (See Chapter 18 for information on appropriate insurance levels.)

- **Maintenance and repair costs:** You can get the oil changed anywhere, but for more extensive maintenance or repair projects, you may have to go to the dealership or a mechanic who specializes in your car make. Parts for some cars may be more expensive, too; even tire prices can be substantially higher for sports cars, for example, than for your basic sedan.

- **Fuel costs:** With gas prices hitting record highs, mileage can have a big impact on your fuel budget. Also, high-performance engines generally require higher-octane gas, which can raise your fuel costs considerably.

Consumer Reports (www.consumerreports.org) has a "cost of ownership" comparison report for different makes and models of cars, which includes such things as depreciation, maintenance and repairs, insurance, fuel costs, and interest and taxes for some 300 vehicles. You can see how much it will cost you to own any one of these vehicles for five to eight years. The report is available online (although you have to subscribe to the site to access it — you can get a one-month membership for $5.95 or a yearly membership for $26).

House expenses

There are many joys in home ownership, and there are lots of expenses, too. Beyond the regular maintenance required, you should plan ahead for major repairs, renovations, and higher tax and insurance costs:

- **Structural issues:** Will you need a new roof, new eaves, or a new gutter system in the next five years? How old are the plumbing and wiring? How long can you reasonably expect the furnace to last? Do the windows need to be replaced?

- **Renovations:** If you add a family room, a garage, a screened-in porch, or any enclosed space, your property taxes and insurance premiums may go up; check it out when you're planning these kinds of projects so you don't get blindsided.

- **Insurance rates:** After Hurricane Katrina hit the Gulf Coast in 2005, the cost of lumber and other construction goods skyrocketed, and that increase translated into higher home-insurance premiums across the country. If you pay your homeowner's insurance through an escrow account, your monthly mortgage payment will go up to reflect higher insurance premiums. If you pay the insurance separately, you'll have to come up with the extra cash whenever you pay your premium.

- **Tax rates:** Local governments nationwide are just as strapped for cash as individuals, and the only way they can get more is to raise taxes. Your tax bill also may rise as the value of your home increases. Either way, you'll pay more on a monthly basis if you have an escrow account through your mortgage company, or you'll have to come up with the extra cash when your tax bill arrives.

Many states have programs that lower your property-tax bill, such as exemptions for veterans and seniors. Check with your local government — the town or city clerk's office is a good place to start — to see if your area has any programs like this and how you can qualify for them.

Child expenses

For such small creatures, children sure use up a lot of resources. Diapers, formula, strollers, car seats, toys, clothes, and accessories are only the beginning; there are also doctor visits and day care, birthday parties and play dates, swimming lessons and music lessons and soccer practice and drama rehearsal and the college savings fund.

There's no way to anticipate every expense you'll encounter on your child's behalf; all you can really do is brace yourself for the unexpected. How? Try setting up a separate savings account specifically for child expenses. That way, when these unexpected bills come up, you won't have to scramble to rearrange your budget.

Chapter 6

Managing Debt and Freeing Up Your Money

*I*t's nearly impossible to live entirely debt free these days. Most people can't afford to pay cash for cars, homes, or college, and businesses large and small rely on credit to get started and grow. And, believe it or not, debt can be a useful tool to help you make your millions.

Unfortunately, many people don't know how to use that tool properly, and, when it's misused, debt can flip from wealth-building ally to overwhelming burden in a heartbeat.

And it's a burden more and more people are carrying. Collectively, Americans have more than 1 billion credit cards with more than $937 billion in outstanding balances. According to the Federal Reserve, average credit card debt has more than tripled since 1990; in that year, the average household carried just under $3,000 in credit card balances, compared with more than $9,600 today. Add to that mortgages, car loans, and other debts, and it's easy to understand why so many people feel like they're drowning in debt.

Part of the problem is that many people don't understand how the credit system works or how their credit histories affect their lives. Your credit score goes far beyond the interest rate you get when you apply for a loan or credit card. It also can affect your ability to get a job, housing, and even insurance.

In this chapter, we explain credit reports and credit scores, showing you what factors affect your credit and what you can do to improve your credit-worthiness. We discuss the difference between good debt and bad debt. We take you through the process of creating a budget so you can manage your debt better (and, thus, improve your credit). And we show you ways to free up more of your money so you can make the financial choices that are most important to you.

Understanding Your Credit

You're probably at least vaguely aware that, whenever you apply for a loan, whether it's a mortgage, a car loan, or a credit card, the lender pulls a credit report to help determine whether you're a good credit risk — that is, how likely you are to repay the loan. But you may not know what's on your credit report, how to improve your credit, how to fix errors, or even that what's in your credit report affects the interest rate you pay on the loans you do get.

Lenders use credit reports to see what kinds of accounts you have and how you've handled credit in the past. If you have a variety of long-standing accounts that are current, and you haven't run up your credit card balances, you're probably a pretty good credit risk. But if you haven't had credit for very long, or if you've got a history of late payments, lenders probably will get a little squiggly-eyed, and if they do approve a loan, you may pay a higher interest rate.

How much difference does your credit score make? Say you're shopping for a $300,000 mortgage. With a high credit score, you may qualify for an interest rate in the 5.5 percent to 6 percent range, so your monthly payments would be between $1,500 and $2,000 on a 30-year fixed-rate mortgage. But if your score is in the lowest range, you'll be lucky to get an interest rate of less than 10 percent, and your monthly payments would be around $2,600 — or between $600 and $1,100 more per month.

The credit bureaus

There are three credit reporting agencies in the United States: Equifax, Experian, and TransUnion. Not all lenders use the same credit bureau, so it's important to check your reports from all three agencies to make sure they're accurate.

Fortunately, it's easy to keep tabs on all three of your credit reports. In 2003, Congress passed the Fair and Accurate Credit Transactions (FACT) Act, which entitles consumers to one free credit report a year from each of the three credit bureaus. You can get your free reports online at www.annualcredit report.com or by calling 877-322-8228.

You can order all three reports at the same time, which is useful to compare the information each agency has. You also can choose to get one free report every four months, which allows you to keep tabs on your credit report (without charge) more frequently and lets you see the most current information.

Any time you're turned down for credit, housing, or employment, you can get a free copy of your credit report from each of the three credit bureaus if you request them within 60 days.

When you have a copy of your credit report, make sure the information on it is accurate. Accounts and payment histories stay on your credit report for seven years; bankruptcy can stay on your report for as long as ten years. So even an account that you closed five years ago can still show up on your report.

If you find an error on your report, you have to ask in writing for it to be corrected. The same is true if there are special circumstances you want potential creditors to be aware of. For example, if you filed bankruptcy because a business failed or you had huge medical bills, you may want to write a brief explanation that can be attached to your report. (Potential creditors are going to ask you about it anyway, so you may as well make it part of your credit report.)

Just because you write to a credit bureau about an error on your report doesn't mean the error will be corrected immediately. Although the credit bureaus are required to investigate any claims of errors and make corrections, the process can take several months. In the meantime, your written objection will be part of your credit report.

Your credit score

Credit reports are pretty straightforward. Credit scores are less so. For one thing, you probably have three different credit scores, because each of the credit bureaus has its own calculation for assigning scores. For another, those scores may fluctuate by 20 points or more. Here's the scoop on the various types of credit scores:

✔ **FICO score:** Equifax uses the FICO score, developed by Fair Isaac Corporation, which is the best-known of the credit scores. Fair Isaac says 90 percent of the country's largest banks use FICO scores to help determine creditworthiness. Scores range from 300 to 850, with higher scores assigned to those with better credit histories. The average FICO score is around 700.

In 2008, Fair Isaac revised the rules for its scoring model. Under FICO '08, you won't be heavily penalized for occasional late payments, and you'll get more points if you have a variety of loan types — mortgage, car loan, and credit cards — because it shows you can manage different kinds of debt.

However, if you're maxed out on your credit cards or close to your limits, your FICO score will be lower. Most experts recommend using no more than 30 percent of your available credit; some even recommend limiting your credit card purchases to no more than 10 percent of your available credit.

Your score also will be lower if you have a history of "seriously delinquent" accounts, defined as payments that are late by 90 days or more. But if you're seriously delinquent on one account and all your other accounts are in good standing, that one delinquency won't hurt you as much.

✔ **Your "FAKO" scores:** The credit scores used by Experian and TransUnion are sometimes referred to as "FAKO" scores — a play on fake FICO scores. Experian calls its version a PLUS score; TransUnion calls its version a Vantage Score, which is a combination of points (ranging from 501 to 990) and a letter grade.

The problem with having three credit scores is that you can never be sure which score potential lenders are seeing when they pull your credit report. And even if you get free copies of your reports from all three bureaus, those reports won't include your credit score, FICO or FAKO. Free credit scores weren't included in the FACT Act, so you have to pay between $6 and $16 to get your score from a credit bureau.

Some credit card companies offer free access to your FICO score online. Others charge for this service, but we don't recommend signing up for it unless it's free, because it'll probably cost less to order your FICO score directly.

Although there are other credit scoring systems out there, FICO is still the most commonly used score, especially for mortgage lenders. So, if you want to buy your credit score but aren't sure which one to get, we recommend buying the FICO. You can buy it directly from www.myfico.com, or you can pay for it when you get your free credit report from Equifax.

Things that affect your FICO score

TransUnion and Experian have their own proprietary formulas for determining credit scores, and the various factors we cover here may be weighted differently than they are for your FICO score. Because FICO is so widely used, this section focuses on how these factors affect your FICO score. No matter which credit bureau a lender uses, though, your credit score affects whether you can get new credit and how much you'll pay for it.

Payment history accounts for 35 percent of your FICO score. If you have a record of paying creditors on time — and paying more than the minimum, especially in the case of credit cards — your score will be higher.

Next, in terms of scoring weight, is how much you owe. The more you owe in total — mortgage, auto and personal loans, and credit cards combined — the lower your score will be. The amount you owe accounts for 30 percent of your FICO score.

Also in the equation is how "thin" your credit history is. If you're young and have only one or two credit cards or loans, or if you haven't had credit for long, your score will be lower; there isn't enough information for a lender to determine how risky a borrower you are. The thinness or thickness of your credit history accounts for 15 percent of your FICO score.

This is why experts recommend you keep credit accounts open, even if you have a zero balance and don't use the credit card or line of credit. Older accounts carry more weight than newer ones. Besides, another factor is how much of your available credit you've used: Those older, unused accounts help lower your debt-to-available credit ratio and bump up your score. (The exception: credit cards that require a yearly "membership fee." If you have a card that charges you such a fee, you may be better off dropping it and switching to a card without a fee — unless you intend to apply for a mortgage or other major loan within the next 6 to 12 months. In that case, the age of the account probably will help you more than the fee will hurt you, and you can cancel the fee-charging card after you get approved for your new loan.

The variety of credit you have accounts for 10 percent of your score, and new credit accounts for another 10 percent. Lenders like to see a mix of fixed loans (mortgages, car loans, and personal loans) and revolving credit (credit cards and lines of credit). But if you've opened a lot of new accounts recently, that can negatively affect your score.

Accounts that are two years old or older will help your credit score; accounts that are less than six months old probably will drag your score down a bit.

Every time you apply for new credit, you knock a few points off your credit score — usually between 2 and 5 points. So you may want to give those store credit offers a miss, even if they offer an immediate discount just for applying. Even those 0 percent balance transfer offers can affect your credit score.

Things you can do to boost your score

There are some things you can do to build up your credit score:

- **Make sure you pay your bills on time.** This is the single most important thing you can do to boost your score. Chronic late payments show potential creditors a pattern of managing credit poorly, and you'll lose points quickly.

- **Make more than the minimum payment.** This applies not just to credit cards but to every kind of loan. If your budget allows, add $5 or $10 to your monthly car payment or mortgage payment. You'll lower the total interest you pay because those few extra bucks are applied to the principal. Plus, you may get a hefty point boost if you pay off those loans a month or two early.

- **Pay down your credit card balances, and don't let them creep back up.** Lenders look at the ratio between how much you owe and how much credit you have available to you. The closer you are to your limits on your credit cards, the lower your credit score goes.

- **Plan ahead for credit applications.** If you know you want to buy a car in the next few months, don't apply for any other credit, and pay down your existing balances as much as possible beforehand. Also, avoid making new charges in the two months before you apply for that loan; that way, payments should be recorded in your credit report, and your balance-to-available-credit ratio will be lower.

- **Make time your ally.** Late payments lose their importance as time goes on. So if you had a rough patch a few months ago but have been making your payments on time ever since, take heart in the knowledge that those late payments won't haunt you forever. The important thing is to build up a history of consistently on-time payments from now on.

Millionaires (and those in the making) think of credit cards as a convenience, not a source of money. Limit yourself to two credit cards, and, if possible, make one of them a cash-back reward card. Charge only as much as you can afford to pay at one time, and pay your balances off in full every month.

Good Debt versus Bad Debt

All debt is not created equal. Good debt is the kind that allows you to leverage your limited assets into more assets — like buying a home or expanding a business. Bad debt is the kind that lets you live above your means (at least until the bills come due) and doesn't produce any assets, like using your credit card to eat out most days or taking a fancy vacation.

If you're like most people, you carry a mix of good and bad debt. Your mortgage is a good debt, because when you're done paying the loan, you'll have an asset that will be worth more than your initial purchase price; real estate boom-and-bust cycles notwithstanding, the average home doubles in value within ten years.

Auto loans also are considered good debt, even though your car will be worth less when you've paid it off. That's because your car gives you leverage beyond its intrinsic worth: It allows you to commute to your job, to shop where you like, to get back and forth to doctors' appointments, and so on. Likewise, college loans are good debt, because chances are good that you can leverage your education into a higher-paying job.

Because cars depreciate so fast — a new car loses as much as 40 percent of its value as soon as you drive it off the lot — the only way to get your money's worth out of any vehicle is to drive it until the maintenance costs get close to what a different vehicle would cost. With car payments averaging between $300 and $400 a month, you're probably better off driving your old car as long as maintenance and repairs don't exceed $2,500 a year.

And debt that allows your money to work harder for you can be good, too. Suppose you have $5,000 in your savings account, and you're trying to decide whether to invest it or use it to make some repairs or improvements to your house. If you can get a loan for a low interest rate, and if you can invest that $5,000 in something that will earn a higher interest rate, it may make sense to get the loan for your home improvement projects and put your cash in an investment account.

Figuring out what your debt costs you

One reason so many people are confounded by debt is that the terms don't always mean what you think they mean. Take 0 percent financing: If you buy a refrigerator or a couch under a plan that offers 0 percent financing for six months, you may think that interest doesn't start accruing until the seventh month. But often, buried in the fine print, is a notice that, if you don't pay the balance in full by the sixth month, you'll be charged interest dating back to the first day of the loan — which means you end up paying interest on the full balance.

A similar gotcha is true for 0 percent balance transfer offers from credit card companies. Most credit cards charge a fee for transferring balances; the average is 3 percent, so if you transfer a $10,000 balance, the fee will be $300. Some cards cap their transfer fees at $75, but this practice is becoming rarer. More commonly, there's a minimum fee and no maximum.

Even with the fee, you may be able to save money by transferring debt from a high-interest card to one with a 0 percent offer. But check the fine print to find out how long the 0 percent interest is in effect and what the interest rate goes to after the introductory offer expires. Of course, the best thing to do is make sure you pay off the transferred balance before the 0 percent interest offer expires.

Making use of online calculators

No matter what kind of debt you have (or are considering), there's a calculator on the Internet that can help you figure out exactly how much it will cost you. Here are some of our favorites:

- **Mortgage-Calc.com (www.mortgage-calc.com):** This site has debt-consolidation and amortization calculators, so you can see how much money you'd save if you made extra payments on your loans.

- **Bankrate.com (www.bankrate.com/brm/calculators/autos.asp):** This site has calculators to let you determine whether you're better off taking a rebate or a financing offer on a car, whether you're better off buying or leasing a car, and depreciation information on new or used cars. Bankrate.com also has a multitude of other calculators for things like mortgages, investments, and other types of loans or savings.

- **Kiplinger.com (www.kiplinger.com/tools):** This site has credit card calculators that show you what you'll pay if you stick with the minimum monthly payments and what you need to pay to get your balance to zero by your target date.

- **CNNMoney.com (http://cgi.money.cnn.com/tools):** The Personal Finance section of this site has a variety of calculators to help you come up with a debt reduction plan, assess how home improvements will affect the value of your house, calculate your net worth or your retirement fund's growth, and compare college costs and even the cost of living in different regions of the United States.

- **CCH Financial Planning Toolkit (www.finance.cch.com/tools/calcs.asp):** On this site, calculators are sorted into categories, including mortgages, auto loans, credit card debt, debt consolidation, savings plans, insurance, taxes, and personal and business finance.

Understanding other kinds of costs

Some people make poor choices in their anxiety to get their debt under control, leaving themselves vulnerable to even worse consequences. It's not that there isn't some logic behind these decisions — but the logic is flawed.

For example, some people are tempted to tap the equity in their homes to buy a car or pay off their credit cards. The logic is simple: Home-equity interest rates usually are lower than the interest rates on other kinds of credit — in the case of many credit cards, a *lot* lower. Besides, the interest on home-equity loans usually is tax deductible (as long as you don't exceed the loan limits set by the Internal Revenue Service).

The flaw is in the worst-case scenario. If you default on a car loan, the lender can take only your car. Credit cards (and personal loans, if you haven't put up any collateral) are unsecured, which means the credit card company can't come after your other assets if you default.

But with a home-equity loan, you could lose your home if you default. (This is why we dislike marketing materials that suggest using a home equity loan to finance a vacation. We've never heard of a vacation so fabulous that it's worth risking the loss of your home.)

The same is true of taking a loan from your 401(k) to pay off debts. True, you pay yourself back with interest, and the interest is lower than you'd pay on any other kind of loan. But you're basically trading a less secure financial future for a more stable financial present. Not only do you miss out on the gains your principal would have made if you'd left it alone, but also, you're being taxed twice on the loan — first because you repay it with after-tax dollars, and again when you retire and start to withdraw those funds.

Getting a handle on your debt

The insidious thing about debt is that it's so easy to get into without even thinking and so darned difficult to get out of unless you think. If you're like most people, you probably aren't exactly eager to confront your debt load and figure out a plan for coping with it. But, believe us, it's the one thing you can do right now that will affect your life for years to come.

Start with figuring out where you are debtwise. List all your debts — mortgage, car, personal, and college loans, and your credit cards. This exercise shows you exactly how much of your income is going toward debt each month, and that gives you an idea of whether you're carrying too much debt.

Most experts recommend that debt payments take up no more than half of your monthly take-home pay, and some even recommend keeping it under one-third of your net income. That's a worthy goal, but we don't want you to panic about your debt load if it's higher than these recommendations. The fact is, your current debt level is a barometer to help you set your financial priorities (getting rid of debt and starting a savings plan are the two critical keys to becoming financially secure) and decide whether adding to your debt load would put you closer to or farther away from your goals.

Next, set aside the debts with fixed monthly payments and concentrate on the cards. Why? Because your credit cards likely have higher interest rates than your other loans, and, for most people, credit card debt is the toughest kind of debt to get under control. Write down each card, the balance, the interest rate, and the minimum monthly payment.

Finally, prioritize your credit card debt. You can do this one of two ways:

- ✔ You can target the balance with the highest interest rate and pay it down first (making sure you pay the minimum balance on the others on time, of course), and then move on to the card with the next-highest interest rate, and so on.

- ✔ You can choose to pay off the card with the smallest balance first. This approach makes sense if the interest rates on your cards are within a point or two of one another. It's also helpful from a psychological standpoint, especially if you have trouble staying motivated and sticking to your plan. Paying off one card, even if it's a small balance, gives you confidence and a sense of accomplishment.

If you're struggling to make the minimum payments, look into debt-consolidation loans or contact a credit counseling center for help. You can find reputable counseling firms through the National Federation for Credit Counseling's Web site (www.nfcc.org).

The key to any debt-reduction plan is to avoid reloading your credit cards with new charges that have to be paid off. If you have trouble resisting the temptation to charge purchases you don't really need or want, take the credit cards out of your wallet and put them in a drawer. They'll be there if you really need them, but if it's inconvenient to get to them, you'll be less likely to use them unnecessarily.

Organizing Your Budget

According to the Pew Research Center, Americans are pretty evenly divided when it comes to using a formal budget to manage money: Forty-eight percent of Americans say they use a budget, and 51 percent don't. This is true of this book's authors, too: Meg uses a written budget religiously, and Bob keeps his finances in his head.

The Pew survey indicated that the people who use formal budgets either have a lot of loans or credit card debt to pay off, or they had problems managing debt in the past. Meg falls into the latter category; before she began keeping track of her income and expenses, she would find herself scrambling to make her car payment or rent because she didn't pay attention to the relationship between when she got paid and when her bills were due. With a written budget, she no longer has that trouble, because she can see at a glance which bills need to be paid out of every paycheck. Now she keeps a written budget for at least the next six months so she can plan for quarterly or semiannual expenses like car insurance and her water/sewer bill. An added bonus: Whenever her checkbook balance looks unusually high, she can check her budget to see if she forgot about an upcoming bill.

Even if you're like Bob and don't need a written budget to keep track of your bills, you can benefit from creating one. It's like cleaning out a storage closet: It gives you a better idea of what you have, what you want to keep, and what you can get rid of.

A written budget is the easiest way to keep track of your spending and make sure you're using your money the way you really want to. A budget also gives you a road map for moving toward your other financial goals and lets you keep track of your progress toward those goals.

Getting started

If you've never made a budget before, it can feel a little intimidating. Let's face it: Most people have a love/hate relationship with money, and it's understandable if you're not exactly eager to pin down your own spending habits. But financial planning is a journey like any other, and you can't possibly figure out how to get where you want to go if you don't know where you're starting from.

First (and easiest), figure out your income. If you receive a set salary, don't include any extras like bonuses; use only what you can count on as your base income. If your pay depends on how many hours you work or commissions you earn, total your last three months of take-home pay and divide by the number of pay periods to come up with an average. If you get paid every week, for example, you'd divide your three-month total by 12; if you get paid every two weeks, you'd divide the total by 6. Don't include overtime here; again, you want to base your budget on what you can count on, not on maybes.

If you overestimate your income, you'll probably overestimate what you can spend, too, and that can cause big problems. If you underestimate your income, any extra is gravy that can be applied to your goals — paying down your credit cards, for example, or saving for that nice digital camera you've always coveted.

Next, figure out your expenses. Collect your receipts and bill payment information from the past three months, and sort them into categories: mortgage or rent payment, car payment, utilities, groceries, gas, insurance, clothing, entertainment, and so on.

If you don't keep receipts, your bank statements can help you figure out where you spent your money the past few months. If you don't have your statements or can't access them online, you may have to keep your receipts and statements for a month so you can come up with the figures you need for your budget.

Creating your budget

There are all kinds of ways to write a budget. When Meg first started writing down her budget, she used a sheet of legal paper with a series of rows and columns. The columns were headed with the month, and the rows were titled with the bills that needed paying; when she paid a bill, she just put a check mark in that month's column for that bill.

Today, Meg uses a Microsoft Excel spreadsheet to manage her budget, which shows her not only which bills need to be paid when, but also how much cash she has left over each pay period.

The best savers treat paying into their savings account like any other bill. Meg's spreadsheet includes contributions to her various savings accounts, so the cash she has left over each pay period really is what's left after paying both her bills and herself.

If you have trouble thinking of your budget — and particularly your estimated expenses like groceries and entertainment — as "fixed," try imagining that your household is a business. If you don't meet your budget targets, your boss is going to have apoplexy. If you do meet your targets, you get a pat on the back and maybe even a bonus — like the ability to buy something you've been saving for.

There are two main purposes behind creating a budget, The first is to identify where your money goes. The second is to give yourself control over your spending. If your budget allows for $100 to be spent on groceries this week, and you have to stock up on expensive items like paper goods and detergents, that may mean you can't splurge on steak until next week. On the other hand, if you're having 20 people over for dinner next week, you may want to buy the bare minimum in groceries this week so you can spend extra next week.

Personal finance software like Quicken and Microsoft Money makes it easy to create a budget, and some software even lets you download your bank statements automatically. You can edit the categories to monitor all your spending or just portions of it (although we recommend monitoring all your spending, at least to start with, because it's easy to overlook potential problems if you just concentrate on one or two specific areas). Some of these programs also use your past spending patterns to provide estimates of your future spending.

Keeping it flexible

The Pew survey found that people who use a formal budget are more likely to review their household expenses on a regular basis. That regular review is especially critical if you have trouble sticking with your plan, but it's also helpful to make adjustments when you need to.

 Just because you've written down your budget doesn't mean you can't or shouldn't tweak it once in a while. Unexpected expenses may require some juggling to your ideal budget, and your financial priorities will change as your life changes. Your budget is your guideline. As you get used to working with it, you may find that you've overestimated some expenses and underestimated others. That's fine. Don't beat yourself up for not following your budget exactly; instead, look at it as an opportunity to fine-tune.

Freeing Up Your Money

Once you have your budget in place, you can start looking for ways to trim your spending so you have more money to put toward your financial goals. Don't be afraid to start small, either. Saving a buck or two here and there gets you in the frame of mind to keep a reasonable rein on expenses, and those small savings really do add up.

There are lots of places where you can squeeze a bit more value out of your dollar — your car; your home; and shopping for everything from groceries to home furnishings, vacations, and services.

Saving money with your car

You may not be able to reduce your monthly payment, but you can make sure you're getting the best value out of your car. Here are some things to look at:

✔ **Fuel and maintenance:** You can save on fuel costs by carpooling and planning your errands to reduce total miles driven. Some gas stations offer discounts for cash; others offer discounts if you use their credit card. If you don't change the oil yourself, keep an eye out for coupons and discounts at lube shops.

You can make a tank of gas go farther by making sure your tires are properly inflated and cleaning unnecessary weight out of the trunk or cargo area.

✔ **Insurance:** Higher deductibles will lower your premiums. Make sure you're getting any discounts you're entitled to for antilock brakes, passive restraints, and antitheft devices, as well as a good-driver discount or a discount for taking a defensive-driving course.

✔ **Car shopping:** New cars are great, but they lose a huge chunk of their value as soon as you sign the contract. Used cars have already depreciated, so you're paying closer to what they're really worth. They're also usually cheaper to insure and may be cheaper to register than new cars.

Bob, whose goal is to drive the same car for ten years, likes to use the Internet to search for "slightly used" cars (ones with 18,000 or fewer miles). His favorite sites are Cars.com, AutoTrader.com, and Edmunds.com; at these sites, you can specify color, options, and the distance from your zip code.

Saving money at home

Running a household is more than just paying the mortgage every month. There are utility bills, maintenance needs, entertainment options — a whole slew of categories where you may be spending more than you need to. Here are some areas to investigate for potential savings:

✔ **Utility bills:** Aside from turning the lights off and yelling at the kids to close the refrigerator, you can lower your utility bills by buying energy-efficient appliances and light bulbs, using curtains and blinds to keep the house cooler in the summer and warmer in the winter, and installing a programmable thermostat so you aren't heating or cooling your home when you don't need to. Using high-energy appliances like clothes dryers and dishwashers during nonpeak times — before 9 a.m. or after 8 p.m. — also saves money.

✔ **Maintenance and repairs:** Been putting off fixing that annoying leak in the kitchen faucet or the broken window in the guest room? Fixing small problems before they have a chance to become big ones can save you thousands down the road. To save money on those small problems, shop sales at your home-improvement center, or look for a discount lumberyard or hardware store where you can buy overstock items for much less than retail.

✔ **Home-based services:** If you're paying someone to mow your lawn, shovel your driveway, or clean your house, you can save money by either doing these chores yourself or cutting back on how often you pay others to do them. If you can't physically do some of these chores, maybe you can work out a trade with a neighbor: If he mows your lawn once a week, you'll babysit for his kids every Saturday night.

✔ **Telephone, TV, and Internet:** Do you need both a land line and a cellphone? If you want or need both, consider a local-only plan for your land line and using your cellphone for long-distance calls (assuming long-distance calls are included in your cellphone plan, of course). Or consider bundling your phone, TV, and Internet service; you may be able to save $20 or more a month — that's $240 a year.

If you're paying for a lot of TV channels you don't watch, consider switching to a less-expensive cable or satellite package.

✔ **Insurance and taxes:** A higher deductible on your homeowner's insurance will lower your premium, and challenging your assessment can lower your tax bill. Also, check to see if your local government offers any property-tax exemptions you may qualify for (see Chapter 14).

Depending on the housing and credit markets where you live, you may be able to save quite a bit of money by refinancing your mortgage. The general rule is, if you can lower your interest rate by at least 2 full points, refinancing may make sense for you. Keep in mind, though, that you may be giving up the equity you've already built in your home if you decide to refinance.

Saving money when you're shopping

You can't avoid spending money sometimes; you've got to eat, after all, and you have to have clothes and the occasional haircut. But that doesn't mean you have to overspend on these things. Here are some ways you can stay within your budget for common expenses:

✔ **Look for sales on items you'd buy anyway, and use coupons for those items, too.** If you save only $10 a week, that's $520 a year. Search the Internet for coupons on the products you use. Try www.smartsource.com, www.grocerycoupons.net (where you place an "order" for coupons that are then mailed to you) and www.coupons.com for a variety of coupons. Or go to brand-specific sites like www.scottcommonsense.com, www.bettycrocker.com, and www.kraftfoods.com for coupons on a specific company's products.

✔ **Check out dollar stores for paper goods and cleaning supplies.**

✔ **Consider joining a warehouse club like Sam's Club, Costco, or BJ's Warehouse to take advantage of bulk discounts.** Just make sure you actually go. Paying a membership fee for a store you never use doesn't make sense.

Don't get suckered into buying anything just because the price is good. It's not a bargain if you're spending money on something you won't use.

✔ **If your grocery store has a free rewards program, sign up for it.** You'll get special discounts that way.

✔ **Buy store brands instead of national brands.** Often, store brands are surplus products from the national companies, so you get similar quality at a better price.

✔ **At the mall, shop the clearance rack.** You may find nothing that interests you, but once in a while you'll find a treasure at a great price. You can save a lot of money by shopping only sales and ignoring anything that isn't on sale. Also keep an eye out for special coupons that give you additional discounts on your entire purchase or the most expensive item you purchase.

✔ **Shop online.** Shopping online can save you even more than shopping sales, because you don't have any transportation expenses. Sometimes you can get free shipping, too, so you're not even paying for the convenience of shopping from home. On big purchases, like furniture, the shipping charges may be lower than the delivery fee that a bricks-and-mortar store would charge. Online retailers often have much better prices, too, and some even have the virtual equivalent of a clearance rack.

Online shopping, like any other kind, can be addictive. If this is true for you, you may want to keep your credit cards in a separate room from your computer; creating a physical barrier between your spending impulses and the means to spend can temper those urges. Also, remember that, if you order something online and decide to return it, you'll probably have to pay the shipping charges.

✔ **Travel during off-peak seasons.** You can get good deals by avoiding the peak seasons for vacation destinations and planning your trip for the off-season or *shoulder season* — the few weeks at either end of the peak season when fewer people are vacationing but most attractions are open for business.

✔ **Shop around for the best prices on services.** Rates for things like dry cleaning, veterinary care, haircuts, manicures, and other services can vary greatly. Your goal is to find the best service for the least amount of money.

Kicking expensive habits, like smoking or buying lottery tickets, can ease the strain on your budget, too. If you can't or don't want to quit, look for ways to cut back on those expenses: Switch to a cheaper brand of cigarettes or tobacco, and spend only half of your usual lottery-ticket money. (Bob calls lottery tickets a tax on the math-impaired, because the odds of winning are so lousy.)

Avoiding Fees and Extra Charges

For many people, the easiest way to free up money is to stop paying unnecessary fees and charges on their bank accounts, credit cards, and other bills. Bob knew one person who shelled out more than $2,500 a year to the bank in overdraft charges, simply because he didn't balance his checkbook regularly.

No one ever got rich spending money unnecessarily. But that's exactly what you do when you get lax about paying bills and rack up late fees and other penalties. Think of it as a game: If you don't pay attention to due dates and the balances in your accounts, the bank or creditor wins extra money. But if you do pay attention, you get to keep that extra money in your pocket, and you win a better credit score — which makes the cost of credit cheaper for you.

Overdraft charges

From the consumer's point of view, overdraft charges make no sense at all. If there isn't enough money in your account to cover the check you wrote or the debit card charge you authorized, what makes the bank think you can afford to pay $34 for being overdrawn?

But from the bank's point of view, overdraft charges are essentially short-term loans. They pay the check or charge for you as a "convenience" (instead of returning the check for insufficient funds or denying the charge) and then apply the fee for this service to your account. And they make a ton of money off these "convenience" fees; according to one report, in 2007, American account-holders paid $38 *billion* in various bank fees, including overdraft charges.

The easiest way to avoid overdraft charges, of course, is to keep a close eye on your balance. But if you have trouble doing that, here are some ways to fool yourself into avoiding those fees:

✔ **Keep a "secret" cushion in your checking account.** For years, Meg kept an extra $50 in her checking account that she didn't record in the check register. This was particularly useful when she and her husband were both tapping into the same account; it reduced the risk that one of them, unaware of what the other had spent, would overdraw the account.

✔ **Look into overdraft protection linked to your savings account.** Meg's credit union will transfer money from her savings account to her checking account up to three times a month for free; fees kick in for additional transfers.

✔ **Ask to have the fee waived.** If overdrafts are rare for you, your bank may be willing to waive the overdraft charge. (They're less likely to do it if you're a chronic overdrawer.) Call your bank's customer service number or go to the bank in person to plead your case — and always be polite.

✔ **Negotiate a reduction.** If you have a lot of fees, you probably won't be able to get them all waived, but you may be able to negotiate with the bank to reduce them by as much as half. Again, this may not work if you're a habitual offender. But then, if you frequently incur overdraft charges, it's time to handle your checking account differently.

✔ **Streamline your accounts.** If your money is spread among several accounts at your bank and you find yourself overdrawn more than twice a year, you may be better off consolidating your accounts. Alternatively, you can use one bank for your regular checking and savings, and put your other money in accounts at a different bank.

Maintenance fees

"Free" checking and other types of accounts aren't always free. At many banks, you have to keep a minimum balance in your checking and savings accounts to avoid monthly maintenance charges. Sometimes banks will charge these fees if your balance dips below the minimum for even a single day during the month. Often the minimums are high: $2,500 is common, and some require $10,000 minimum balances.

No-minimum accounts are a better deal, especially because few checking accounts pay interest these days. If you've got an extra $10,000 lying around, you'd be better off investing that money (in a CD or money market mutual fund, if nothing else) than letting the bank sit on it indefinitely.

The trade-off for truly free accounts usually is that you'll get very little to no interest. On the other hand, your balance won't be gouged by fees every month, either.

Credit unions often charge lower fees than banks, and many of them now have extensive ATM networks and other services that make them attractive alternatives to commercial banks. Check out the fees and requirements for credit unions in your area, and see if you could save money by transferring your accounts.

Late fees

Earlier in this chapter (in the "Understanding Your Credit" section), we discuss the havoc that paying late can wreak on your ability to get future credit at a decent interest rate. But there's another, more immediate reason to pay your bills on time: It saves you money.

Credit cards get the most attention for their late fees, but the truth is that nearly everybody charges a fee if you don't pay the bill on time — the electric company, the cable company, the trash collection company, the telephone company, everybody. And even though the late charge for each bill may be small — often just a couple of bucks — they add up. If you're late on five bills and each bill carries a $2 late charge, that's an extra $10 you didn't have to spend this month. If you do that every month, you're giving away $120 a year of your own hard-earned money.

If that isn't enough motivation, consider what happens when you're late with your credit card payment. The average late fee is now $39. If you have to pay that fee every month, you're giving your credit card company an extra $468 a year. If you have two credit cards, you're turning over $936 a year in late charges. Three cards, $1,404 a year; four cards, $1,872 a year; and five cards, $2,340 a year — nearly $200 a month in late fees alone.

But you don't stop paying there. Most credit card companies will hike the interest on your account to their "default" rate if you pay late twice in any six months (some even go to their default rate after only one late payment), and those default rates can be as high as 34 percent.

Let's put that 34 percent in perspective. If you have a credit card with 8.9 percent interest and a $1,000 balance, and you pay the minimum $10 each month, it'll take you seven years and three months to pay it off and cost you a total of $270 in interest. If you have that same $1,000 balance at 34 percent interest, your minimum payment stays at $10, but it will take you more than *50 years* to pay it off, and you'll pay a total of — are you sitting down? — $10,762 in interest. (If you don't believe us, check it out for yourself at www.calculatorweb.com/calculators/creditcardcalc.shtml.)

Paying bills online can save you from late fees; many companies allow you to make same-day payments without triggering a convenience charge or processing fee. If you're uncomfortable using this method, make sure you mail your payments at least four or five days before they're due so they can be posted to your account on or before the due date.

Many credit card companies and other businesses will charge you a fee to make a payment over the phone (and some will charge you a fee for a same-day online payment). If you're otherwise going to be hit with a high late fee, it may make more sense to pay the phone-pay fee.

The best way to avoid late fees is to make sure you pay your bills well in advance of the due date. Using a written budget can help you keep on top of your payments. Another handy method is getting a sorter that has slots for each day of the month; every bill that's due on the 17th, for example, goes in the slot marked "17." You also can use a calendar to write down due dates for various bills or a divided folder labeled with each payday or the days of the month.

If you have trouble paying bills on time, for whatever reason, add "Paying bills on time" to your list of goals (see Chapter 3). Writing it down makes it more likely that you'll remember to pay your bills on time, and every time you pay a bill before it's due, you can give yourself a pat on the back.

Chapter 7

Starting on Your Savings Plan

. . . .

In This Chapter

▷ Preparing for life's curveballs

▷ Learning to enjoy the act of saving money

▷ Identifying your savings priorities

▷ Figuring out how you can attain your goals

. . . .

*A*mericans are lousy at saving. Even those who do have regular savings plans say they don't save enough, and that's true for both the wealthy and the poor (although, naturally enough, more of those with lower incomes say they don't save enough). How bad is the savings situation? According to a 2008 survey by the Pew Research Center's Social & Demographic Trends project, 75 percent of American adults say they don't save enough.

Other surveys are just as discouraging. The Consumer Federation of America, which sponsors an annual America Saves Week with other consumer and social groups, reported in 2008 that only 40 percent of Americans have separate savings accounts for emergencies. Of those who do have rainy-day funds, one-third of Americans have less than $2,000 set aside for unexpected expenses.

Wealthier households are more likely than poorer ones to set aside some of their income in savings; 60 percent of those who make more than $75,000 have emergency funds, compared with only 25 percent of those who make $25,000 or less. Overall, though, the U.S. Commerce Department says, Americans are saving less today than they have at any time since the Great Depression.

So, if you're among those who aren't saving enough, or even at all, you can stop beating yourself up: You've got plenty of company.

But that doesn't mean you should continue to hang with the nonsavers. Saving is the first and most basic step in taking control of your finances. You can't build wealth if you don't have anything left over at the end of the week, the month, or the year to build on. In this chapter, we discuss why saving is important to your quality of life, how to start your own savings plan today, and how to make saving a regular habit.

Understanding Why Saving Matters

There's this to be said for a poor economy: It motivates you to cut back on spending and focus on saving. It's simple psychology, really. In flush times, your brain leaps to the conclusion that things will always be at least this good, so saving for a rainy day drops to the bottom of your to-do list (if it doesn't disappear from your list altogether). But when the economy slows down, your brain kicks into survival mode, and you start thinking about what you'll do if things get even worse.

Regardless of what the economy is doing, though, saving matters, because there are no guarantees that today's circumstances will be the same tomorrow. You may be blindsided by unexpected expenses or sudden, major changes in your life. Without a cash cushion, these things can wreak havoc on your finances, and their effects may linger much longer than you'd expect.

Unexpected expenses

Here's your mantra to remind you why saving is important: You always need car-repair money.

It's not just that your muffler might drop off on the highway tomorrow or that you really should get new tires before next winter. Suppose you hit a deer on your way to work, or someone hits you in the grocery-store parking lot? Even if your auto insurance covers most of the damage, you'll have to come up with the deductible — which, depending on your policy, could be $500 or more. If you don't have collision coverage, your out-of-pocket expenses will be even higher.

Even if you don't have a car, you're still vulnerable to unexpected expenses:

- ✔ Home maintenance and repairs
- ✔ Computer or electronics repairs
- ✔ Doctor visits and prescription co-pays
- ✔ Unplanned travel (getting to your parents in an emergency, for example)
- ✔ Veterinary bills for pets
- ✔ Rate hikes in utilities, insurance, services, or taxes
- ✔ Helping family with *their* unexpected expenses

Life is unpredictable. You may not run into any unexpected expenses for months or even years. On the other hand, you may go through a phase where one darned thing after another strains your finances. It's much better — and much less stressful — to have an emergency fund that you don't need than to need an emergency fund and not have one.

Major life changes

Nearly every time something big happens in your life, it comes with a price tag. Sometimes you can save up for these things ahead of time — for weddings and graduations, for example. But sometimes you'll have to dip into your emergency fund to tide you over until you recover your financial equilibrium.

Here are some examples of major life changes that an emergency fund can help with:

✔ **Adding to your household:** Having a child is one of those financial events you can often plan ahead for, although children *do* have a peculiar talent for draining your wallet in ways you'd never expect. But there are other ways your household might expand, even if only temporarily, and those times can stretch your budget to the breaking point. You'll probably spend more on groceries and entertainment if you have houseguests for a week. Your utility bills might go up if you take your cousin in for a month or two while he looks for his own place.

✔ **Losing an income:** If you get laid off, or your spouse or partner loses her job, a decent emergency fund can see you through until the income starts flowing again. And if the replacement income is lower than what you used to make, your emergency fund can help make up the difference.

In most states, if you become disabled or unemployed, you have to wait at least a week before you can start collecting worker's compensation, disability, or unemployment benefits. And, especially in the case of worker's compensation and disability, you may have to wait much longer before you see either a lump-sum check or regular benefits.

✔ **Medical emergencies:** Healthcare costs have been rising at triple or more the rate of inflation for years now, and there's no indication that the trend won't continue. Even if you have an excellent health-insurance plan, a medical emergency or illness can throw a whole series of monkey wrenches into your financial plan.

And it's not just your own health that can cause such problems. If your child, spouse, or parent gets sick and you have to miss work — or, in a worst-case scenario, leave your job altogether — to care for him, how will you pay your regular bills?

✔ **Divorce or death:** No matter what stereotypes say about one spouse taking the other to the cleaners, divorce is expensive for both parties. So is death. You can pay bills and other expenses out of your emergency fund until things get straightened out and back to normal — or settled into a new version of "normal."

✔ **Disasters and cataclysms:** As with car insurance, you probably have a deductible on your homeowner's insurance, so if a storm sends a tree crashing through your roof or fire destroys your garage, you'll be responsible for some out-of-pocket expenses. Then there are the things your insurance policy won't cover. Flood damage, for example, isn't covered in a typical home-insurance policy; you have to have a separate policy or a flood rider on your regular policy.

Even if you have insurance coverage for most of what you lose in a disaster, it can take a while to get the money. In the meantime, you may have to shell out for things like clothing, food, a rental car, or even temporary shelter.

If you still don't think having an emergency fund is important, you can skip the rest of this chapter — we can't help you. But if you're convinced that you need to start saving as soon as is humanly possible, read on. We've got lots of tips and suggestions to get you started.

An emergency fund is a basic tool of self-sufficiency and independence. When the unexpected happens — and it will — your emergency savings allow you to deal with it yourself. You don't have to rely on banks or credit card companies or relatives to bail you out, and you aren't forced into outrageous terms.

Developing a Saving Attitude

There may be such a thing as an "accidental saver," but we've never met one. Saving money is nearly impossible if you don't think about money. You have to know what you need and what you want — and the difference between needs and wants — and you have to make continual choices between what you want now and what you want for the future.

The first step is setting immediate, midrange, and long-term goals (see Chapter 3 for more on setting goals). When you know what your goals are, you can decide which of them takes priority — and you can adjust your priorities as circumstances warrant. Then you can make deliberate choices about when and how you spend the money you have. And — *voilà!* — you've developed a saving attitude.

Finding pleasure in saving

Starting on your savings plan can be a tough mental and emotional challenge. But after you've done it for a while, you'll find that you actually get a charge (no pun intended) out of saving. According to the Consumer Federation of America, new savers experience a psychological boost after just a few months; self-confidence in your ability to save grows as your savings balance grows.

Saving also becomes a fun mental challenge, like a treasure hunt. When Meg and her husband were decorating their new home, they shopped at yard sales and auctions for furniture, wall décor, and knickknacks. Not only did they find unique pieces, but they *never* paid retail — and the joy of finding their treasures was even greater because they didn't go over their budget. Bob and his wife have used the same strategy to find the things they wanted at prices they were willing to pay.

A key part of finding pleasure in saving is knowing what something is worth to you. Not what the price tag says, mind you, but what your head and your gut tell you your dollar limit is. When you overspend, you may get a headache or a sick feeling in the pit of your stomach — the physical manifestations of "buyer's remorse." But when you make a conscious decision about how much something is worth to you, you're willing to walk away (without more than a twinge of regret) when the price is too high, and you get more enjoyment out of your purchase when the price is right.

And this pleasure isn't limited to major purchases. When you get into the habit of assigning your own value to the things you want or need to buy and enjoying the feeling of saving, you'll find yourself seeking out ways to save on everyday items, too.

Fortunately, there are lots of options for you:

- ✔ **Dollar stores and deep-discount stores can save you lots of money on paper goods, cleaning supplies, cosmetics, holiday decorations, and a slew of other products.** They aren't always generics or brands you've never heard of, either; very often, these stores get overstocks of national brands that sell for three, four, or more times the price in "regular" retail stores.

- ✔ **Thrift shops and secondhand stores offer great deals on used furniture and clothing.** They're an excellent resource for new or practically new baby clothes, for example. You can often find quality goods at a fraction of the price you'd pay in a regular retail store.

> ✔ **Estate auctions and auction houses also are great places to seek out treasures at a reasonable price.** You'll pay a buyer's premium — usually 10 percent of the winning bid — and you have to be careful not to get carried away with your bidding, but, if you have the discipline to stop bidding when the price exceeds your predetermined limit, you can get some real bargains.

Need money to seed your savings account? Consider having your own yard sale. You can clean out the clutter in your home, shed, or garage and make a few bucks — maybe even considerable bucks, depending on what you have to sell. Then use the proceeds from your sale to start your savings account.

Saving for specific things

When there's a big-ticket item you want, you have three choices:

> ✔ You can whip out the credit card (or apply for in-store financing).
>
> ✔ You can walk away and push the thought of the item out of your mind.
>
> ✔ You can start a special savings plan for the item.

This may be the toughest part of developing a saving attitude, because saving for purchases is a bit too much like being a 6-year-old waiting for Christmas morning. And you're not just fighting your own emotions and impatience — you're up against our culture of conspicuous consumption and those tempting buy-now-pay-later offers that seem to accompany everything except a $4 latte. Small wonder that the seductive coaxing of the debt devil sounds so much louder in your ear than the whispers of the solvency angel counseling prudence.

On the other hand, there are few experiences more fulfilling than proving to yourself that you really do have control over your finances. Saving for a coveted purchase isn't always easy. But imagine the sense of accomplishment you'll feel when you come up with a plan that will allow you to buy what you want without jeopardizing your financial stability, and then see that plan through to the day when you can walk into the store with a full wallet and a clear conscience to buy the thing you've been saving for.

Changing your life

Financial experts often despair of Americans' motivation to change their money habits. No one is going to start saving a few bucks a week, they worry, if they don't see a link between saving and their quality of life.

So let's assume for a moment that you're one of those people the experts wring their hands about. Let's say you could save $10 a week pretty painlessly. How is $10 a week going to change your life?

Let's start with the numbers. Ten dollars a week is $520 a year. If you put that $10 a week into a savings account that pays 3.5 percent interest, you'd have $531.47 at the end of a year. It's not a fortune. But it might be enough to cover those unexpected car repairs we mentioned earlier in this chapter. And if you don't have any unexpected expenses, that money can just sit there, doing its job for you — earning more money.

If you keep saving that same $10 a week for 5 years in the same account with the same interest rate, you'll have $2,852.65. In 10 years, you'll have $6,248.27; in 15 years, you'll have $10,290.22; and in 30 years, you'll have $27,645.73. All from $10 a week earning quite a modest interest rate.

Is saving $520 a year, in itself, going to change your life? Probably not. But getting into the habit of saving surely will. Today, maybe all you can manage to put away is a few bucks a week. But after you get your credit cards and other debts paid off, you'll have more money to put aside — and you'll already be mentally primed to actually do that, because you've trained yourself to save.

Figuring Out Where to Start

Okay, you're all fired up to start saving right now, and you're ready to go down to the bank, plunk down your money in front of the teller, and say, "I want to open a savings account."

"Wait a minute," the accountant in your brain says. "You've got bills to pay with that money. You can't afford to put anything into savings."

The truth is, you can't afford *not* to put anything into savings. But you have to be realistic, too. First, you have to identify your priorities. Then you can figure out ways to get started on your savings plan and stick with it.

Setting your priorities

Talk to five different "experts" about what your financial priorities should be, and you'll get at least three different answers. Some say you should pay down your credit card debt before you start on a savings plan. Some say you should put money away for retirement before you worry about building an emergency fund. Some even say you should consider making extra payments on your mortgage first, instead of putting money in a savings account.

The reasoning is that, if you pay off your credit cards, you'll be able to use them in the event of an emergency; likewise, if you prepay on your mortgage, you'll build up more equity that you can tap if you need extra cash. There's also the number-crunching argument: You can't make as much interest in a savings account as you're paying in interest on your credit cards or mortgage, so, from a strict accounting point of view, it makes sense to use any extra cash to get rid of expensive debt. And, of course, the earlier you start saving for retirement, the bigger your nest egg will be when you punch the clock for the last time.

Unfortunately, this advice, though common, is ridiculous. Certainly, paying down your credit card debt and saving for retirement are important, and making extra payments on your mortgage can save you thousands of dollars in interest in the long run. But doing these things at the expense of building a cash cushion today makes no sense. Why? Because, if you don't have an emergency fund and you do have a money emergency, your only option is to go back (or further) into debt to deal with the emergency. That's not financial progress — that's an endless trip on a hamster wheel.

If you're struggling to make the minimum payments on your credit cards, don't add to your stress by trying to start a savings plan, too. Instead, look for ways you can put a dent in your credit card debt (the first step is to stop using them), figure out how long it will take you to get that under control, and set a target date for launching your savings plan.

If your employer offers a 401(k) plan, join it. Your contributions are taken out of your pay before taxes are calculated, so the difference in your take-home likely will be only a few bucks, and you'll never miss it. But if you have to choose between starting an emergency fund and starting an IRA on your own, we recommend building your emergency fund first.

Your priorities will change as your circumstances fluctuate. There's nothing wrong with having a larger-than-usual savings goal this month and a smaller-than-usual one next month; maybe your car-insurance premium is due next month, or maybe you have to buy birthday or graduation gifts, and that will eat up the cash you normally would put in your savings. That's okay. The key to taking charge of your finances is doing what you can with what you've got.

Paying yourself first

Paying yourself first is a fundamental axiom of financial security. But what does it mean, exactly? And how do you go about it?

The principle behind this is that, instead of attacking your finances on the spending end so you can find the money to save, you decide first how much to save and then adjust your spending habits to fit in with whatever you've got left. Payroll deductions for 401(k) plans are a pay-yourself-first mechanism, because you never handle the money you're putting in your 401(k).

That's the advantage to paying yourself first. If you never see the money in your checking account, you're less likely to want to spend it. And it's easier to avoid spending temptations when your savings are taken out first. When you pay yourself last, chances are, you'll pay yourself less — or not at all — because you won't have the same mental brake on your spending. This is true whether you plan to save a little or a lot. When the money hangs out in your checking account or as cash in your wallet, it's easier to rationalize spending some or all of it.

Say you intend to save $10 a week, and you tuck that $10 in your wallet until you can get to the bank to deposit it. Then a friend asks if you want to go out to lunch. You don't have much money left in your checking account, but you've got that $10. "Sure, let's go to lunch," you say, because part of your brain is thinking (a) "It's only $10, so I'm not really hurting myself that much" and (b) "I'll make it up next payday." Only, of course, you never do make it up next payday.

What if you've got $100 a week to save? You don't like carrying that much cash around, so it's in your checking account until you get around to transferring it to savings. Your friend asks you to go out to lunch. You say, "Sure," and maybe you go someplace that's a little more expensive because, hey, you've got that money in your checking account. And your brain is busy rationalizing that (a) you'll still have money left over to put in your savings, even if it's not as much as you planned, and (b) it's one little lunch bill that you can make up any time. Only, of course, you probably won't ever make it up.

In either case, you end up sabotaging your own savings plan, which is why financial experts — and we — recommend paying yourself first.

Making it automatic

Paying yourself first is easiest when it happens automatically. If you have to transfer funds yourself, you may find it slipping to the bottom of your to-do list. Fortunately, most banks and credit unions allow you to set up automatic transfers that can be tied to certain dates (if you get paid on the 1st and the 15th, for example) or paydays. If you sign up for direct deposit, you probably won't even have to pay a fee for the automatic transfer.

You can set up automatic transfers between accounts at different institutions, too. If your main account is at your local bank or credit union, but you can get a better interest rate from an online-only savings account like those offered by HSBC (www.hsbc.com) and ING Direct (www.ingdirect.com), you can set up both regular and one-time transfers.

Make sure you don't have to pay any fees for transferring funds. Especially if your account pays a low interest rate, fees can easily eat up any gains you may get on your deposits.

Start your automatic transfers at a rate you know you can live with — even if it's only $5 a week. When you get comfortable with paying yourself a small amount first, you can increase it to maximize your savings rate.

Putting it beyond temptation's reach

Saving is most effective when you have to put some effort into taking your money *out*. The effort makes you stop to think before you spend, so you're less likely to blow your savings on an impulse.

Here are some techniques to make accessing your savings more difficult but not impossible:

- ✔ **Ask your bank or credit union to link your ATM or debit card *only* to your checking account.** You should still be able to transfer funds in person or through the institution's Web site, so you can get to your money if and when you need it. But you won't be able to withdraw cash from your savings at an ATM.

- ✔ **Keep the ATM or debit card for your online savings account at home.** If you don't carry the card in your wallet, you won't be tempted to use it on a whim.

- ✔ **Use different institutions for your checking and savings accounts.** If you have to go to a different bank to access your savings, the lack of convenience will force you to make a conscious decision about whether you really want or need to spend the money.

Filling your emergency fund

The beauty of starting your savings plan today, no matter how little you can reliably save, is that, when your emergency savings account is fully funded, you can redirect your savings into other vehicles, like CDs or mutual funds, that will earn higher interest for you.

So how do you figure out how much you need in your emergency fund? There are lots of different measures. Here are some of the most commonly recommended ones:

- **Enough to cover living expenses for a period of time:** Most financial experts recommend having the equivalent of three to six months of living expenses in your emergency fund. If your monthly expenses — housing, food, transportation, loan and credit card payments, and everything else in your monthly budget — are $3,000, you should aim to have between $9,000 and $18,000 in your emergency fund.

- **Enough to cover out-of-pocket emergency expenses:** You should always have enough in your emergency savings to cover at least the deductibles you'd have to pay in the event of a car accident, damage to your home, or a medical emergency. Figure out the maximum you'd likely have to pay — deductibles usually range from as low as $250 to $2,500 or more — and set your emergency fund goal to match.

- **A sum that will let you sleep well:** Will you worry if you have only $1,000 in your emergency fund? Will you feel secure if you have $7,500? Figure out how much of a cash cushion you need to feel comfortable — and, by that, we mean that you aren't holding your breath, fearful of something unexpected happening — and set that as your target.

After your emergency fund is full

When you've achieved your goal for your emergency savings, you can start working on your other savings goals — putting more into investments, or your retirement funds, or saving for your dream home, or financing your own or your children's education.

Funding your cash reserve for emergencies is excellent training for more ambitious savings goals. Not only do you establish the saving habit for yourself, but the confidence you gain from reaching your first goals helps motivate you to work on your next goals. And, before you know it, you're well on your way to making your dreams of financial security happen.

Chapter 8

Getting the Most from Your Job

. . . .

In This Chapter

▶ Divvying up your paycheck

▶ Understanding employer stock plans

▶ Taking full advantage of benefits

▶ Planning for a job change

. . . .

*T*here are three key ingredients to building wealth: making money, invest-ing money, and holding onto money. If you're like many people, you may think of your job just in terms of the pay you get — a way to pay your bills. That's certainly important, but, although pay may be tops on the list of ben-efits, it's not the only way you can profit from your job.

The first step is to divide your paycheck in a way that makes sense for you and your goals. Next, you should make sure you're taking advantage of every benefit your employer offers, whether it's a retirement savings plan, a stock plan, or even pretax health-insurance benefits.

Finally, if you're like most Americans, you'll change jobs several times over the course of your working life. Having a plan for those changes will help you avoid major financial mistakes that can deplete your wealth alarmingly fast.

In this chapter, we show you how to make the most of your job in each of these crucial areas.

Allocating Your Paycheck

If most (or all) of your paycheck goes to paying your current bills, the idea of allocating it differently may strike you as absurd. But income isn't the same as wealth. If you want to build wealth, you have to divide your income into separate pots:

- ✔ **Current expenses:** The bulk of your paycheck probably will go here; refer to your budget to figure out how much you need from each paycheck to cover your bills.

- ✔ **Emergency savings:** If you don't have three to six months' worth of living expenses saved yet, this should be your top savings priority. Put at least half of your total savings in this account until you've reached your goal.

- ✔ **Planned major purchases:** This is where you put money for your next vehicle, that living room set you want, or the trip you want to take next fall.

- ✔ **Savings for future needs:** This could be your retirement fund or the kids' college fund.

When you've decided how much you have to put in your savings accounts, figure out which category of savings is your top priority. Put half of your savings in the account that has the highest priority, and divide the other half evenly among the other savings pots.

Your savings priorities can change as circumstances change. Even if you have a comfortable amount in your emergency fund, for example, you may want to bolster that account if you're worried about you or your spouse losing a job.

Divvying up your paycheck for specific things is an easy way to stick to your budget and get started on your making-millions plan.

Using direct deposit to augment your savings

Most larger employers offer direct deposit these days, which saves you (and your employer, and even the bank) time and money. You don't have to actually go to the bank to deposit your pay, and you aren't tempted to cash your check at a convenience store or grocery store, which may charge you a fee for the service. Some banks, and especially credit unions, also waive monthly account fees when you have direct deposit.

Perhaps one of the best features about direct deposit, though, is that you can set it up so your saving becomes automatic. If you have the four pots we discuss earlier, you can split up each paycheck so some goes into each pot. Making it automatic serves two purposes: (1) It's convenient, and (2) you don't have to remember (or exercise the self-discipline) to do it yourself.

If your employer isn't set up to do the split for you, see if your bank can do it.

If your bank charges a fee for automatically transferring your money among different accounts, look for a bank or credit union that will do it for free. If you can't find one that offers this service, you'll have to do it yourself, either online or at an ATM.

When you're starting out on your savings plan, how much you save isn't as important as getting into the habit of saving. Even if you can spare only $10 or $20 a paycheck for your savings pots, putting that money aside — and allocating it appropriately for your savings priorities — is worthwhile.

If you're easily tempted to dip into your savings for nonemergency reasons, try setting up your savings accounts through online banks. You can still make your savings automatic — plus, you'll probably earn a higher interest rate, and you'll have to make a real effort to get it out, which can curb those spending impulses.

Taking advantage of pretax deductions

Some of the benefits your employer may offer are paid before taxes are calculated on your wages. The effect of pretax payroll deductions is twofold: Your taxable income is lower, and, because these things don't come out of your take-home pay, you don't notice much difference in your pay. The most common pretax deductions are for health insurance and 401(k) plans.

Health insurance

Most employers who offer health insurance split the premiums for the plan between themselves and the employee, and the employee's share usually comes out of pretax dollars.

If you pay for health insurance, or a health savings account, with post-tax dollars, you may be able to claim a deduction for these expenses on your tax return (see Chapter 17).

If your employer doesn't offer a health-insurance plan, you can get your own. To get tax savings, look into health savings accounts (HSAs). These are similar to IRAs in that you can invest the money to make it grow, and you can use the money only for specific expenses, or else you'll pay a penalty. Also, to have an HSA, you have to be covered by a high-deductible health plan (HDHP), sometimes called a *catastrophic plan*. These plans generally require you to pay $1,000 or more before coverage kicks in; that's what the HSA is for. Your bank or credit union may offer HSAs; insurance companies also offer them.

401(k) contributions

Most employers who offer retirement plans take the 401(k) route rather than offering traditional pension plans. Until recently, employees often had to sign up for their 401(k) plans, but since December 2007, employers have had more freedom to automatically enroll their workers. The goal was to get more employees saving for retirement, and it appears to be succeeding. However, there are some downsides to automatic enrollment:

- ✓ **Workers who are automatically enrolled often stick with the automatic contribution.** Most employers with automatic enrollment funnel 3 percent of your pay into the 401(k) plan to begin with. But if your employer offers a match that's higher than the automatic contribution, you're missing out on free money if you don't increase your own contribution.

- ✓ **Your employer is limited in investing your automatic contribution.** If you don't change the investments, your 401(k) plan may be too risky or too conservative for your needs. Unfortunately, studies have shown that workers who are automatically enrolled are less likely to rebalance their 401(k) funds and less likely to actively choose their own investments.

- ✓ **Your contribution rate may not change.** Some automatic plans start at 3 percent of your pay and increase 1 percent a year until you're automatically putting 6 percent of your wages into your 401(k). But some plans don't increase the savings rate, and, for most people, 3 percent a year isn't nearly enough to fund the retirement you want.

- ✓ **Fees for automatic 401(k)s may eat up a lot of your returns.** Some plans charge as much as 3 percent a year, which gets taken out of your savings whether you've actually made money on your investments or not.

Here's how to make the most of your employer's 401(k) plan:

- ✓ **Find out what the employer match is, and max it out.** If your employer will give you 50¢ for every $1 you contribute, up to 5 percent of your salary, for example, you should contribute 5 percent to get the full match benefit.

If your employer doesn't offer any match to your contributions, you may be better off putting your money in a traditional IRA or Roth IRA, especially if your employer's plan has high fees or limited investment options.

Even if the fees are high, you should max out your employer match, as long as the matching contribution is greater than the fees you'll incur. This involves crunching some numbers, but here's an example: Say your employer matches 1 percent of your $25,000 salary. That's $250 from your employer in your 401(k), plus another $250 that you contribute.

The fee will be based on the balance in your account. For our purposes, we'll assume you didn't make or lose any money during the year, so your balance is $500. If the fee is 3 percent (which is obscenely high), you'll be charged $15. But you're still $235 ahead because your employer gave you $250 ($250 – $15 = $235).

✔ **Choose funds with low or no fees, so your returns don't get eaten up.**

✔ **Rebalance your 401(k) investments at least once a year to make sure you have the right mix of stocks and bonds for your goals.** (See Chapter 16 for information on finding the right mix for your goals.)

You can contribute up to 10 percent of your salary to your 401(k), plus "catch-up" contributions if you're nearing retirement. Some financial advisors recommend increasing your contribution percentage every year until you reach that 10 percent threshold. After all, it's easy, and this strategy fits in with the "pay yourself first" philosophy because you never see the money.

But it won't necessarily give you the best returns. After you've maxed out the employer match, you probably can find better investments with fewer fees through a traditional or Roth IRA for that extra savings.

If you're in an automatic 401(k) plan, you can get any contributions back without penalty if you opt out of the program within 90 days of the first payroll deduction. It may make sense to do this — and put the money in an IRA instead — if your employer doesn't offer a matching contribution.

Pensions

The days of company pensions are fast disappearing, and even if you qualify for a pension plan now, there's no guarantee it will be around — or be worth as much — by the time you're ready to collect it. Most employers have made the move from traditional pensions — also called *defined benefit plans,* because they typically guarantee a specified monthly payment for life after you retire — to 401(k)s and IRAs (called *defined contribution plans,* because the only specific number is how much you and/or your employer contribute, not how much you'll get in retirement).

If you do qualify for a company pension, chances are, you don't have any control over it. Pension plans usually are invested in the company's own stock, and employees don't have much, if any, say in its management. But, because pension plans so often depend on an individual company's performance, your wisest move is to augment your expected pension money with your own savings in a well-balanced IRA.

Your monthly pension benefit may not go nearly as far when you retire as it would today. Find out if your plan has a cost-of-living adjustment (COLA) and whether that adjustment is high enough to keep up with inflation. If not, you'll definitely need additional retirement savings.

Stock Plans

Stock plans (unlike pensions) are still pretty popular ways for employers to offer additional money to their workers and, at the same time, build company productivity and loyalty among employees. There are several ways to structure stock plans, and your best move depends on the structure of your employer's plan. Here, we give you an overview of some of the most common plans: stock options, employee stock purchase plans, restricted stock awards, and restricted stock units.

Tax rules for employee stock plans differ, so consult your tax adviser for specific advice on how to take advantage of your employer's plan without incurring heavy taxes.

Stock options

Stock-option plans give you an opportunity to buy your company's stock at a preset price, regardless of what the stock is selling for on the open market when you exercise your option. Usually, there's a vesting period — that is, you have to wait, say, two or three years — before you can exercise your option; most plans also have an expiration date, and if you don't exercise your option by that date, you lose out on the opportunity to buy stock at that preset price.

Here's an example of how this works: Say you were given a stock option on January 1. The preset price (also called the *grant price*) is $5 per share. You have to wait three years until you can exercise your option — until you can buy your company's stock at the preset price. If you don't exercise your option within five years, you lose the right to buy the stock at $5 per share.

So, after the three years are up, but before you hit the five-year mark, you have to decide whether you're going to exercise your option. If the company's stock price on the open market is lower than $5, there's no point in exercising your option. But if the market price is higher, you have to decide when to make your purchase. Like any other form of investing, this is a bit of a gamble. You can wait until you get close to the expiration date, betting that the stock price will go up, but it's also possible for the price to go down.

Ideally, you want to exercise your option when the stock price is on its way up, but if you wait for it to peak, you may miss out on some profit.

If your plan is a nonqualified stock option (NSO), you pay your regular income tax rate on any profit you make from buying the stock at your option price and selling it at fair market value. You also have to pay Social Security and Medicare taxes on your profits.

Incentive stock options (ISOs) get special tax treatment. However, in order to qualify for those tax benefits, you have to hold your stocks for at least a year from the time you exercise your option and at least two years from the time the preset price was established.

Employee stock purchase plans

Employee stock purchase plans (ESPPs) work a little differently from straight stock options. Typically, your employer will offer you an opportunity to buy the company's stock at a discount — up to 15 percent — through payroll deductions. If your company's ESPP is a qualified 423 plan, you won't have to pay taxes on the discount, but you'll have to hold onto your shares for at least a year to get more favorable long-term capital-gains treatment on your profits when you do sell the stock. (See Chapter 17 for more on long- and short-term capital gains taxes.) Nonqualified ESPPs don't have any special tax benefits.

Most plans allow you to change your payroll deduction for the ESPP at any time. Check with your human resources or benefits office to find out how your plan works.

Restricted stock awards

Under restricted stock award plans, your company grants you stock but you can't sell the shares until the restriction period, sometimes called the *vesting period,* expires. Typical restriction periods are three or five years; sometimes the restriction period is based on the company's performance rather than a straight timeline.

At the end of the restriction period, your employer may issue shares to you, which you then own outright just as you would any other stock. Or you may receive the cash equivalent rather than shares. Some plans require employees to pay the grant price when the shares are issued (or, if you get cash instead, the grant price will be deducted from your award check).

You can choose whether to pay taxes on your restricted stock award immediately or to defer taxes until the restriction period ends. If you defer taxes, you may end up paying more in taxes if the stock price rises significantly. But if you choose to pay taxes from the beginning, and you leave your employer before the restriction period ends, you forfeit not just the restricted stock award, but also any taxes you've already paid on it.

Restricted stock units

Restricted stock unit plans are similar to restricted stock awards, except that no shares are issued at the time of the grant. Instead, the "unit" is based on the value of company stock when the grant is made. After the restriction period — which can be time-based or linked to company performance — the company issues either shares or the cash equivalent.

You may have to decide whether to accept or decline a restricted stock unit grant. If you accept, your employer may require you to purchase the grant, usually at a discount from the fair market value. Generally, you aren't liable for taxes until after the restriction period ends; then, as with other stock plans, you'll be taxed on the difference between the fair market value of the units when the restriction period expires minus whatever you paid when the grant was made.

Using What You've Earned

Most people focus on what their job pays and ignore the less tangible, or less regular, rewards their employers offer. To get the most out of your job, you need to look at the whole picture — paid time off, raises and bonuses, and any other benefits that can either help you now or lay the foundation for meeting your goals.

Holiday, vacation, and personal time

Americans are notorious for failing to take time off from work, even when they can get paid for it. Three out of every four workers in the United States get some paid time off, but most of them fail to use all the time off they're entitled to. According to one study, the average worker "gives back" three paid days off. Multiply that by the entire U.S. workforce, and Americans fail to take 438 million days of paid vacation time every year.

The problem is, working like that can hurt your physical and mental health. And employers, who are starting to notice that productivity tends to fall and healthcare costs tend to rise when their staffs don't take time off, are increasingly moving to a "use it or lose it" system of paid vacation, holidays, and personal time. (Part of the reasoning behind this also involves the bottom line: Employers who allow workers to roll over or accumulate vast stores of paid time off have to count that as a liability on their balance sheets.)

Even under "use it or lose it" systems, though, workers are sometimes reluctant to take the time they've earned. There are lots of reasons: Maybe the nature of your work makes it hard to plan vacations for slow times, or maybe you feel you should keep your vacation days on ice in case the kids get sick or you have to stay home to deal with a household emergency of some kind.

On the other hand, paid time off can actually improve your own bottom line. How? You can use your vacation days to research the business you want to start or the invention you want to market. You can set up your investment accounts or meet with your financial or estate planner. And your employer is paying you while you do it — as opposed to doing it on your own time, which nobody is paying you for.

You know the saying "Time is money." And you know how much you get paid for your time at work. If you don't take your vacation time, you're essentially sacrificing the equivalent of a day's pay — more, if you can use that time to further your financial goals.

Raises

Allocate your raises the same way you allocate your paycheck: some to current expenses, and some to each of your savings "pots" — emergency fund, special purchases, and investments. After all, if you're making more money, you can both spend and save more, too.

If you're in a 401(k) plan, your contribution will automatically increase when you get a raise because it's figured as a percentage of your salary. But if you have a set amount of money automatically transferred from your checking to your savings accounts, you'll have to change that amount to reflect your increased pay.

Bonuses

Depending on how your employer's bonus program is structured, you may be able to make specific plans for that money. But even if you don't know how much you'll get in your bonus envelope, you can figure out ahead of time how you want to use it. In general, we recommend planning to set aside at least half of your bonus money for your various savings accounts (see "Allocating Your Paycheck," earlier in this chapter). If you're carrying a balance on a high-interest credit card, though, you may be better off dedicating that bonus money to paying down your debt.

Setting your priorities before you receive your bonus will help you use it to get you closer to your financial goals. Otherwise, you may end up blowing it and kicking yourself later.

Other perks

Look into other benefits your employer provides and see if you can take advantage of them to make money, save money, or lay the groundwork for making more money down the road. Things like training classes and tuition reimbursement, for example, can improve your marketability to other companies, even if they won't lead to an immediate promotion or pay raise at your current job.

Sometimes employers arrange discounts at other local businesses for their employees, too. Don't use the discount as a rationale to buy things you wouldn't purchase otherwise, but do see if you can use any discount programs to save money on things you already were planning to buy. These programs may include things like discounted (or sometimes even free) admission to attractions like ball games, amusement parks, and museums; free or discounted software for your home computer; and even substantial discounts on high-ticket items like electronics and even cars.

Changing Jobs

The days when you could count on staying with your current employer for your entire career have long since faded away. According to the U.S. Department of Labor, the average American will hold 10 different jobs in her first 20 years in the workforce — an average of 2 years per job.

There's nothing wrong with changing jobs. In fact, most workers get better pay, better hours, and more job satisfaction with each new job. But you do need to tie up loose ends whenever you make a move out of one job and into another.

What to do with your 401(k)

One of the biggest questions you'll have to answer when you change jobs is what to do with your 401(k). Even if you haven't been in your current job long enough to be vested in the employer match, you have to decide what to do with the money you've put into your retirement account. Your options are to cash it out, leave it alone, or roll it over into an IRA. Each option has consequences you should consider carefully in making your decision.

Cashing out

It's tempting to look at that pile of money and think how you could spend it — to finance your own business startup, pay off bills, create an emergency fund, or take the trip of a lifetime. But before you tell your company to cut you a check, think about how much it will cost you to cash out your 401(k).

First, if you're not at least $59^{1}/_{2}$ years old, your employer is required to withhold 20 percent of your balance for taxes. If you've got $50,000 in your 401(k), that cuts your take to $40,000 right off the bat.

Then there's the 10 percent penalty for withdrawing the money before you're $59^{1}/_{2}$. That, too, is figured on the entire balance, so take another $5,000 off the amount you'd receive in our example.

Now you're down to $35,000 in cash, but when it comes time to file your taxes, you'll have to declare the entire $50,000 as income. The $10,000 your employer withheld will be credited against the taxes you owe, but the $5,000 penalty for early withdrawal won't be. So you could end up owing an enormous amount to the Internal Revenue Service, especially if you have other income during the year you cashed out.

Sometimes you just have to take the hit and work on recovering your losses later — if you're laid off and don't have any other way to cover your expenses while you're looking for another job, for example. But, because you lose so much of your own money this way, cashing out before retirement should be absolutely your last resort.

Leaving it there

Many employers allow you to simply leave your 401(k) account behind when you switch jobs. Your principal won't grow, because neither you nor your employer is contributing to the account any more, but you'll still earn interest and dividend returns from your investments.

However, you may lose the ability to rebalance your investments, which means they may become too risky or too conservative for you over time. Leaving your 401(k) money where it is may be the path of least resistance, but it won't necessarily help you build the wealth you want.

Millionaires don't like giving anyone else control over their money; they prefer to take charge of it themselves. It may be easier to leave your 401(k) in the hands of your former employer, but remember that you are the best judge of how to invest that money to meet your own goals.

Rolling it over

Rolling your 401(k) money over to a qualified IRA is your best option whenever you switch jobs. If you authorize a direct rollover — that is, your 401(k) fund transfers your money directly to your IRA account — you don't incur any tax liabilities or penalties for the switch.

If you have your money sent to you, you have 60 days to deposit it in a qualified IRA account to avoid the early withdrawal penalty. However, your former employer still has to withhold the 20 percent for taxes, and if you don't make that 20 percent up with other funds, you'll have to claim it as income on your tax return. In that case, the 10 percent early-withdrawal penalty will apply only to the 20 percent rather than to the entire balance.

So, on a $50,000 account, you'll actually receive $40,000 ($50,000 × 0.20 = $10,000 and $50,000 – $10,000 = $40,000). If you deposit the $40,000 in an IRA within 60 days, you'll have to declare the remaining $10,000 as income, and you'll pay a $1,000 early-withdrawal penalty ($10,000 × 0.10 = $1,000). The only way to avoid this is to come up with $10,000 to deposit in your IRA in addition to the $40,000 you got from your 401(k) — and you have to do it within the 60-day window.

You don't have to worry about taxes and penalties when you choose a direct rollover, because the money never passes through your hands.

Unless you're in dire financial straits (as in, you'll lose your home if you can't access your 401(k) money — not as in, you really, really want a new car), a direct rollover is your best option. You preserve all your funds that way, and you retain control over how to invest them.

Severance pay

Whether or not you leave your job voluntarily, you may be offered a severance package that could include two or more weeks' salary, payment for any unused vacation or sick time, a grace period on health insurance, and perhaps even buyouts on any stock or pension plan you participate in. Your employer may offer all this as a lump sum, or it may be structured so you receive a specified payment on staggered dates.

Have a plan for handling your severance package before you leave your current employer. Even if you don't know how much you might receive, you can still identify your priorities for what you do get. If you're anticipating a layoff, for example, you may want to add any severance pay to your emergency fund to help you meet expenses while you're looking for another job. If you're planning to leave on your own terms, maybe that money will serve you better in one of your other savings pots.

Health insurance

For more than 20 years, federal law has required employers to give former employees the chance to continue their health insurance coverage for up to 18 months after they leave their jobs. Most people refer to this coverage as COBRA (it stands for Consolidated Omnibus Budget Reconciliation Act, the 1986 legislation that contained this health-insurance provision). You have 60 days after your employment changes to decide whether you want COBRA coverage; if you do choose to continue your healthcare coverage, you're responsible for the entire premium, which can be quite expensive.

In general, COBRA applies to employers with 20 or more workers, employee organizations (like unions) that provide health-insurance plans, and state and local governments. COBRA can take effect under a number of conditions, including situations where your hours are cut so that you no longer qualify for your employer's regular health plan. The U.S. Department of Labor has a useful FAQ section about COBRA on its Web site: Go to `www.dol.gov/ebsa/faqs/faq_consumer_cobra.html`.

Part III
Paths Paved with Gold

The 5th Wave   By Rich Tennant

HANDBASKETS TO HELL *Mfg.*

"I tried to find something the whole world could use."

In this part . . .

There are many ways to realize your financial dreams: You can inherit wealth or marry it, for example, or you can start a business and work to make it profitable. You can invent something that strikes a chord with millions of consumers, like the Pet Rock of the 1970s, and spend the rest of your days endorsing the checks. You can play the lottery or gamble at casinos and take in a big haul. You can invest in real estate or in the stock market.

Not all these strategies will appeal to you. In this part, we break each one down to give you a better idea of the common challenges and opportunities along these separate paths.

Chapter 9

Starting Your Own Business

*L*ance Vella is tall and lean and not prone to standing still. Nearly any day of the week, you can spot him striding purposefully through his small-town grocery store with a case of something in his arms or donning a white coat and paper hat to cut fresh steaks in the meat room. He says hello hundreds of times a day to friends and neighbors — regular customers all — and, if there isn't anything really urgent demanding his attention, he'll stop and chat a while. Often, it's the only chance he has to catch up with these friends and neighbors.

"It's nothing you want to get stuck doing if you don't enjoy it," he says with a wry smile. "This is 70, 80 hours a week. It has to be a labor of love."

Lots of people dream of dumping their day jobs and striking out on their own. They have fantasies of being their own bosses, working their own schedules, taking charge, and turning their business in the direction they know it should go. And, in truth, there are lots of advantages to owning your own business — the potential to make millions being just one of them.

Owning your own business is also a lot of hard work. Still, that shouldn't scare you off: As Vella says, if you love what you're doing, it doesn't feel like work.

In this chapter, we give you an overview of entering the world of business ownership by starting your own, buying a franchise, or taking over an existing business. We show you what you need to know before you start and what to consider while you're weighing your options. And we direct you to other resources that can help you make your decision and make the best of the opportunities available to you.

Owning your own business is a huge topic — we cover the basics in this chapter, but if you decide owning a business is right for you, we recommend adding one or more of the following books (all published by Wiley) to your personal library:

- *Small Business For Dummies,* 3rd Edition, by Eric Tyson, MBA, and Jim Schell

- *Entrepreneurship For Dummies,* by Kathleen Allen, PhD

- *Business Plans Kit For Dummies,* 2nd Edition, by Steven Peterson, PhD; Peter E. Jaret; and Barbara Findlay Schenck

- *Retail Business Kit For Dummies,* by Rick Segal

- *Small Business Financial Management Kit For Dummies,* by Tage C. Tracy, CPA; and John A. Tracy, CPA

- *E-Commerce For Dummies,* by Don Jones, Mark D. Scott, and Richard Villars

- *Business Contracts Kit For Dummies,* by Richard D. Harroch

You also can get free information online from the Federal Trade Commission (go to www.ftc.gov and click the Franchises & Business Opps link), the Small Business Administration (go to www.sba.gov and click the Small Business Planner, Services, and Tools links), and from FindLaw (go to www.findlaw.com and look for the "Small Business Issues" headline under Learn about the Law).

Before You Jump In

Going into business for yourself is *not* something you want to do on a whim. There's too much at stake in owning your own business to jump into it lightly; missteps could cost you not just your business opportunity, but also everything else you've worked so hard to build. So before you let your imagination get too far ahead of you, rein it in by doing your research and understanding just what it is you're contemplating.

In our opinion, the best place to start your research is with an accountant. It is vital — *absolutely vital* — that you have a good, experienced accountant who knows the pitfalls and dangers of various business ventures. Experience is key here; an accountant who's just starting out won't have the wealth of experience to share with you. But someone who's been in the field for many years will have all kinds of stories to tell about businesses that failed for lack of proper funding, proper management, or due diligence. And, thanks to that experience, this veteran accountant can alert you to the realities of owning your own business that books, magazine articles, and business contacts may gloss over.

Perhaps the most useful thing a good accountant can give you is a reality check about financing a business venture. A big chunk of businesses fail simply because they're underfunded; entrepreneurs as a class have a tendency to underestimate expenses and overestimate revenues. Your accountant can tell you, realistically, how much money it'll take to run your business (and support yourself) during that first year of operation when, typically, there's no profit.

No matter what kind of business you get into, expect it to take twice as much money and twice as much time as you estimate.

And that brings us to the question of financing your business. We don't recommend going into debt to finance 100 percent of your business. That just increases the risk for you. We also don't recommend using borrowed money to correct an underfunding issue; there are better ways to come up with the money you need. You can work another year or two to save the cash you need, or you can moonlight for extra money to put in your business startup fund. And you can use that extra time to complete your research for your business.

The less debt you have when you start your business, the sooner you can expect to see profits. Besides, if you don't have the discipline or drive to stash your own cash for your business, that could be a sign that your business idea isn't really right for you.

Going into business for yourself is a risky proposition, balanced by potentially enormous rewards. You need to be willing to lose what you invest, and at the same time take every action possible to make sure that doesn't happen. You also have to protect your core assets — your home, your retirement savings, and so on — so that, if your business fails, you don't have to rebuild everything from the ground up.

Vella says doing your research before you get into business for yourself is a critical element for success. "I've never done one thing where I thought I'd have to cut my losses," he says. "Everything you do has to have value, and the best way to make sure it has value is to come in with a plan. Going into business is always a risk, but you can make it a calculated risk if you do your homework."

Starting from Scratch

The key to any successful business is finding a need and filling it. Lance Vella's grandparents did that when they opened a general store in the tiny village of Cleveland on the north shore of New York's Oneida Lake in 1949. Once a thriving glass-factory town, Cleveland's industry had long since faded away, and the nearest grocery store was 15 miles distant. Lance's father and uncle began running the store after they finished their military service during the Korean War, and Lance and his cousin Joe (also the lottery winner from Chapter 12) grew up with the business in their blood. Today, the cousins operate three locations — Lance's grocery store; Joe's hardware store and lumberyard in the nearby hamlet of Constantia; and a convenience store in Cleveland, run by Lance's wife, Lisa. The three businesses together are worth more than eight figures — all in a town with about 5,000 residents.

Determining the kind of business you want

Talk to virtually any business owner, and she'll tell you that the best business for you is something you're good at and something you love. The passion is important, because building a business from the ground up takes hard work and dedication — and lots of long workdays. If your business doesn't excite you — if you don't look forward to the challenges and opportunities it presents every day and wake up eager to tackle them — chances are good you'll burn out early.

So when you're thinking about what kind of business you want, think about what inspires you. And then think about whether you can make a living doing it.

This is a good time to go over your list of goals (see Chapter 3). Even if you didn't include "starting a business" there, reviewing your goals can give you insight into your passion.

Also, consider what you're good at it. Don't be bashful about this, either; be honest with yourself about what your real talents and gifts are. Some people are gifted organizers; some are exceptional public speakers; some have a knack for throwing great parties, or creating financial statements, or working with animals. Make a list of your particular talents — the things that you're good at and that seem to come easily to you.

Just because something is easy for you doesn't mean everyone can do it. And, if other people need what you can offer, you could turn your talent into a money-making business opportunity.

Assessing your skills

After you've identified what you're good at, it's time to figure out what you're not so good at. Doug Carson, the inventor from Chapter 10, frankly admits that he's not good at overseeing the day-to-day operations of his company. He's an idea man, and the details of running a business bore him. So he hired people with the skills and interests he lacks.

Lance and Joe Vella did the same thing when they divvied up responsibilities for the family business. Either of them could run the entire operation himself. But Lance loves the grocery business, and Joe always has been more interested in the hardware store and lumberyard. So they've structured the businesses so that each can pursue what he enjoys and what he's good at.

Here are some common areas where new business owners often find they need help:

- ✔ Financial tracking and organization, including accounting, taxes, and insurance
- ✔ Employment law and employee relations
- ✔ Clerical work, including filing, recordkeeping, and billing
- ✔ Computerization and automation
- ✔ Sales and marketing

You may have to handle all these things when you're starting out and building your business. Or you may be able to hire outside help on a temporary or as-needed basis to handle some of these things. The important thing is to be objective about what you are and aren't good at or interested in, and create a plan to bring those skills in another way.

Figuring out what you'll need

No matter what kind of business you're interested in starting, you'll need some basic things to get going: financing, technical assistance, equipment, and a marketing plan that identifies who your customers are and how you'll reach them.

Financing

Lots of businesses — especially those that are home-based — don't require much outside financing, if any. You can use your current computer to start an e-commerce site, for example, or to do freelance work at home. Home printers often combine fax, scan, and copy capabilities, and they aren't very expensive. You can get basic office supplies at good prices at dollar stores or discount retailers.

But if you're looking to rent space, hire employees, or buy specialized equipment, you may have to look outside your own bank accounts for seed money. When this is the case, you have several options. You can

- ✔ **Ask friends or relatives for a loan.** The advantage here is that friends and family probably won't require a formal business plan to give you the loan, and they'll probably cut you some slack if you're late with a payment or two. There are potential disadvantages, though. Your friend or relative may feel he has a say in how you run your business, because he put up the money for it. And, if you have problems repaying the loan, it can seriously damage your relationship.

  If you do borrow money from friends or family, make the transaction as businesslike as possible. Ideally, you should both sign a promissory note that details the amount of the loan, the interest to be paid, and the repayment schedule. This ensures that everybody knows what the deal is and can help you avoid misunderstandings down the road.

- ✔ **Ask a bank for a loan.** If you choose this route, you'll need a formal business plan. Banks want to see how you intend to make money from your business, and they want assurance that you'll be able to repay the loan. Your business plan has to show that there's a need for the service or product you intend to offer, who your target market is, how many people in your target market are in your service area, and how large a share of that market you expect to be able to capture.

  Your local Small Business Development Center (SBDC) can help you craft your business plan. It also can refer you to any special financing programs available in your area. Go to http://sbdcnet.org to find your local SBDC, and, while you're there, check out the tools and information for small-business owners and aspiring owners.

  Depending on how much startup cash you need, you may have better luck getting a personal loan to finance your business. Most banks will lend up to $5,000 without collateral, assuming your credit is good (see Chapter 6).

  You also could look into using your home's equity to start your business, but this can be extremely risky. If you can't repay the loan, you could lose your house. Also, if you don't use your home equity loan to make improvements to your home, there may be limitations on the amount of interest you can deduct on your income tax. (IRS Publication 936 details the rules on deducting home-equity-loan interest for purposes other than home improvement or purchase; you can get the publication online at www.irs.gov/publications/p936 or by calling 800-829-3676.)

If you get a bank loan for your business, you'll have to pay it back as you would any other loan. Most commonly, you make set monthly payments for a set term, and the payments cover principal and interest. But you can also get loans that require you to pay only the interest or a lower percentage of the principal for a certain period, and then you owe a *balloon payment* — essentially the remaining balance of the loan — at the end of that period.

✔ **Sell ownership interest in your business.** The advantage to this approach is that you don't have to make monthly payments on the loan, the way you do with a bank loan. However, when you sell ownership interest, you're selling part of your future profits. You also may be courting unwanted interference in the running of your business.

If you decide to sell shares in your business, you're leaving the realm of the sole proprietorship — the simplest business structure — and getting into the more complex structures of general partnerships, corporations, limited liability companies, and limited partnerships. Each of these structures has its pros and cons, so make sure you do your homework thoroughly before you decide whether to raise money this way. (Check out *Incorporating Your Business For Dummies,* by The Company Corporation, and *Limited Liability Companies For Dummies,* by Jennifer Reuting [both published by Wiley], for more information.)

Raising money by courting investors also can subject you to federal and state securities laws, further complicating this fund-raising option.

Technical assistance

Beyond your business plan, you may need legal assistance in setting up your business — especially if you decide to form a corporation, partnership, or other complex type of business. You may need to comply with state and local health and environmental laws, federal securities laws, or other regulations. Unless you're an accountant yourself, you'll likely need the services of one to make sure your taxes — withholding, sales and use, gross receipts, and income taxes, among possible others — are filed properly and on time. You may need a payroll service to make sure you're withholding taxes correctly.

As always, the amount of outside help you need depends on your own skills and training. Your SBDC can help you with referrals; you can also ask your own circle of acquaintances for referrals.

Equipment

If you're opening a restaurant, you'll need ovens and fryers and freezers and coolers, among other things. If you're opening an accounting business, you'll need office furniture, computer hardware and software, telephones, copiers, and other business equipment.

You can save a lot in startup costs by shopping around for whatever you need. Auction services often sell used equipment and furnishings that are in good condition; specialty supply stores sometimes have good deals on new, refurbished, or consigned furnishings and equipment. You can also look online for good deals on things like computers and furniture; you may even be able to find what you're looking for on eBay (www.ebay.com), craigslist (www.craigslist.org), or similar sites.

You can depreciate equipment and furnishings against the income from your business, and that has significant tax advantages. This is another area where you need to consult your accountant.

Marketing plan

Your business won't flourish if your potential customers don't know about you. Your marketing plan identifies your target customers and how you'll reach them. Will you have a Web site? If so, what kinds of services will you offer on your site — shopping, requests for information, electronic newsletters, a blog? And how will you direct people to your Web site?

If you're focusing on a bricks-and-mortar operation, how will you get the word out? You may be able to get the local newspaper or TV station to do a feature on you when you open, but how will you keep your business name in front of your customers? Direct mail? Radio, television, or print advertising? Word of mouth? It'll probably be a combination of lots of tactics, but you have to have a plan for how much of your resources you'll devote to each approach.

Building it into the black and beyond

The average profit margin for a grocery store that's part of a chain is between 1 percent and 2 percent. Lance Vella's store is an independent concern and has a profit margin of 4 percent to 5 percent. "But that's only because I'm here all the time," he cautions. "You have to want to work. And I don't mean just be here, but be immersed in it."

Balancing business and family

If you have a family, expect to feel torn between your responsibilities to your business and your desire to spend time with your spouse and kids. "You put in your mind that family's always first, but sometimes it doesn't happen that way," Vella says. "It's sad to say, but sometimes you can't put family first."

Vella, the father of five, had to figure out a way to make time for his family, even as he was building his business. His solution? "I tried to make it home for dinner. Even if I had to go back to the store after, at least I had that hour a day to spend with my family." When his children were involved in sporting events, he couldn't always get away for the entire game. "But I'd try to see at least a couple innings of the softball game," he says.

The good news is, it's worth it, Vella says. He loves the business, and the business has given his children the option to pursue their own dreams. Besides, he says, he's only gotten better at his job over the years.

Learning from the competition

When a Wal-Mart Supercenter opened in a neighboring town, Vella's grocery felt the impact. "We took a 10 percent sting that stuck for a while," Vella says. "But it actually was good for us. It made me hungry. It made me a better operator."

Competition keeps you from getting complacent or smug, Vella says. When you have to respond to a competitor's moves, it unleashes your creativity and allows you to find new and better ways to do things.

Experience is a great teacher, too. Vella declined to go into specifics, but he acknowledged that he's been had a time or two. Now, he says, he makes sure he has a controlling interest in everything he does. "I don't buy 49 percent of anything. And I'll never be an absentee business owner."

Conventional wisdom advises you to learn from your mistakes. But we recommend learning from your successes, too. When something in your business works, figure out why it worked, and see if you can replicate that success. That's how million-dollar businesses are built.

Buying a Franchise

The franchise route has some definite advantages over going it alone in starting your business. *Franchisors* (those who sell franchises) usually have a proven business plan and often have national or even international name recognition, which can help enormously in driving business to you. They also often offer technical support and ongoing training.

But success with a franchise isn't automatic. The Vellas' hardware store used to be a True Value franchise, and Lance Vella said the national chain's business model didn't translate well to the rural area where the Vellas' businesses are established. "We were paying a lot of money for not a lot of benefit. They'd send out their mailers, and it wouldn't bring anybody into the store for us," he recounts.

Now the hardware store is part of the Do It Best co-op — a different business structure that offers cafeteria-style services better suited to the Vellas' needs.

Their convenience store is still a franchise, though, operating under the Mobil brand name. The profit margins are lower, Vella says, because franchise fees and royalties are added expenses. But, for the convenience store, the franchise model makes sense.

Weighing the pros and cons

"It's all about weighing the pros and cons," Vella says. "Franchises are a good place to learn, and if you don't have a lot of business experience, there are advantages to going with a franchise."

Among the pros, he says, are the following:

- ✔ An established business model that provides a blueprint for running the business
- ✔ Technical assistance for things like financing, marketing plans, site selection, and so on
- ✔ Management and product training
- ✔ Advertising support

On the flip side, Vella lists

- ✔ Lack of control over how the business is run
- ✔ Additional expenses for things like advertising that may not help your specific location
- ✔ Inventory requirements that may not suit your location
- ✔ Restrictions on innovation

There are two main forms of franchising. One is called *product* or *trade name franchising,* and the other is called *business format franchising.* Business format franchising is usually more restrictive in terms of how you run the operation, but you also usually get more support from the franchisor.

Focusing on funding

Investing in a franchise is generally pretty expensive. There's an initial franchise fee, which can range from a few thousand to tens of thousands of dollars and is sometimes nonrefundable. Your expenses to build or rent a location and equip it in accordance with the franchisor's requirements also may be much higher than if you went the independent route. You'll have initial inventory costs (which you would have if you were an independent, too, but the franchise costs may be higher). You may even have to pay a "grand opening" fee to the franchisor in exchange for promotion of your business.

You may have to pay other fees, too. The most common franchise fees are

- ✔ **Royalties:** Royalties are based on your location's gross income, but sometimes you'll have to pay them even if you don't have significant income; the royalty payment is for the right to use the franchisor's brand or name, and you typically are required to pay royalties for the life of the franchise agreement.

- ✔ **Advertising fees:** Advertising fees are sometimes charged to help pay for national advertising. Sometimes these are co-op arrangements, where your location is advertised in your area or in rotation with other locations. Often, though, advertising fees pay for general advertising of the brand, not your specific location, or to attract new franchisees.

Franchise terms usually run between 15 and 20 years, but there's no guarantee that you'll be able to renew your franchise agreement then. The franchisor also can cancel your agreement if you fail to pay the required fees or meet the franchisor's standards for operation. If that happens, you lose your investment.

Be wary of any franchisor who fills your head with how much you can make from a franchise or how well other franchisees are doing. The Federal Trade Commission (FTC) requires franchisors to back up what they say about performance and profit potential with written proof. When a franchisor says he doesn't have the written proof or refuses to provide it, that's your cue to walk away.

Determining the best opportunity for you

Deciding whether to pursue a franchise opportunity requires the same kind of examination you'd give to opening an independent business. Look for a field that interests you and that you have skills for, or that you can learn easily. Think about how much time and money you're willing to commit to make a franchise successful. And think about whether you'll be able to carry on the business if the franchisor goes out of business — which sometimes happens.

Here are some other things to consider:

- ✔ **Do you want the franchise to provide your main source of income or extra income?** This is related to the time and money commitment you're willing to make. If you're only looking for supplemental income, make sure your investment won't outweigh your returns.

- ✔ **Do you envision running the business yourself or hiring a manager?** There's nothing wrong with either approach, but hiring a manager may cut into your profits, while running the franchise yourself may cut into your time.

- ✔ **Can you see yourself running this business for the next 15 or 20 years?** When you sign a franchise agreement, you're making a long-term commitment. If you don't know whether you'll be happy in this situation years down the road, you may want to keep looking for an opportunity that really inspires you.

Beyond knowing yourself, you need to do your due diligence in investigating franchising opportunities. That means assessing the value the franchisor is offering in return for your investment in terms of the following:

- ✔ **Demand:** A franchise that's been successful in other areas of the country (or even your state or city) won't necessarily be successful in yours. Do people in your community or neighborhood want the franchisor's product or service? Is the product or service seasonal, like lawn care or tax preparation? If it is, will it generate enough profit during the season to support you through the off season?

- ✔ **Competition:** What other businesses offer the same product or service, or even similar ones? How many of the franchisor's locations are in your area, and is there enough demand for the franchisor's name to spread around all the franchises?

Franchise agreements sometimes provide territory boundaries to prevent locations of the same franchise from competing directly with each other. But those boundaries may not include the same market mix, meaning your territory may not be as lucrative as another franchisee's.

When you're investigating the competition, look at price points and value, too. You may be able to compete with a lower-priced business if yours provides significant added value. But if your products or services are substantially the same, getting customers may be more challenging.

Also look into how long the competition has been in business and how it's perceived in the community.

✔ **Growth:** Look at not only the growth potential of your own location, but also the growth history of the franchisor. In general, growth is a good thing; it means there's a demand for the product or service and usually means better name recognition for the franchise. But if the franchisor grows too fast, there could be problems with providing promised support or keeping territorial boundaries intact.

✔ **The experience of the franchisor:** An entrepreneur who's just starting to franchise her business may not have the experience or skills to parlay a successful business into a successful franchising operation, whereas a chain like McDonald's pretty much has the franchising thing down pat.

✔ **The reputation of the franchisor:** If the franchise name is associated with value and service, that's a good thing. But a franchisor's poor reputation can spell failure for your investment, even if you do everything right.

You probably don't want to invest in a franchise with a poor reputation, but it could represent an opportunity for you to open a business that competes with the franchisor. The essence of a successful business is doing it better than anybody else.

Franchising can be a complicated business. For more information, check out the FTC's Web site (`www.ftc.gov`), the SBA's site (`www.sba.gov`), and *Franchising For Dummies,* by Michael Seid and Dave Thomas (Wiley).

Taking Over an Existing Business

The advantage in buying an existing business is that the seller has taken the business through the often-rough beginning stages, doing the market research and implementing a marketing plan, building a customer base, and establishing a reputation that keeps people coming through the door.

These things are an advantage, though, only if you have the experience and skills to capitalize on the groundwork the previous owner has done. If you're entering an unfamiliar field, you'll have a sharp learning curve that could jeopardize your ability to keep a going concern going well.

Another big advantage with existing businesses is that you're not working from projections; you're dealing with actual performance and figures. This makes it a lot easier to evaluate the potential return on your investment.

That said, you still have to do your homework. You need to know exactly what you're getting into, good and bad. And that means you have to review financial statements, understand contract issues, investigate potential or ongoing litigation, and spot other pros and cons of the business.

Reviewing financial statements

Aside from the cash flow and profit/loss statements of the business, you'll need to review other records that can affect its long-term profitability. These records include accounts payable and receivable; if there are a lot of outstanding bills or invoices that haven't been paid, either going out or coming in, that could be a warning sign that the business isn't quite as stable as other records may make it appear.

Ask for a list of ownership of all the company's assets and any loans or other financial obligations attached to those assets. This will give you a good idea of what the business owns outright and what it is merely leasing or renting, as well as any liens there may be against the assets it owns.

Review employee records, too, to see what benefits the business provides, whether there seems to be an inordinate amount of overtime, whether worker's compensation and other insurance policies are paid up, and any contracts with employees. You'll also want to know about any worker's compensation and unemployment claims.

If there are employee contracts, you'll have to find out whether they're binding on you if you buy the business. You may not want to be tied to a manager or required to buy out his contract if you and he don't share the same vision or philosophy for the business. On the other hand, you may want noncompete or nondisclosure agreements made with the previous owner to be binding when you take over.

Keeping an eye on contracts and leases

Other contracts and leases must be reviewed to see if you can benefit from them when you take over ownership. Some contracts with vendors or customers don't allow the seller to transfer the contract to a new owner without the vendor's or customer's consent. If you or the current owner can't convince the other party to the contract to transfer its terms to you, you could face the immediate loss of a significant revenue stream.

The same goes for leases. If the business is renting space, you'll have to find out whether the landlord will offer you the same terms. If not, that could have a big impact on the expense side of the ledger.

Look into the details of utilities and phone service, too. You don't want to have to change the business phone number or get socked with bills the previous owner didn't pay.

Other contracts you'll want to examine may include

- ✔ Any joint venture, partnership, or similar agreements
- ✔ Any outstanding loans, lines of credit, or other financing arrangements
- ✔ Any installment agreements, whether the business is buying or selling on such a plan
- ✔ Any agreements with sales staff, distributors, advertising outlets, and other vendors
- ✔ Any stock options or stock purchase agreements
- ✔ Any records relating to mergers, acquisitions, or sell-offs, especially within the last five years

Paying attention to potential or ongoing litigation

If the business you're eyeing has any legal issues, you could inherit them when you buy. Be sure to check out any threatened lawsuits or ongoing lawsuits, as well as any past settlements or other court actions involving the business. You'll also need to check for *unsatisfied* (that is, unpaid) judgments, and you'll need to review any insurance policies that may provide coverage for litigation.

You don't have to — and you shouldn't — take the seller's word about any litigation. After they're filed, lawsuits and judgments are public record. Even if settlements are confidential, they have to be filed with the court, and the filings are public record. Mechanic's liens, also a matter of public record, can tell you whether the owner has left unpaid bills.

Investigating other areas

There's a lot of research involved in buying an existing business. Here are some other areas you should look into before you sign the purchase agreement:

- ✔ Tax issues, including whether there are any unpaid taxes, and what the business's total tax liability is
- ✔ Zoning laws, building codes, and other local or state regulations
- ✔ Intellectual property like patents and trademarks
- ✔ Trade secrets and other proprietary information, including protection measures
- ✔ Environmental or health issues
- ✔ Business licenses, including whether any licenses can be transferred
- ✔ Audits and credit reports
- ✔ Customer information, including mailing or e-mail lists, purchasing and credit policies, and any information explaining the gain or loss of major customers

Twenty-three states have "business opportunity disclosure laws" that require business sellers to provide certain information to prospective buyers. Even if your state doesn't have such a law, you can get help investigating a business opportunity from your state government. FindLaw (www.findlaw.com) has a list of contacts for every state and notes those that have disclosure laws. You can find the list at http://smallbusiness.findlaw.com/starting-business/starting-business-more-topics/starting-business-buying-state-disclosure.html.

Chapter 10

Inventing a Better Mousetrap

*D*oug Carson isn't a household name. But we bet you've got lots of examples of his work in your home. If you own CDs, DVDs, or an Xbox game, you're using technology that Carson invented and licensed to the companies — including Microsoft — that produce those things.

Carson got into the optical media field in 1981, two years before CDs hit the market. He had been working as vice president of engineering for a company that was using equipment from Philips, and he was modifying that equipment to store digital data. "Philips grilled me on the modifications, and when I passed the 'audition,' they asked our company to assist with the launch of CD-ROM," Carson said. Until 1988, the company Carson worked for supplied all of Philips's equipment for global CD-ROM production.

Unfortunately, in 1988, the company he was working for "just didn't see any future for themselves in that aspect of optical media. That's when Philips asked me to start my own company and help them solve more problems," Carson says. That company, DCA, now has locations in Japan, Malaysia, and Germany, in addition to its headquarters in Oklahoma. DCA has about 50 issued and pending patents related to optical media and digital data storage and protection techniques. They created high-speed mastering; network mastering; and the trademarked Disc Description Protocol (DDP), the industry standard for CD and DVD mastering.

Wanna be like Doug? Read on. In this chapter, we discuss the ways that innovation can make you rich — if you know how to make your idea make money for you. We take you through the steps from coming up with your idea to finding a market for it to protecting it so it can continue to make money for you. And, along the way, we give you a glimpse inside Carson's innovating (and moneymaking) mind.

This chapter is just an overview of the world of inventing and making money with inventions. For a thorough grounding in this topic, check out *Inventing For Dummies,* by Pamela Riddle Bird, PhD (Wiley), and *The Inventor's Bible: How to Market and License Your Brilliant Ideas,* by Ronald Louis Docie (Ten Speed Press).

Coming Up with Your Big Idea

Carson, who credits his faith in God as the basis for his ideas, calls innovation "nothing more than revealed creation."

"There's nothing new under the sun, so it's really a matter of discovering what was waiting there all along," Carson says. "If you put yourself in a position to hear that small, still voice, that's where ideas come from."

Many innovations are improvements on existing ideas. The board game we know as Monopoly started out as The Landlord's Game, patented by Elizabeth Magie in 1904. Charles Darrow played The Landlord Game, made improvements, and named his version Monopoly; when he sold it to Parker Brothers in the 1930s, Darrow became the first person in history to join the millionaire club by designing a game.

The best ideas aren't always completely new. Sometimes they're simply significant improvements that can make an existing idea or product more efficient or more user-friendly.

Pairing problems and solutions

The iconic Pet Rock of the 1970s aside, the most valuable ideas generally are those that solve a problem. (The Pet Rock, incidentally, was marketed as solving a problem — the problem of renters who weren't allowed to have live pets and people who didn't have the time or resources to care for one. In the six months that Pet Rocks were hot, Gary Dahl, the advertising executive who came up with the idea, became a millionaire. By the way, Gary also wrote *Advertising For Dummies,* 2nd Edition [Wiley].)

"You have to satisfy a need — that's where innovation comes from," Carson says. "Unless you're solving someone's problem, they're not going to open their wallets and give you money."

That's how Carson got involved with Microsoft Game Studios. "We got a call from Microsoft asking if we could make a disc that couldn't be copied. We said, 'Yeah, we can do that,' and now the Xbox antipiracy system is licensed from us." It's a good antipiracy system, too. Since the first-generation Xbox was released in 2001, no one has figured out a way to create counterfeit Xbox games that can be sold at full retail value (a huge potential problem, as the movie and music industries can attest).

Of course, you can't expect to get a call from Microsoft asking you to solve a problem for them. So where do you start? Look within your own experience:

- **Around your home:** All those closet organizers on the market were invented by people who saw the problems cluttered and overstuffed closets cause. Stain removers, dusters, even power strips all were designed to solve a common household problem.

- **At your workplace:** These days, most employers are eager to cut costs and improve productivity and efficiency. Look for things that annoy you or delay completion of your work, and see if you can come up with an alternative.

  The most lucrative ideas are the ones that can be applied broadly. A solution that applies only to your employer or your division is unlikely to make you wealthy; look for innovations that can be applied more universally.

- **In your hobbies:** Think of all the gadgets out there that make it easier to learn needlepoint, or proper putting in golf, or a foreign language, or a musical instrument. If you can come up with a way to make your favorite hobby, or an element of it, easier and more enjoyable, you may have a winning idea on your hands.

Checking out your idea

Once a brainstorm has struck, the next step is to find out if anyone else has already come up with your brilliant idea. That means searching through the records of the U.S. Patent and Trademark Office (USPTO), which, fortunately, you can do online at www.uspto.gov. The site allows you to search all patents from 1790 on.

Since 1790, when the first patent laws took effect in the United States, some 7 million patents have been issued in this country, and in recent years patent applications have consistently set new records. So it's entirely possible that someone else has beaten you to your great idea. Don't let that discourage you, though. ***Remember:*** If you can make an existing idea significantly better, you still have a shot at turning your idea into a moneymaker.

Complete patent searches are highly technical. Seek out a professional to do this for you if you decide to proceed with your idea. The technique we recommend here is really a *preliminary* patent search — a way to help you evaluate the quality of your idea and learn about potential competitors.

The McKinney Engineering Library at the University of Texas has an online tutorial that takes you step by step through the preliminary patent search process. Find it and more patent information and tools at www.lib.utexas.edu/engin/patent-tutorial.

According to the McKinney Engineering Library's Web site, the average preliminary patent search takes 25 to 30 hours. A full search — the one you hire a pro to do — takes even longer, because it involves not only the search you can do, but also a review of international patents, patent literature, and other resources beyond the easy reach (or, frankly, interest) of most inventors.

Although it's time-consuming, a preliminary patent search is worth it. Reviewing others' patents will help you understand competitors' ideas and avoid patent infringement and will give you an idea of how to write your patent application if you decide to proceed. Looking over other inventions in your field also can teach you more about the field as a whole.

Getting Paid for Your Big Idea

Thomas Edison wouldn't have tried to make an incandescent light bulb 2,000 times if he didn't think there was a market for it. "Anything that won't sell, I don't want to invent," Edison is often quoted as saying.

Doug Carson agrees with that philosophy and says that figuring out how to get paid for your idea is more important, at least at first, than protecting it with a patent or other mechanism.

"If you've got a great idea, yes, you want to protect it. But the real question — and this is where a lot of innovators get their priorities turned around — is, 'Can you outcommercialize the competition?' Any idea is only a good idea if you can monetize it," Carson says.

Seeing the value in your idea

Carson says lots of inventors don't really understand the value of their ideas, especially those who are most interested in the technical side. He counts himself among that class of innovators, too, noting that he hired a president for DCA eight years ago to handle the daily operations of his company.

"I'm not good at that, and I'm not good at the financial side either," Carson says. "I don't even check on the financial side on a monthly basis, because I hired the best guy in the world to take care of that for me. I have the innovative conversations — that's what I'm good at and where my strengths are."

He says there are two classes of innovators. "Commercial innovators know the value of their ideas. Technical innovators often don't, because the commercial side doesn't appeal to them as much." Bill Gates is a commercial innovator, Carson says. Gates saw the value in creating a standard for personal and business computer software but didn't invent the technical innovations that made it possible. On the other hand, Pearle Waite, the inventor of the fruit-flavored gelatin dessert that we know as Jell-O, didn't have the manufacturing or marketing expertise to capitalize on his invention, and he sold the formula to Orator Frank Woodward in 1899 for $450; three years later, Jell-O sales hit the $250,000 mark.

Don't run away with the idea that your first invention will make you rich. Only a tiny fraction of all patented inventions make money, and they're usually ones that have been worked and reworked for years. Carson warns about innovators and finances: "Innovators are extremely enthusiastic and will spend themselves into bankruptcy. If you're running a business, you have to have someone who's completely risk-averse running the financial side to balance that out."

To figure out whether your idea is commercially viable, you have to know the answers to these questions:

- **Who can use my invention?** Are you aiming to help businesses or individuals? Who are these businesses or individuals?

- **What problem does my invention solve for my potential customers?** Remember what Carson says about satisfying needs: If your invention doesn't solve a problem, no one's going to pay you for it.

- **How big is my potential market?** No matter how great your idea is, "everybody" is not your potential market. "Everybody" doesn't even own a telephone, a home computer, or a TV — inventions that arguably have universal appeal. So be realistic about what kind of consumer will actually be interested in your idea.

  The broader your potential market, the more likely it is that you'll be able to make money from your invention. But you still need to identify your core market — long-distance truckers, for example, or pet groomers, or skydivers, or what have you. You'll also need data like gender, income level, and education for your target customers.

- **Will my invention generate profits for everyone involved?** Whether you plan to manufacture your invention yourself or license it to another company, your invention has to be able to deliver profits at every point along the distribution chain — the manufacturer, the distributor, and the retailer. As a general rule, the cost of making your invention needs to be no more than a quarter of the retail price in order to be profitable. So if you plan to sell your invention for $100 in a store, it can't cost more than $25 to make; conversely, if it's going to cost $25 to make, you need to be able to sell it for at least $100.

✔ **Who's my competition?** You need to know what the products are and how much they sell for, as well as who makes them and who distributes them.

You can find professional services that perform assessments for a fee. Check out the Innovation Institute at `www.wini2.com`; they offer assessment services for $200 for U.S. customers ($220 for those outside the United States) and an extensive section of FAQs to help you learn more about the process. Your local Small Business Development Center (SBDC) also may be able to offer assistance and referrals; you can find yours by going to `www.sba.gov/aboutsba/sbaprograms/sbdc/index.html` and clicking SBDC Locator. We also recommend checking out the United Inventors' Association (UIA; `www.uiausa.org`), which has a lot of information on its Web site. The UIA also offers invention assessment services for a fee.

You'll spend some money to get a professional evaluation of your idea, but it's an investment that could save you thousands later on. Carson says the patent process, from initial application to approval, costs about $50,000 — money you definitely don't want to spend on an idea that won't earn it back several times over.

Don't have $50,000? Check out `www.asktheinventors.com` or read *Inventing on a Shoestring Budget,* by Barbara Russell Pitts and Mary Russell Sarao (Second Sight Publishing).

Outcommercializing the competition

Sometimes ideas that are technically superior fail because their competition reads the market better. That's what happened with Sony's Betamax video format. Although it was arguably a better format, it had serious limitations compared with JVC's VHS format. For one thing, Betamax tapes were only 60 minutes long, not enough to record a movie or more than a one-hour TV show; VHS allowed for up to six hours of recording. And by the time Sony introduced longer Betamax tapes, it was too late. Plus, VHS machines were significantly cheaper to make than Betamax machines and, therefore, cheaper in the stores. Eventually, movie rental stores saw that most of their customers owned VHS machines and began stocking fewer and fewer Betamax movies. Betamax aficionados held on tenaciously, but U.S. production of Betamax ended in the early 1990s, and the last Betamax machine in the world was produced in 2002.

This is a cautionary tale for all of today's inventors. It's not enough to just come up with a great idea. You also have to be able to make your idea more appealing to the market than your competitors'. Cost and ease of use often trump technical superiority. You can charge a premium for better quality, of course, but if someone else comes along with similar advantages at a lower price, you can easily lose out on making your fortune.

Licensing versus producing and selling outright

For the first 10 to 15 years, Doug Carson's company was focused on manufacturing their products. "We just sold products as fast as we could make them," Carson says. "But the problem we got into was that production was getting crowded. There was a lot of competition on that end of things." So DCA changed its strategy and starting applying for patents on its products. "We moved away from being production-based to being licensed-based, and that turned every customer into a revenue-generator for us," Carson says.

That's the essence of licensing. Instead of selling your invention to everybody who wants one, you license another company to use your invention. The company takes on the issues of making, marketing, and selling the product, and you get paid for letting that company do all that work with your idea.

Why is this better? For one thing, it creates a passive income stream for you. You do the work once — coming up with your invention and licensing it to others — and get paid for it over and over again.

You can license your idea before you have a patent, and even before you apply for one. You'll have to take different steps to protect your ownership rights until you do apply for or receive a patent; an attorney who specializes in intellectual property rights can advise you on ways to do this.

Licensing also opens up much greater markets for your idea. Consider OnStar, the General Motors onboard communication, security, and diagnostic system. As of this writing, OnStar is available on 50 GM model vehicles. But if GM licensed the OnStar system to other automakers, their market wouldn't be limited to GM customers or potential customers; they'd also be reaching customers of Toyota, Honda, Nissan, Ford, and so on — in theory, they could reach every single car buyer in the world. And, also in theory, they'd get a cut of every single car sale in the world.

"You read all the time about inventors who sold their ideas outright for ridiculously low sums when they could have been making money on them for the rest of their lives," Carson says. "To me, licensing is the only sensible way to go, unless you just want to give your ideas away."

In fact, Carson says, he decided to switch to licensing for precisely that reason. "There was a niggling feeling that I was just giving it away. And without this kind of revenue stream, we'd be seriously hurting — our industry has been terrible for the past five years from a production standpoint."

If you sell your idea or invention outright, you get a one-time payment, and you forfeit any future royalties because the idea or invention becomes the property of the buyer. If you decide to produce and market your invention yourself, you'll be responsible for those expenses, and you'll spend a lot of time and energy on those tasks — time and energy that may be better spent working on your next great idea. But licensing allows you to make money from one idea while you're working on your next one.

A licensing agreement lets you "rent" the right to make, use, or sell your invention to someone else. Licensing can be exclusive; that is, only the company you make the agreement with has the right to use your invention. Exclusive licensing agreements usually fetch more than nonexclusive ones; the licensee expects your invention to add value to its product and, therefore, expects to make more money if it's the only one offering your invention.

Nonexclusive licenses can be more profitable in the long run, though. That's because your invention can reach an entire market (like all potential car buyers, from the OnStar example earlier in this section) if you license your invention to several companies in the same market sector.

Licensing agreements usually involve either a flat fee or *royalties* — that is, a set percentage per unit sold — or, often, a combination of both. Royalties usually are small, or at least smaller than most inventors expect them to be; often they're less than 3 percent for first-time licensers. But even 2 percent or 3 percent can put you well on your way to making millions if your invention is useful enough to capture a wide market. Remember, too, that the licensee company is taking the financial risk off your shoulders; if the invention fails or doesn't sell as well as expected, it's their money, not yours, that's on the line.

License agreements usually are *time-limited,* meaning they expire after an agreed-upon period. Often, these agreements give the licensee company the right to renew its license, perhaps at a better royalty rate or upon payment of a renewal fee, or both. The length of license agreements varies greatly but most often involves a period of several years. This makes sense, because, in many cases, it will take years to fully develop and market a product based on your invention; the company wants and needs assurance that it'll have the right to use and profit from your invention once the development is done. Lengthy agreements also provide some certainty of income for you.

Not all licensing timeframes are reasonable. A 99-year license (most often used in leasing mineral and timber rights for land but sometimes encountered in other fields) may look like a lot of security for your invention. But suppose your invention really takes off five or ten years into the agreement. If there's a renewal clause in your licensing agreement, you could renegotiate your royalties based on your invention's performance in the marketplace. But if you can't renew your licensing agreement for 99 years, you (and your heirs) could miss out on truly fair compensation.

Protecting Your Big Idea

When you know you can make money on your idea, it's time to take steps to protect it. Depending on what you want to protect, you can use patents, trademarks, or copyrights to formally protect your work. Confidentiality agreements also have a role to play as you begin shopping your idea to potential licensees, and good recordkeeping can help you prove that your idea is really yours.

Patents, trademarks, and copyrights

U.S. and international law provide for the protection of *intellectual property* — anything that comes from your imagination into actual being. Intellectual property is an asset the same way your home or investment account is an asset. You can profit from intellectual property rights; you can lease, sell, and bequeath them; and you can protect them against theft and misuse through patents, trademarks, and copyrights.

For a thorough discussion of intellectual property rights and protections, check out *Patents, Copyrights & Trademarks For Dummies,* 2nd Edition, by Henri J. A. Charmasson and John Buchaca (Wiley).

Patents

Patents issued by the USPTO provide protection within the United States; other patent organizations protect international patent rights. A patent gives you the exclusive right to produce and market your invention for up to 20 years; no one else can make it, license it, use it, sell it, or even offer to sell it without your permission.

The patent application process is lengthy and expensive, and there's no guarantee that you'll get a patent when you apply for one. In 2007, USPTO issued 93,691 patents. The office received nearly 485,000 applications that same year.

Patents are divided into three broad categories:

- ✔ **Utility patents,** which cover processes, machines, and the composition of items (such as prescription drugs)
- ✔ **Design patents,** which protect the appearance and design for things like clothing, protective gear, and characters (like Mickey Mouse or Dora the Explorer)
- ✔ **Plant patents,** which protect hybrid and genetically engineered plants as long as they're reproduced asexually

Sometimes these types of patents overlap; for example, you can apply for both a utility and a design patent for the same invention.

There are things you can't patent. You can't patent a philosophy or other abstract idea — but you can protect these with copyright if you write them down. You can't patent anything that's designed for illegal purposes, or any law of nature or physical element like water or rocks. You also can't patent a perpetual-motion machine, because the USPTO considers it to be impossible.

To qualify for a patent, your idea or invention has to meet these criteria:

- ✔ It has to be new.
- ✔ If it's based on something that already exists, it has to be different enough — and not just in obvious ways, like changing the size or materials — to be considered new.
- ✔ It has to be useful. (This may be one reason why the Pet Rock wasn't patented.)
- ✔ It has to be able to perform the way it's supposed to (which is why perpetual-motion machines aren't considered patentable).

If your invention is based on something that already exists or has been described elsewhere, you have only one year to file a patent application. If you don't file your application within that deadline, your application will be denied — even if you're the one who described your idea in print (and that includes the Internet). It also will be denied if you started your inventing *after* the publication or presentation of a similar idea anywhere in the world.

Patents that were applied for on or after June 8, 1995, last for 20 years from the earliest filing date, and your heirs can inherit valid patents from you.

Trademarks

Trademarks are words, names, logos, even sounds and colors associated with goods and services. Trademarks are issued for ten-year terms and can be renewed indefinitely as long as they're being used in business. You can't renew a trademark for your company if your company is no longer operating.

Trademarks prevent competitors from confusing consumers by using your symbols, company name, or other protected items. For example, in the mid-1990s there was a bar and grill in Dover, Delaware, called The Outback. They had to change their name to The In-Back (referring to their location in a strip mall) after the Outback Steakhouse chain objected. Because the Dover bar and grill was a similar business to the chain, it had to be renamed.

Trademarks don't protect you from competition. They only prevent competitors from using similar symbols, names, or other elements that could confuse consumers. Your competitors can still sell the same goods or services that you do.

Trademarks you own can be sold or assigned to someone else, either during your lifetime or after your death.

Copyrights

Copyright protects written works and any other artistic work that's in *fixed form,* including music, prose and poetry, videogames, puzzles, photographs, paintings, movies, and even choreography as long as it's written down. You can register copyrights through the U.S. Library of Congress, although copyright protection takes effect as soon as the work is created in fixed form. That means you can't copyright an idea that's been rattling around in your head, but the doodle you make on your notepad while you're on hold with the cable company is, technically, protected by copyright.

Copyright lasts for your lifetime plus 70 years for works created after January 1, 1978, and for a maximum of 95 years for works created before then. You can assign copyrights you own to your heirs, your estate, or other beneficiaries.

Confidentiality

Confidentiality is critical in the stages before you apply for — and receive — a patent for your invention. Public disclosure of your idea starts the clock ticking on how long you have to apply for a patent, not to mention the danger that a competitor will slip in ahead of you.

Nondisclosure agreements are a good way to protect that confidentiality. When you're seeking the advice of experts or shopping your idea to potential licensees, you should have them sign a nondisclosure agreement (drawn up by your attorney, of course).

A good nondisclosure agreement can compensate you if your idea is stolen or otherwise used without your permission or proper compensation. Bob knew someone who, thanks to the strong nondisclosure agreement she insisted upon, won a judgment of nearly $50 million from a company that turned down her invention and then produced and marketed it as their own.

When you apply for a patent, you don't need confidentiality agreements; the application itself is public record, available to anyone who cares to read it.

Because confidentiality is a concern, at least in the beginning stages of getting your idea to market, you should discuss details only when you absolutely have to. When you're researching your idea and the competition, do it in the most general terms you can get away with.

Recordkeeping

Good records can help you prove when you thought of your invention and the work you've performed on your idea. Use a logbook to record the date when you first came up with your idea and any activity you undertook to bring your idea to fruition. Test results, drawings, and any other information related to your idea should be included in your logbook.

The integrity and validity of your logbook could come into question during the patent application process. Use a bound journal, not a loose-leaf binder, to record your information; pages can be added at any time to a loose-leaf binder, which can make your entire logbook suspect.

Inventors used to be able to file a *disclosure document* with the USPTO that preserved their rights to file a formal patent application for two years. But that program was discontinued in 2007. Now the USPTO allows inventors to file a *provisional patent application,* which provides more protection than a disclosure document. However, you have to file your formal application within one year of the date you file your provisional application. For more information on provisional applications, go to www.uspto.gov/web/offices/pac/provapp.htm. You can also call the Inventors Assistance Center at 800-786-9199.

Chapter 11

Inheriting Wealth

. . . .

In This Chapter

▶ Understanding the emotional toll of inheriting

▶ Managing your inheritance to meet your financial goals

. . . .

The old joke is that the super wealthy made their money the old-fashioned way: They inherited it. A century or two ago, that may have been true, or at least mostly true. But these days, you don't have to have blue blood to collect a lot of green. Numerous studies by a variety of institutions show that inherited wealth represents only a tiny fraction of most millionaires' assets in the 21st century. The vast majority of today's millionaires have earned their money — which means that, although the rich may indeed be getting richer, more people are rich than ever before.

So, if most wealthy people earn rather than inherit most of their wealth, why are we devoting a chapter to inherited wealth here? Because we are on the brink of the largest transfer of wealth in U.S. history. Today's retirees have more personal wealth than any previous generation. They and their children, the Baby Boom generation, are expected to leave at least $41 *trillion* to their heirs by 2052. (Before you start counting the zeros, though, keep in mind that, according to AARP, only one in five people inherits significant sums, and the median inheritance — the exact midpoint — is $50,000.)

Few people are prepared to deal with the inheritance they receive when a parent or spouse dies, and the combination of grief and responsibility for an inheritance can be overwhelming.

We both have personal experience with this. Bob's first wife died in 1985; Meg's husband died in 2005. Although our situations were different, both of us had to figure out how to handle our emotions and our changed financial circumstances simultaneously. In this chapter, we discuss dealing with common feelings of guilt and fear and explain why it's so important to take the time you need before making any decisions about your inheritance. We take you through the also-common, but potentially dangerous, spendthrift phase of grief and inheritance. And we show you how to find your way back to the values and principles that guide your own making-millions efforts so you can apply them to your inheritance as well.

Thinking about how you might deal with an inheritance and experiencing it are not the same thing. We don't expect this brief chapter to prepare you for the reality of losing a loved one, and you shouldn't expect that, either. Rather, this is an overview of some issues that commonly attend inheriting even modest wealth.

Dealing with the Emotional Impact

Grief, shock, and mental paralysis — a sense of not knowing what to do or being afraid of making the wrong decision — are all common reactions to the death of a loved one. When the death is accompanied by an inheritance, these feelings often are compounded by even more confusing emotions. You may feel relieved if your inheritance eases financial pressures for you. But if you feel relieved, you may also feel guilty about feeling relieved. You may feel angry if a parent divides his estate unevenly between you and your siblings, or you may feel angry if your financial need is greater than a sibling's but each of you gets an equal share. You may be inclined to view your loved one's bequests as something akin to a performance review, where the size of your inheritance reflects the breadth and depth of your loved one's love and respect for you.

Wrestling with all these emotions isn't easy. When you add the responsibility of managing your inheritance, the mixture can be positively overwhelming. You may feel trapped, depressed, and isolated, and you may spend hours or days wishing it would all just go away.

Unfortunately, there's no way around your grief and all the other emotions and responsibilities you face; your only choice is to slog through it at your own pace until the world makes sense to you again. But it helps if you understand what you feel, because then you can step back from your emotions and let the logical part of your brain do its work, in its own time.

Understanding what you feel

When inheritors say, "I don't want the money," that isn't always precisely what they mean. What they're rejecting is the idea that anything good — like financial security — can come from something so heart-rending as the death of a loved one.

In the months before he died, Meg and her husband were just treading water financially. They had a mortgage and two car payments; he was paying child support for his son; and they were still recovering from an earlier period when he was unemployed, which had depleted their savings. They were making ends meet, but only just. Meg, who was in charge of their finances, used to joke that their emergency fund was the $20 bill she keeps tucked away in her wallet.

Then her husband died of a heart attack, and, thanks to the two life insurance policies he left, Meg was suddenly in better financial shape than she had been for years. She was relieved that she could pay off the cars and other debts, but that relief was colored with anger and guilt — anger that widowhood was the price she paid for this new financial security, and guilt that any aspect of her husband's death elicited feelings of relief.

On its own, money strums our most basic emotional chords. Attach it to a death, and it's not surprising that many inheritors feel as though they've been stuffed in a washer set to the spin cycle. The more complex and ambivalent your relationship with the deceased, the more complex and ambivalent your feelings about your inheritance are likely to be.

One technique for sorting out all those tangled emotions is to write them down. Some people are reluctant to do this, fearful of what others will think. But this isn't for public consumption. This is an exercise to help you articulate for yourself what you feel and why you think you feel the way you do. If you have trouble getting started, try asking yourself these questions:

- ✔ What was my relationship with this person like?
- ✔ What does my inheritance represent to me?
- ✔ Do I deserve this inheritance?
- ✔ Do I feel embarrassed about or ashamed of my inheritance?
- ✔ Am I afraid to manage this inheritance?

Issues with the rest of the family over inheritance can compound your emotional turmoil. We don't have space to address these issues here, but we do recommend seeking help — financial, legal, or counseling assistance — if a relative's death strains your family relationships.

Other books may help, too. We recommend *The Wise Inheritor: A Guide to Managing, Investing, and Enjoying Your Inheritance,* by Ann Perry, heiress to the royalties from the original Go Fish card game. If you've inherited enough to put you in the super-wealthy category, check out *Navigating the Dark Side of Wealth: A Life Guide for Inheritors,* by Thayer Cheatham Willis.

It's not unusual to feel like your inheritance is more of a curse than a blessing. Acknowledging that you don't want the responsibility is the first step in preparing yourself to accept it.

Identifying and examining your emotions automatically shifts your internal focus from what you're feeling to what you can, or should, do about it. Sometimes a specific course of action will pop right out at you. Sometimes, though, the best thing to do is just ride it out, having faith that you won't always feel the way you do right now.

Taking your time

Grief counselors advise not making any major decisions about things like selling your house or quitting your job for at least a few months after the death of a spouse or other close relative; some recommend waiting a year before making any decisions like that. Time has a unique way of clearing your head, and options and strategies that never occurred to you immediately after the death are likely to show up quietly, without fanfare or fuss, months later.

Time also can do much to heal the mental paralysis that inheritors often experience. Money represents choices and opportunities, but if your inheritance is more than you've ever managed before, the sheer multitude of options can shock you into doing nothing. In the short run, that's a good thing; doing nothing prevents you from making irreparable mistakes.

In Meg's case, doing nothing was easy. The insurance companies put the proceeds of her husband's life insurance policies in money market accounts and issued her checkbooks to access the money. After she paid off their car loans and other outstanding debt (except the mortgage), Meg let the money sit in the money market accounts, earning a modest-but-safe 3.25 percent, until she was mentally ready to consult a financial planner about her options.

But not all estates are so easy to manage immediately after a death. Sometimes it takes years to sort out various policies, retirement and investment accounts, and other assets. If you have to take control of cash before you're ready to decide what to do with it, we recommend opening a money market account for the time being. That's what money market accounts are for: a place to park your money until you decide what to do with it.

Your accounts with banks and credit unions are insured for a maximum of $100,000, and some smaller institutions aren't equipped to handle huge deposits. If your inheritance is more than $100,000, consider parking the proceeds in a money market mutual fund until you're ready to put it to work for you. Mutual funds aren't insured, but money market mutual funds are extremely safe, and the likelihood of losing any of your inheritance is negligible.

Although not rushing into decisions that you may regret is important, you shouldn't put off your decision-making indefinitely, either. The longer you delay dealing with your inheritance, the more likely you are to keep ignoring it. And, unless you take charge of your inheritance, it probably won't work as hard as it can to help you meet your financial goals.

Thinking of your inheritance as yours

Sometimes the emotional baggage that accompanies an inheritance prevents you from developing a sense of ownership over the assets you receive after a loved one's death. Many inheritors are reluctant to sell their parents' investments, for example, even if those investments don't fit well with their own financial plans and goals. And sometimes inheritors feel an overwhelming sense of obligation to their benefactors. They don't want to make a mistake or let their loved one down somehow, so they never take full charge of the money they've been left.

Time can help you get over these natural early feelings. But if you still have trouble thinking of your inheritance as your own after, say, six months, you may benefit from professional counseling. A grief counselor can help you sort through the emotional maelstrom of losing a loved one, and that can help you get your financial planning and management feet back under you.

What was suitable for your parent or spouse isn't necessarily appropriate for you when it comes to investment choices. Your plan for building wealth depends largely on your stage of life, which can affect both your financial responsibilities and your tax liability.

Managing Your Inheritance

Inheriting is the most common financial windfall people experience. Wisely managed, an inheritance can increase your wealth by 25 percent or more. Unfortunately, inheriting a sizable amount of money can have the same effect on you as winning the lottery: a tendency to believe the money is unlimited, which sparks a spending spree. Grief is a co-conspirator in this dynamic, too. Studies show that when people feel sad, depressed, hopeless, or purposeless, they spend more than they do when their emotions are on an even keel.

When Lutheran Brotherhood, a financial products company, conducted a survey to find out how people would spend a good-size windfall, only 2 percent said they would pay off debt, and only 1 percent said they would invest it. Ten percent would take a vacation, 9 percent would buy a car, and 3 percent would use it to help their children or other relatives. A third would buy a home (or a bigger home), and another third would use it to pay for education.

Inherited money spends the same as any other money you have. You may have to reorganize your goals and develop new strategies to match your hopes and expectations with your new financial reality, but the basis of success is the same — identifying your goals and coming up with a plan to achieve them.

Recognizing the tax implications

Depending on the form your inheritance takes and how much it's worth, there may be significant tax implications for you. The rules governing an inherited IRA, for example, are complex, and, if you don't handle it correctly, you could see as much as 35 percent of that asset go straight to the IRS.

If you're the executor of the estate, you'll have to take an inventory of the estate's assets — real estate, personal property, cash, bank accounts, investments, life insurance policies, and retirement funds. If you're not the executor, you can ask the executor for a copy of the will, if there is one, and a list of assets, along with an estimate of your share. Then, armed with this information, you can consult an accountant or attorney, who can explain the tax considerations and help you identify your options.

Inheritance laws are different in every state. Before you do anything with your inheritance, consult an attorney who specializes in wills and probate or an accountant who has experience with these issues.

Breaking out that list of goals

When you're ready to think about managing your inheritance, your first step is to review your list of financial goals (see Chapter 3). Think about the things you wanted to accomplish before you received your inheritance, and consider how this windfall can help you achieve those goals.

If you don't have an emergency fund, or it's not as robust as you'd like, use your inheritance to start one or fatten it up. If you've been struggling with credit card debt, pay it off with your inheritance. If you've been praying your old clunker will last another winter while you save money for a new car, put some of your inheritance toward reliable transportation.

If you find yourself overwhelmed by grief or guilt when you start thinking about how to use your inheritance, remember that the entire purpose of estate planning is to provide some measure of help to those we leave behind. Proceeds from life insurance and other assets are tools to meet those estate planning goals, and when you inherit them, they become your tools to help you meet your goals.

As with any other unexpected money, consider splitting your inheritance into separate pots, allocating a certain percentage to the goals you've already set for yourself. Alternatively, set priorities for your inheritance. This approach is particularly useful if there isn't enough money to fund all your goals. Meg's priority was to pay off debts other than her mortgage. Then she had to decide whether to use the remainder to refinance her home or to set up an IRA and an investment account. After considering the pros and cons, she opted for the IRA and investments; refinancing the house was a lower priority.

Matching goals and strategies

An inheritance can open up possibilities that didn't make the cut when you originally set your goals. You may be able to tolerate more risk in your investments, for example, or you may reach some of your goals more quickly than you anticipated. In either case, it's time to reassess your current strategy and think about what else you'd like to accomplish.

The death of a loved one often brings the concept of making provisions for your own heirs into sharp relief, so you may feel a sense of urgency about doing your own estate planning. (Chapter 19 discusses estate planning in detail.) Your financial planner can help you devise a strategy to meet these new goals, and your attorney can help you set up the legal structures to make sure your wishes are carried out after your death. (See Chapter 15 for information on finding professional advisers you can trust.)

Review your original financial goals and allocate your inheritance to meet those priorities before you take on new ones. An inheritance is like any other windfall: It can bring you closer to the financial security you've worked so hard to build, but only if you stick with your plan.

Blowing it — or at least some of it

There's nothing wrong with spending some of your inheritance on indulgences. Problems arise, though, when you don't put any brakes on lavish spending. In this respect, lottery winners and inheritors often have the same experience: They spend as though the money will last forever, and before they know it, it's gone — along with their opportunity to make great strides toward financial security.

Put 5 percent of your inheritance in a "mad money" fund, even before you decide what to do with the rest of it. This is money you can play with guilt free, for whatever strikes your fancy. Putting it in a separate account helps limit your spending, which in turn preserves the rest of your inheritance for your real goals and priorities.

Chapter 12

Winning Wealth

*A*ccording to the Consumer Federation of America, one in five Americans thinks winning the lottery is the "most practical" way to build wealth. For those who make less than $25,000 a year, almost twice as many see the lottery as their best hope for making millions, or even just hundreds of thousands.

If you've read other chapters in this book, you know that, no matter what your financial situation is now, there are plenty of things you can do to make it better, both now and for the future. But the lure of "a dollar and a dream" is strong, and some people really do win the lottery. With the proliferation of slots parlors and full-scale casinos over the past 20 years, some people also win big at bingo, blackjack, one-armed bandits, and countless other games of chance.

One of the catches, though — and there are many catches, if gambling is a key part of your wealth-building strategy — is handling the big bucks when you win them. Too often, sudden wealth makes normally prudent people reckless; within a few years, the money is gone, and the winners are in worse financial shape than they were before they got "lucky."

Then there's the personal side of sudden wealth, which can take just as great a toll as — or an even greater toll than — the practical side.

In this chapter, we show you the pitfalls that can accompany winning big and how to avoid them. We spell out the odds — nearly always miserable — against winning in any game of chance so you can better assess how much of your hard-earned money you want to risk. And we discuss the emotional aspects of winning wealth and how those aspects can either help or hurt your financial future.

First, though, we introduce you to one lottery winner who did it right so you can gain some wisdom from his example.

Coping with Sudden Wealth

In 1985, when he was 27, Joe Vella came back from his lunch break and checked his numbers on the lottery machine at his family's hardware store. Within seconds, he learned that he had won a share of the $10 million New York Lotto jackpot.

"I was looking at the machine and saying, 'Okay, I got one number. Oh, I got two. Oh, good, I got three — I won something. Wait, four. What? Five? Really? Five?' You don't believe it at first," Vella says. "I think I was a little different from most people, though, because (a) I had to get back to work, and (b) I had everything my parents had taught me about business and money whispering in my ear."

Vella signed his ticket, put it in a safe-deposit box, and talked to an accountant and an attorney before he went to Albany to claim his prize. His share of the jackpot was $2 million, doled out in annual installments over 20 years (because New York didn't offer the option of taking a lump-sum payment at the time). His yearly payments were $100,000 before taxes, and, for most of the time he received the checks, taxes weren't automatically deducted from his checks.

"That's something a lot of people didn't realize. Yeah, I got a check for $100,000, but I had to give $50,000 of that back at the end of the year. Plus, the money I got from the lottery put me in a higher tax bracket for earned income," Vella says. "By the time all the taxes were accounted for, I got about $47,000 a year from the lottery."

That's a decent salary, especially in the mostly rural area of central New York where Vella lives, but "I couldn't call myself a millionaire with that," he says.

Two years after Joe Vella won the lottery, he and his cousin Lance added a lumberyard to the family hardware business. Everyone assumed Joe had used his lottery winnings to finance the lumberyard, but that wasn't true. "Not one dime" of the lottery money went into building the business, Vella said: "We did what everybody does. We went to the bank and got a loan, and the rest of it was all sweat and blood from the family."

The lottery winnings — after taxes were paid — were invested for the future, and that's where they remain today, Vella said. He never tried to live off his lottery proceeds, and he didn't use the money to buy the trappings of wealth — or even most of his grown-up "toys."

"Of course, the money helped me. It made my life easier, and I have nice things in part because of it. But I also attribute a lot of it to hard work," he says. "It took a lot of the worry away about being able to afford a house and help my daughters with college and that kind of thing."

Word of Vella's lottery win spread quickly in his small community, and he got a lot of unwanted attention, especially at first. A Baptist minister came into the hardware store a week or two after Vella won and urged him to give most of the money away — ideally, he said, to the minister's church. "He thought I had won the whole $10 million, and he said, 'Nobody needs more than $1 million,'" Vella recalls. "I had to tell him that I hadn't won that much. And then I told him, 'I'm Catholic, so if I were going to give the money away to a church, I'd give it to my own church.'"

That wasn't the end of the solicitations for money. In the first two years after winning, Vella got hundreds, perhaps thousands, of calls and letters from people who wanted him to educate their children, pay for their medical care, or just hand money to them for their bills. Old classmates and acquaintances surfaced magically, full of talk about classes and shenanigans Vella barely, if at all, remembered. He was pestered by people who wanted to manage his money for him and people who wanted him to invest in their funds or companies. Firms that specialize in converting annualized payments into lump-sum ones were frequent callers, as were various churches and charities.

The hardest ones to deal with, though, were his friends, Vella says. "I can honestly say I didn't change. The people around me did," he says, echoing a sentiment common among lottery winners. "I lost some friends over this."

There were the inevitable requests to borrow money — "and it was never $10 or $20 — it was $500 or $1,000" — followed by the failure to repay the loan. Vella got angry. Then he started saying, "No."

"They didn't realize that when I gave them $500, it wasn't lottery money — it was money I worked hard for," Vella says. "The lottery money is in investments and trusts. The cash I have on me is what I work for. But everybody thought it was lottery money, and I guess they figured that since it was 'found money,' they didn't have to pay me back."

He stopped socializing for a while because every time he was out with his friends, they'd introduce him to others as a lottery winner. "I didn't like that," Vella says. "I've always been a low-key kind of guy, and I wanted to stay low-key. When strangers know you won the lottery, you can never tell whether they want to hang out with you because you're a cool guy or because they think you've got money."

Eventually, his friends stopped labeling him as the lottery winner, either in public or in their own dealings with him. "They got over it eventually," Vella says. "But it took a good couple years."

Building Wealth from Winnings

Like most lottery winners, Joe Vella (see the preceding section) was touted as a new millionaire when he claimed his prize. But, because of the way his winnings were structured, he had only about $47,000 a year from the lottery — hardly an unlimited sum of money.

Unfortunately, many lottery winners (and casino jackpot winners, for that matter) are dazzled by the celebratory hype that always accompanies a big win, and it's hard to see the boulders in your path when stars — or dollar signs — are in your eyes. If everybody around you keeps saying, "Congratulations, you're a millionaire!", you can be forgiven for thinking, "Hey, yeah, I'm a millionaire!" After all, that has a much nicer ring than "Hey, I'm a 47,000-dollar-aire!"

But, nice ring or no, the second phrase is closer to reality than the first. Even if you win a $1 million jackpot and take it in a lump sum, you'll get only about $500,000 after taxes. And although that's nothing to curl your lip at, it's a far cry from being independently wealthy.

So, how do you let the inevitable hype swirl around you without letting it go to your head? Take your time, get professional advice, talk to your family, and implement a management plan.

Taking your time

Joe Vella did the smart thing when he put his winning lottery ticket in a safe-deposit box and went back to work. Instead of rushing off to Albany to claim his money, he gave himself time to think about what winning the money meant.

Experts recommend this do-nothing approach for everyone who comes into money suddenly. Especially if you're not used to having money, the sudden onset of wealth can overwhelm your emotions and thought processes. You're in a uniquely fragile state, and it's easy for others — even family and friends — to take advantage of you under these conditions.

If you have a winning lottery ticket, sign it and make a copy of it. Unsigned lottery tickets are like cash; if there's no signature, anyone who finds or takes your lottery ticket can claim it as her own.

After you've signed the ticket and made a copy, put the original and the copy in separate safe places. That way, if you lose the original, you'll have proof that you did purchase the ticket.

Lump sums versus annual payments

When you play the lottery, you usually have to decide when you buy your ticket whether you want any winnings in one lump sum or in annual payments. There are advantages and disadvantages to both. With a lump sum, you have control over how the money is invested when you win, and you may want to take a more aggressive approach to build more wealth faster. On the other hand, it's easy to let a lump sum go to your head, and you could end up spending more of it faster than you intended. Annual payments offer you the security of a guaranteed income for a number of years (usually, 20 years), but, if you intend to quit your job and live off your winnings, annual payments may make that more difficult.

Whichever route you choose, financial experts recommend investing your lottery proceeds and spending only the earnings, not the principal, of those investments. That's the best way to ensure your winnings will still be around to give you security and independence years from now.

If you can't do what Vella did and wait a few days before claiming your prize — for example, you have to take your winnings from the casino or slots parlor right away — do the next best thing and park the money in a separate account at your bank. Don't link it to your regular checking or savings account, and don't sign up for an ATM or debit card linked to it. Just deposit the money and let it sit for a while until you've come up with a plan.

This is also the time to find out whether you have the option of keeping your winnings private. Joe Vella didn't have any choice about the publicity surrounding his lottery win; the news conference and public revelation of his identity was a requirement to claim his prize.

But some lottery winners do manage to keep their identities out of the public eye. They set up trusts, and a representative of the trust — often, a bank officer or an attorney — collects the prize money on the winner's behalf.

Obviously, there are advantages to keeping your lottery win a secret from the general public. You won't have to deal with the news media, and people are less likely to recognize you as a lottery winner in the grocery store or call you at all hours asking for a share of the pie. The smaller the circle of people who know about your winnings, the fewer hassles you have in beginning your new life with money.

If staying unknown isn't an option — each state lottery has its own rules about this — figure out how you'll cope with the publicity. Some winners assign a relative or other representative, like an attorney, as a spokesperson to respond to media requests. Many experts recommend changing your phone number to an unpublished one (not just unlisted, because persistent folks can still find your number through a variety of venues) and getting out of town for a few weeks or months, until the hubbub dies down a bit.

Getting professional advice

Before you take any steps with your winnings, consult an accountant, a financial planner, or an attorney to make sure you understand both your options and the legal ramifications of your sudden wealth. (See Chapter 15 for information on selecting professional advisers.)

Joe Vella says talking with an accountant and an attorney before he claimed his winnings helped him understand exactly what he could do with the money — and what he couldn't. "There's a lot of responsibility to managing that money," he says. "If you don't have the right guidance, I can see how people run through their winnings and don't even know how it happened. It could really ruin your life."

A professional adviser can help you get a handle on the number-crunching aspect of your new wealth — your tax obligations and how the winnings will affect your "regular" tax situation, the responsibilities you'll have if you buy a bigger house, and so on.

Talking to your family

Sudden wealth can have a devastating impact on your personal relationships. You've heard stories of lottery winners whose spouses or significant others sued for a share of the winnings, of relatives who tried to hire hit men in hopes of inheriting the lottery winner's money, or of relatives who convinced the lottery winner to invest in shaky business deals or other poorly conceived moneymaking schemes. These things really do happen, mainly because money strikes such deep emotional chords in most people.

After you've gotten some perspective from your professional adviser, it's time to sit down with your partner — and perhaps your children and other relatives, too — to discuss what the money means and how it changes your plans.

Your family likely will suffer some degree of sudden-wealth shock, too, and they may have unrealistic ideas of what you can do with all this extra money. That's why we recommend talking to a financial professional first; then you can educate your relatives about how much money you actually have to play with.

This is a good time to break out your list of goals (see Chapter 3) and review them together. Talk about which goals your winnings can help you accomplish and whether you want to add any other goals to your list now that you have more money.

Here are some things to consider when you have your family discussion:

- ✔ **Budgeting:** Think about splitting your winnings into separate pots — for example, using part of the money for debt reduction, saving or investing part of it for the future, and maybe using part of it to satisfy immediate needs or fancies like a more economical car or new furniture.

- ✔ **Priorities:** Your values don't change just because your income does. If you find yourself (or your family members) slipping into the seduction of sudden wealth, you can realign your internal compass by reviewing what your priorities were before you won the lottery. If getting out of debt was your top priority the day before you won the lottery, buying a personal jet shouldn't be your top priority the day after.

- ✔ **Indulgences:** Part of the joy of "found money" is being able to splurge on things you couldn't or wouldn't buy before. There's no reason you can't enjoy spending some of your winnings, as long as you don't overspend. This is where many lottery winners get into trouble: They spend as though they have limitless funds, and sooner or later the well runs dry.

When you're trying to figure out how much of your money you can "blow," try thinking in terms of percentages. If you spent 10 percent of your winnings on nonessentials, would that leave enough to fund your priorities? How about 5 percent?

Implementing a management plan

After you've taken the time to adjust to the idea of your newfound wealth and gotten the input you need from your family and professional advisers, you're ready to start on your management plan for your winnings. Having a plan in place can help you stay on track with your priorities and learn to say no to people who want you to shower them with money.

Protecting your assets

Joe Vella put his lottery winnings in investments and trusts for two reasons: He wanted that money to grow for the future, and he wanted to limit any temptation — on his part or his family's — to spend it.

Putting your money aside in these kinds of accounts — as opposed to a basic savings account or checking account, accessible with an ATM — forces you to think before you spend, and that alone can help protect you against both your own whims and the requests of others.

Anticipating requests

At the obligatory news conference often arranged for lottery winners when they claim their prize, lots of winners announce that they intend to help their extended families and give to charity. These are laudable intentions and make for great sound bites on the evening news, but they may not be practical.

Suppose you have a sibling, an in-law, or another relative who always seems to be in shallow financial water or who comes up with crazy schemes that never pan out. You can be pretty sure this relative will have his hand out when you collect your winnings. How will you handle it?

What about a friend who wants to continue her education but doesn't have the money? Or a relative whose car is on its last legs? Or someone who needs a new furnace before winter? If you decide to help out with these things, will it be a loan or a gift? If it's a loan, how will you feel — and how will it affect your relationship with that person and anyone else involved — if the borrower doesn't pay you back?

As of 2008, you can give up to $12,000 a year to any individual as a gift without incurring tax liabilities either for yourself or for the recipient.

Thinking about these scenarios before they arise — and talking about them with your spouse or partner — can help you avoid giving into guilt or other emotional manipulation.

There's nothing wrong with helping out others, and we're not saying you should meet every request with deaf ears. But money issues have ruined countless relationships, and this is especially true for people who experience sudden wealth.

You can't anticipate every solicitation for money, but you can develop a general plan for considering these solicitations when they come your way. Whenever someone wants you to write him a check, whether it's a relative, a friend, or a charity, ask yourself these questions:

- ✔ **Is this what I consider a good use of money?** You shouldn't feel obligated to finance something for someone else if it strikes you as foolish, wasteful, or unnecessary.

- ✔ **What would I give up if I gave away this money?** If you have to sell investments or otherwise sacrifice something you've planned on, the trade-off may not be worth it.

- ✔ **What if this person doesn't pay me back?** Think not just about the effect on your relationship, but the effect on your pocketbook, too. If you don't get repaid, would that cause difficulties for you? Sometimes you can give others money without expecting to get it back, and that's okay. But don't cut yourself short to help out someone else.

Learning to say no

Joe Vella learned the hard way that, when people know you have money, they're not shy about asking you to share it with them. Sometimes they even act as though they're entitled to a portion of your money, especially in the case of winning the lottery, which requires more luck than skill.

It's one thing, and hard enough to say no, when friends and acquaintances try to help themselves to the contents of your wallet. When family members do it, the emotional burden can make it nearly impossible to refuse. Lots of lottery winners — often, those who end up broke within a few years — report that they gave money away to friends and family to try to keep the relationships on an even keel. But that seldom works.

Here are some things to remember if you ever find yourself feeling guilty about or ashamed of your winnings:

- **By definition, winning the lottery (or any other kind of gambling) isn't fair.** You can't make it fair by giving away your winnings.

- **Winning the lottery only gives you additional resources to build your financial security.** It still requires work and responsibility to manage those resources wisely.

- **Having money doesn't make you any more responsible for others' financial well-being than you were before you had money.** Your first responsibility is, as it always has been, to yourself and your immediate family.

- **Wanting to help is a natural desire, but giving away money isn't always the best way to help.** Share your knowledge, your experience, and your advice freely to help others learn how to help themselves.

Treating Gambling as What It Is

The average lottery player spends $150 a year on drawing and scratch-off tickets. Casual casino visitors — those who gamble once or twice a year — spend an average of around $250 per visit. The vast majority of them win nothing and so have nothing to show for their wagers.

On the other hand, if you took that same $150 a year and put it in a 401(k) or IRA earning 8 percent, it would be worth $28,000 in 35 years. That doesn't count any employer contributions to a 401(k) plan or any other money you might put into an IRA over the years. If you saved $250 a year — slightly more than $20 a month — you'd have $51,800 in 35 years.

Naturally, we like investing better than any lottery or other game of chance. That's because we know, stories of the rare big winner notwithstanding, that your odds of scooping in the big jackpot in any venue are closer to none than to slim.

Gambling is not an investment strategy. If you're serious about building wealth, concentrate your efforts on things you can control: reducing debt; saving money; and making conscious, wise investment decisions. Play the lottery or the slots if you like, but don't count on it to make your financial dreams come true.

Understanding the odds

Ever wonder why poor people always seem to win the lottery? It's simple: Poor people play the lottery more often than wealthy folks. The well-to-do tend to buy lottery tickets when the jackpot is big, but studies show that only 20 percent of lottery players kick in more than 80 percent of lottery revenues, and those 20 percent are disproportionately low-income people, often minorities, without a college education and, in many cases, without a complete high-school education. This is what fuels many vocal antilottery movements — the fact that the most frequent players tend to be those who can afford to squander their money the least.

Why do we call it squandering? Because the odds against winning are astronomical, especially in multistate games like Powerball and Mega Millions. If you buy one Mega Millions ticket, your odds of winning are 1 in more than 135 million. (You're almost 200 times more likely to get struck by lightning this year.)

Buying more tickets doesn't significantly increase your odds of winning. If you buy ten Mega Millions tickets, your odds of winning are 10 in more than 135 million. Twenty tickets, and your odds are 20 in more than 135 million. And so on. That 135 million figure doesn't change, and, unless you can afford to buy hundreds of thousands of tickets, your odds don't change significantly. But then, if you can afford to buy hundreds of thousands of Mega Millions tickets, why on Earth are you playing the lottery?

Joe Vella, our smart lottery winner, understands the odds. He still plays occasionally, but only a buck at a time. "There's no reason to spend $20 on lottery tickets," he says. "Even if you have different numbers on each ticket, your odds are still 1 in something horrible for each ticket."

What about other games of chance, like blackjack or slot machines? There again, the odds are stacked against you. Every casino, every slots parlor, and every bingo hall is structured so the house always gets its share. Depending on the game and the type of bet you place, the house "edge" can be as high as 22 percent or more.

For slots, the house edge is between 5 percent and 15 percent, depending on the type of game and the denomination of the machine; casinos and slots parlors pay out more on the $5 machines than they do on the nickel machines. If you know how to play basic strategy in blackjack, and you actually do it (many players abandon basic strategy when they get to the tables), you can cut the house edge to as little as 0.6 percent. But if you plunk a dollar down on the money wheel, the house edge is more than 11 percent.

The problem is, there's not much you can do to improve your odds of winning in any game of chance. Sure, you can make sure you buy only scratch-off tickets from the newest games; that at least ensures that there are, indeed, prizes to be claimed. And you can educate yourself about the house edge on various types of bets in casinos and limit your gambling to the wagers that give you the best odds. But even so, you're more likely to lose money than to win it.

Taking the right attitude

We aren't opposed to gambling per se, but we do advise extreme caution. Gambling can be addictive for some people, and, even if you don't have a gambling problem, it's easy to get carried away by the atmosphere at a slots parlor or the illusory promise of riches when a lottery jackpot hits eight or nine figures.

Gambling is a form of entertainment. That means you should budget for it and stick to your budget — no buying $50 worth of lottery tickets when your budget calls for $5, and no hitting the ATM at the slots parlor after you've spent the $25 you planned to spend.

Chapter 13

Investing for Wealth

*W*hat if you don't want to start your own business, have no aptitude for inventing, don't expect to inherit money, and have never won the lottery? Where do you go to build wealth if none of these other ways are a good fit for you?

Answer: The stock market.

Don't panic — it's not as scary as it seems. Even when the economy is hurting and the markets slump, the stock market is one of your best options for amassing a fortune. In fact, that's just when it makes the most sense to get *in* the stock market, because you'll find some great bargains when the bears are running Wall Street.

No one really knows how the terms *bear market* and *bull market* came about, but you can remember the difference this way: Bulls stampede in groups, creating a lot of energy, and bears hibernate alone, conserving their energy. Likewise, bull markets are full of moving-forward energy, and everybody wants to be in the stampede; bear markets move sluggishly, and investors take on an everyone-for-himself attitude.

Even with the prevalence of 401(k)s and individual retirement accounts (IRAs), many people just aren't comfortable enough with the stock market to jump in. In this chapter, we pull aside the veil of mystery and show you how to take advantage of the best the stock market has to offer. First, we take you step by step through the process of investing, from developing your investment philosophy to deciding whether to go through a broker or invest yourself. We show you which investments make the most sense for the average investor and tell you why. And, finally, we highlight the pitfalls to watch out for and tell you how to avoid them.

We define financial terms throughout this chapter, but if you want handy resources for additional terms, go online and bookmark these two sites: InvestorWords.com (www.investorwords.com) and Raymond James: Glossary of Investment Terms (www.raymondjames.com/gloss.htm). Then, whenever you run across an investing term you aren't familiar with, you can look it up instantly.

Developing Your Investment Philosophy

The beauty of investments is that you can create a portfolio that suits your values, your financial goals, and your comfort level when it comes to risk. (A *portfolio* is your entire collection of investments and financial vehicles, including stocks, bonds, and insurance.) There aren't really any hard-and-fast rules here, unless you count Warren Buffett's basic tenets of investing:

> Rule #1: Don't lose money.
>
> Rule #2: See Rule #1.

Other than that, how you fill out your portfolio is up to you. To figure out what your philosophy is, though, you need to know a few things: how much risk you're willing to take with your money, how to learn from investing's whiz kids, how to decide whom to listen to, and how to take (and keep) control of your investments.

Determining your risk tolerance

Financial advisers use different terms for risk tolerance — *investor profile, risk temperament,* or *risk profile,* for example — but they all seek to answer the same question: How comfortable are you with the possibility of losing money?

The answer is important because it will dictate the kinds of investments that are right for you. If losing 10 percent of your savings would turn you into an instant insomniac with chronic indigestion, you probably don't want to plow a lot of your money into an investment that carries a high risk. But if you're one of those people who gets a thrill out of the ups and downs of the stock market, a portfolio full of safe government bonds earning a staid 3 percent will be singularly unsatisfying.

Stock is ownership interest in a company or mutual fund. Stock can be designated as *common, capital,* or *preferred.* Ownership rights and earnings may vary depending on which type of stock you buy; common stock often offers greater rewards in the form of earnings. Common stock shares profits with you, the investor, in the form of higher dividends. With preferred stock, dividends are fixed, so the price of preferred stock grows at a slower rate. If the company fails, holders of preferred shares are in line ahead of common shareholders to get paid (although they may get pennies only on the dollar).

Unlike stocks, which represent partial ownership of a company, *bonds* represent a loan to the issuer. The issuer promises to pay back the principal and a set rate of interest on a specific date. When you buy government bonds, you're loaning the federal government money in exchange for a guaranteed return. The return is lower than you can earn on stocks because the risk of losing your initial investment is virtually nonexistent. (*Munis,* short for *municipal bonds,* are bonds issued by state and local governments, or state agencies and authorities. Often, interest earned on munis is exempt from federal income taxes, but sometimes it's subject to the alternative minimum tax. See Chapter 17 for more on income taxes.)

Mutual funds are investment vehicles run by *fund families,* which may be companies or trusts. These fund families (Fidelity, Vanguard, and Putnam are all fund families) use their money to invest in other companies; your shares in a mutual fund actually represent fractions of shares in a variety of companies. Fund families typically categorize their mutual funds according to market sector — health, transportation, energy, and so on.

Different advisers also have different classifications of risk tolerance. Some use only three categories: conservative, moderate, and aggressive (see the following sections). Some use as many as seven, ranging from very defensive (or very conservative) to very aggressive.

Tons of risk tolerance calculators are available on the Web. If you just want to know how much of your money should be invested in stocks, check out the Tools & Calculators section at www.kiplinger.com. We like the calculator at www.calcxml.com/do/inv08 because it asks you about several scenarios in just ten questions, and then rates your risk tolerance and offers additional resources (other calculators on asset allocation, for example, and articles on various types of investments) based on your results.

Risk tolerance: Conservative

Conservative investors don't like the idea of losing money. Some are extremely conservative; for them, opening a monthly statement and seeing a lower balance than there was the previous month is the equivalent of reading a Stephen King novel: nerve-wracking and horrifying. If this describes you, most, if not all, of your investments should be tucked away in cash, cash-equivalent accounts like CDs and money markets, and *gilt-edged securities* (the bond equivalent of blue-chip stocks) like government bonds. Your returns won't make headlines, but you probably won't lose capital, either.

One problem with conservative investment strategies is that your money may not keep up with inflation. So even if the number of dollars you have doesn't go down, your purchasing power will. When you factor taxes into the equation, a too-conservative strategy could mean a lower standard of living for you in the long run.

There are lots of reasons why you may want to take a conservative approach to your investments. If you're close to retirement or already retired, you're more interested in income from your investments than in growth; you want to preserve the capital as much as possible. If you can't go back to work or your health is poor, hanging on to what you've got may be a much higher priority than going after bigger yields.

If you can tolerate a little risk, you can take a moderately conservative approach to your investments. The vast majority of them probably will remain in cash or cash-equivalent accounts, but you may want to divert a certain percentage of your portfolio — say, 10 percent to 25 percent — to high-quality stocks that can help you come out ahead after taxes and inflation. Moderately conservative investors typically are those who are retired or near retirement and who need their money to produce income for them for at least ten years.

Risk tolerance: Moderate

Most investors fall into the moderate category — some leaning a little to the conservative side, some a little to the aggressive side, and a whole bunch plumb spang in the middle. These are people who want to see their money grow significantly, and they have time — at least 15 to 20 years — to ride out the market's ups and downs before they have to rely on their investments for income.

Moderate portfolios are well-balanced and *diversified* (spread among several different companies, types of investment, and sectors — like healthcare, technology, domestic stocks, foreign stocks, and so on). They typically hold a few ultra-safe bond funds on one end, a few high-risk stocks on the other, and a mix of virtually every other major asset class in the middle. These portfolios won't go up as much as the markets in good times, but they won't decline as much in bad times, either. Their performance often is compared to the S&P 500 or another whole-market index; when the index goes up, the moderate portfolio should go up, too (although not quite as much), and when the index goes down, the portfolio should decline, too (but, again, not as much). Moderate-risk investments produce middle-of-the-road growth and earnings.

Moderate-risk portfolios aren't going to make you a millionaire overnight. But your returns will stay ahead of taxes and inflation. And, when the markets are good, you can easily see your investments earn double-digit returns.

Risk tolerance: Aggressive

Aggressive investors go for the growth. When you take an aggressive approach, your portfolio likely will slide further than the markets during down times, but it also will post bigger gains during good times. Depending on how aggressive you are, you may lose 40 percent or more of your money when the markets are down, but you also can see returns of 15 to 35 percent when the markets are up.

The younger you are, the more aggressive you can afford to be in your investment strategy, because you have more time to recoup your losses before you have to rely on your investments for income. If you've already got enough money to cover your living expenses, and your emergency fund is full, you also may be inclined to take more risk than someone who's already on a tight budget or close to retiring.

Risk and yields are directly proportionate. The higher the risk, the greater the potential earnings. The lower the potential earnings, the safer your principal is.

Most people think they're very risk tolerant when their investments are doing well. But when the stock market takes a dive, so does your tolerance for risk. Neuroscientists think this behavior is hard-wired into the human brain, which explains a lot of the panicky behavior you see in the markets. For a full explanation of how your brain responds to investing, check out "Are You Wired for Wealth?", an excellent article from the October 1, 2002, issue of *Money* magazine. You can read it online at `http://money.cnn.com/magazines/moneymag/moneymag_archive/2002/10/01/328637/index.htm`.

Getting advice from the big guns

There's no shortage of investment advice out there. There are newspaper columns, radio shows, Web sites, newsletters, seminars, books, magazines, TV shows, and even entire cable channels devoted to the art of investing. Note that word *art.* There is no hard science in the investing world, because there are too many variables — not the least of which is human nature — to draw a universal model capable of predicting what the market will do at any given time.

Investing giants like Warren Buffett know this. At the 2008 Berkshire Hathaway stockholders meeting in Omaha, Buffett told the crowd that he and his team "have no idea" what will happen with the stock market. "We're not in that business," he said. Why not? Because, by and large, it's a fool's game.

If even the Oracle of Omaha doesn't know what the markets will do next, how can you figure out your investment strategy? Focus on the fundamentals: Look for value, educate yourself, and know what you don't know.

Looking for value

Value investing is nothing new. It was proposed by Benjamin Graham in the 1940s, and Warren Buffett was so influenced by Graham's perspective that he built his own investment philosophy on Graham's foundation. In simple terms, Graham said that, although many people view the stock market as a popularity contest, chasing after stocks that others covet, the smart investor views the market as a set of scales. Over the long run, Graham said, the true value of any stock will be weighted appropriately by the market.

Graham also distinguished between investment and speculation. If you understand how a business works and its true financial condition, risk is minimized, and putting money into its stock is an investment. If you don't do your homework, and you buy stock simply because it seems to be hot right now, that's *speculation* — and much more risky, because you don't really know whether the company has the financial wherewithal to perform well.

Millionaires-in-the-making take the long view about investing. They know that down times present opportunities for spotting value, but they also know it may take a while for them to realize any gains. Get-rich-quick hucksters try to time the market — something no one has been able to do reliably in more than 300 years — which is nothing more than speculating.

The easiest way to quickly assess the value of a stock or mutual fund is to look at the *price-to-earnings (P/E) ratio,* the price of a share of stock divided by its earnings per share for the past 12 months. If a stock sells at $10 per share, and each share earned $1 over the past year, the P/E ratio is 10 (10 ÷ 1 = 10). Both stocks and mutual funds have P/E ratios. Our general rule: If the P/E ratio is higher than 22, the stock is pretty expensive in relation to its earnings and may be overvalued at the current market price.

Educating yourself

With the resources available today, there's really no excuse not to learn as much as you can about how money and the markets work. Aside from this book, here are other sources we recommend:

- ✔ **BobBrinker.com (www.bobbrinker.com):** Bob Brinker is the host of the nationally syndicated radio show *Money Talk,* and you can listen to it from his Web site. You also can read dozens of articles about money management and investing, and, if you're so inclined, you can subscribe to his *Marketimer* newsletter. *Note:* Although much on the site is free, the newsletter costs $185 a year within the United States — but you can get one free copy through the Web site, to see if you're interested in subscribing.

✔ *The Intelligent Investor,* **by Benjamin Graham (HarperBusiness Essentials):** Warren Buffett has called it the best investment book ever written, and he often refers to it in his public talks. At the 2008 Berkshire Hathaway annual meeting, he recommended it again, saying, "You can't go wrong following [Graham's] advice." The book originally was published in 1949, and it's now in its fourth edition.

✔ *Investing For Dummies,* **5th Edition, by Eric Tyson, MBA, and** *Value Investing For Dummies,* **2nd Edition, by Peter J. Sander, MBA, and Janet Haley (both published by Wiley):** These two books have the space we lack to get into all the nitty-gritty about investing in today's market and economy, and, like this book, they spell it out in plain, easy-to-understand English.

✔ *The Science of Getting Rich,* **by Wallace D. Wattles (Tarcher):** A classic from the early 20th century (originally published in 1910), this book discusses ways to use your own will to direct your thoughts and actions so you can achieve your goals.

✔ *Think and Grow Rich,* **by Napoleon Hill (Wilder):** Originally published toward the end of the Great Depression, this inspirational book describes the power of thought, especially when it comes to your finances.

In addition to the resources listed here, we recommend you make a habit of reading the financial and business sections of your local newspaper and your favorite online news sites, like CNNMoney.com, CNBC (www.cnbc.com), and Bloomberg.com.

Knowing what you don't know

Charlie Munger, Warren Buffett's right-hand man at Berkshire Hathaway, thinks diversification is overrated — a tactic for "know-nothing investors," not professionals. Buffett, recognizing that not all investors are pros, says reassuringly that there's nothing wrong with being a "know-nothing" investor, and if you fall into that category, diversification is a good strategy.

The trick here is knowing what you don't know — and being okay with not knowing everything, or even much, about investing. If we were gamblers, we'd be willing to bet that this describes the majority of people who know they should put money in their 401(k)s and IRAs but who can't by any stretch be considered investing experts.

Although it's important to educate yourself about finances so you can reach your goals, you don't have to become an expert to do it. Learn as much as you're willing to learn, and don't be afraid to keep things simple.

Lack of confidence can be just as costly as overconfidence. Don't let your lack of knowledge, or your fear, keep you from taking action. Sure, you may make a mistake or two by acting, but the cost of failing to act at all can be much, much higher.

At the 2008 Berkshire Hathaway meeting, Warren Buffett was asked how he would invest $1 million if he (a) weren't a professional investor and (b) were just starting his investing career. Both he and Charlie Munger, Berkshire Hathaway's vice chairman, recommended a low-cost index fund for the "casual" (that is, "not an expert") investor. (*Index funds* are mutual funds that attempt to replicate whole-market performance by purchasing stocks in the same proportion as the index the fund is matched to — for example, the S&P 500.)

Choosing whom to listen to

Not all those who offer you financial advice are doing it out of the goodness of their hearts. There are many honest, honorable people in the financial-services profession, but there are also many who see your money as a paycheck and you as a mark.

Stock brokers and commission-based financial planners make money every time you do business with them. Sometimes what they recommend makes sense. But sometimes their recommendations do more good for their bottom lines than for yours.

Likewise, people who want you to pay a big subscription fee for their investment newsletters are making money telling you how to make money. They may have sound advice. But we can almost guarantee they don't have any "secrets" that you can't uncover on your own. In most cases, you're better off using the resources you can get for free or for relatively little outlay, such as books and financial magazines like *Forbes, Money,* and *Fortune.*

Whenever you hear advice — not just on financial matters, but on anything — bring your critical-thinking skills to bear. Does the advice make sense to you? Does it fit with your situation or your goals? Would you share this advice with someone you cared about? If you hesitate when asking yourself these questions, trust your hesitation — not the advice.

Fee-based financial planners charge an hourly rate to go over your portfolio and make recommendations. The rate is often high — in the hundreds of dollars or more for a consultation — but you can expect an honest assessment of your options without the competing interest of the planner's commission.

Taking control of your investments

Taking control of your investments doesn't begin and end with deciding which stocks and funds to buy. It consists of what the financial and legal professions call *due diligence* — doing your homework before you invest. Look into the stocks or funds you want to buy, and find out as much as you can about the company's history, reputation, and performance record.

Thanks to the Internet, it's easy to research potential investments before you shell out any money at all. Here are some of our favorite online resources (and most of them are free):

- **Bloomberg.com (www.bloomberg.com):** You can get news, market data, and investment tools here, including an economic calendar that tells you when government reports on things like housing, employment, and other topics are due. Some research requires a subscription fee, but much of what you need is free.

- **Hoover's (www.hoovers.com):** Use the search box on the site's home page to get information on specific companies.

- **U.S. Securities and Exchange Commission (www.sec.gov):** Under the Filings & Forms (EDGAR) tab, you can access all the financial filings of a publicly traded company. The site offers a tutorial to show you how to use the EDGAR system, too.

Keep records of your investments organized. It's easier to keep track of your money's progress if you have all your statements in one place, in chronological order. Keep copies of the *prospectus* (a publication required by the Securities and Exchange Commission, which explains, often in highly technical language, how the investment works and the expenses associated with it) and any other pertinent research, too.

Investing in the Stock Market

If you have any kind of retirement account, you're in the stock market. Individual retirement accounts, 401(k)s, and other retirement savings vehicles were created to give workers an incentive, in the form of tax breaks, to put away their own money for retirement instead of relying on Social Security or the old-fashioned (and quickly disappearing) company pension.

And, by the way, if you do have a company pension, you also have a stake in the stock market, because most, if not all, pension plans are largely funded by company stock. When Bear Stearns succumbed to the subprime mortgage mess in 2008 and its stock price dropped to virtually junk status, thousands of employees lost millions in retirement savings because most of it was invested in Bear Stearns stock.

There are limits on what you can put in an IRA or 401(k) every year. But that doesn't mean you can't get into the stock market with other funds. After you've maxed out your IRA and your employer's 401(k) match, and you've got enough cash on hand to meet any money emergencies that might arise, it's time to consider putting some money to work on Wall Street.

No matter what your financial goals are, your goal in the stock market is to minimize risk and maximize returns. For most people, this means diversifying your investments and forcing yourself to be patient. It also means knowing what kinds of investments to look for and what to avoid.

The importance of diversifying

If you're not a professional investor, diversifying your portfolio is the easiest way to minimize risk. Your overall returns may be smaller in the long run, but your overall losses will be smaller, too.

We like simple investment choices that, put together, balance risk and return potentials: index funds, small-business funds, value funds, high-quality bond funds, and high-yielding cash accounts. Funds offer instant diversification because they invest in a variety of companies either within a market sector or in the market at large, saving you the effort and (possible) anxiety of selecting individual stocks. These investments offer good earnings, low fees, and low tax liabilities, making them perfect for your long-term financial goals.

Index funds

Index funds are mutual funds — that is, every share you own in an index fund is actually a collection of fractional shares of every company listed on the index the fund is linked to. Most commonly, index funds attempt to imitate the performance of the S&P 500, but some funds are linked to other indices (such as the Dow Jones Industrial Average, the NASDAQ Composite Index, or the Nikkei average). Expenses on index funds are low, usually less than 0.2 percent of the fund's assets — compared with up to 3 percent, or even more, for actively managed funds (which buy and sell stock more often).

Index funds are a passive investment. They hold on to stocks longer, so capital-gains taxes don't eat into your returns as much. And, because index funds follow a buy-and-hold pattern, they beat four out of five actively managed funds on returns alone. Add in the tax efficiency, and it's hard to beat index funds for total returns.

S&P 500 index funds are blue-chip U.S. stock funds. *Blue chips* are high-quality stocks or companies that have a long track record and have proved their ability to make a profit and pay dividends to their shareholders. Sometimes dividends are paid in cash; sometimes a company will issue a *stock dividend,* in which shareholders get additional stock based on how many shares they originally held.

You also can purchase international stock index funds — a smart strategy, because nearly two-thirds of the world's economic activity takes place abroad.

Small-business funds

Small-company funds have a higher risk than blue-chip funds, but they also can generate significantly higher returns — especially because, when blue chips are down, small companies tend to go up. Over the long term — ten years or more — your small-company fund can beat the rest of your portfolio by 1 percent to 3 percent.

Some small-company funds are passive index funds, and some are actively managed. For actively managed funds, the fees will be higher, but sometimes it's worth paying a little more (only a little, mind you) for a better-performing fund.

Value funds

Some of the best deals in the market come from stocks that are underpriced or simply overlooked by investors. Over the years, value stocks tend to outperform *growth stocks* (stocks issued by companies that have a history of increasing their stock earnings at a faster-than-normal pace). But who has time to do all the research to figure out which stocks are really bargains? Value index funds let you take advantage of the bigger dividends offered by underpriced companies without having to be an expert.

Watch the fees on value funds. Some, like the Vanguard Value Index, have low fees that make them true values. But the higher the fees, the less value there really is in a value fund.

Bond funds

Bond funds won't generate nearly the returns of your stock funds, but they provide a nice counterweight to the ups and downs of the markets. Historically, investing just $1 in bonds for every $4 you put into stocks can reduce your overall risk substantially without cutting too deeply into potential returns.

Average fees on bond funds run a little over 1 percent, and, because bond funds only return around 5 percent, getting the best deal on fees is important to your long-term growth. Keep in mind, too, that taxes and inflation will cut further into your bond returns. Look for a fund with annual fees at 0.3 percent or lower.

Make a place in your portfolio for inflation-protected bond funds, too. These funds invest in Treasury Inflation-Protected Securities (TIPS), which pay a preset yield *and* tweak the bond's principal value to prevent a loss in purchasing power.

High-yield cash accounts

Cash reserves aren't just for your emergency fund. You also should have a separate cash stash earmarked for further investments. Cash in a money-market account may (or, more likely lately, may not) earn enough to keep up with inflation, but its real purpose is to sit by patiently, waiting for the right market opportunity to appear. If you can't get at some cash, you'll either have to pass on an investment you want to buy or sell some of your current investments — thus exposing yourself to capital-gains taxes.

As with all investments, shop around for the highest yields and the lowest fees. Because you won't make a lot of money in cash accounts, keeping fees low is critical to maintaining your liquidity.

Cultivating patience

If you're like most people, you're much less tempted to mess around with your investments when the markets are doing well. It feels good to look at your statements and see how they've grown, and your inclination is to let your investments continue to do their good work.

But when the markets are down, your stomach sinks with every statement, and maybe with every piece of bad economic news. You start arguing with yourself about whether you should just pull your money out now and wait for things to get better. The problem with that strategy is that, if you follow it, you end up worse off than before because you're selling low — possibly lower than when you got in — and, if you get back in, you'll be buying higher than when you got out.

A little perspective can go a long way toward easing the jitters that so often accompany turbulence in the market. When you're wringing your hands over the state of your investments, remember these things:

- **A typical U.S. recession lasts about eight months.** When we're in a recession, the stock market often drops dramatically, but it usually bottoms out pretty quickly and begins to climb back up before other economic indicators start rebounding.

- **After the market loses, it tends to come back stronger.** In the past 40 years, there have been 7 bear markets, and stocks have lost as much as half their value during those times — but blue-chips still have an average annual gain of almost 11 percent.

- **Stocks do much better than commodities when you adjust for inflation.** In the last 100 years, the inflation-adjusted value of gold has just more than doubled. Stock values during the same period have grown by a factor of 8 after inflation.

Few people think of it this way, but a down market is the equivalent of a sale at your favorite store — a chance to buy the things you want at a better-than-usual price. This isn't the time to get *out* of the market — it's the time to get *in*.

Things to look for

Your investing mantra should be "Keep it simple." Look for opportunities that don't require a lot of oversight. Passive index funds, for example, are simpler (and cheaper, and often more profitable) than managed funds because they don't involve much buying and selling of stock.

Simplicity comes in other forms, too. Look for investments you understand. If you don't know how they work or how they generate profits for you, pass. Stick with what you know. As a farmer, Bob has invested in John Deere, Monsanto, and UPS because he knows something about those companies and how they work. He doesn't invest in limited-partnership securities because they're extremely complicated and unfamiliar to him.

Look for reasonable returns, not the-sky's-the-limit promises. An investment that has the potential to earn you 7 percent, 8 percent, or even 10 percent a year is much more reasonable than any investment promising to double your money. (Besides, except when it comes to investments like CDs, you should distrust *promised* returns of any kind.)

Things to avoid

 There are some things the average investor should run, not walk, away from. Some will get you into financial trouble. Some could get you into legal trouble. Either way, they're not worth your time, and they're definitely not worth your money.

Stay away from tax shelters, limited partnerships, and anything called a *proprietary investment product*. Ignore the slick marketing that often accompanies these products; that slickness is designed to distract you from the high fees and potential liabilities, which you want no part of.

If someone mentions *minimum income* or *principal protection,* your response should be not just "No," but "Hell, no!" These are insurance products masquerading as investments. They also go by the aliases *equity-indexed annuity* and *living benefit guarantee.* They charge high commissions and fees, which means unacceptably low returns for you. If you want principal protection, invest in TIPS. Like other bonds, TIPS pay a preset yield, but they also adjust the principal value to guard against inflation.

Annuities are insurance products, not investments; annuities promise either a fixed (defined) benefit or a variable one. Avoid them. You may have to pay a hefty exit fee — often, 6 percent to 8 percent — if you want to get your money out in the first few years of the contract. Even if you stay in it, you pay high commissions and fees that eat up most of your returns.

Never buy on *margin* — you're basically borrowing the brokerage's money to purchase stock, which is fine when the stock goes up but gut-wrenching when it goes down. You have to maintain a certain level of equity — at least 50 percent — and if the price of the stock falls, you'll get a *margin call* to pony up enough cash to get back to your preset equity level. (See the "How margins work" sidebar for more on margins.)

Getting a broker

If you're skittish about plunging into the stock market on your own, you may want to consider getting a broker. A broker can help you assess your risk tolerance and identify the best investments to meet your financial goals. An experienced broker — and we don't recommend going to one who's just starting in the business — should understand how the markets work and should be able to explain your investment options to you in language you understand.

Choosing a broker isn't a decision to be made lightly, though. You should put the same thought and time into selecting a broker that you put into any other major financial undertaking, like buying a house or starting a business. Meet your broker in person; if possible, visit the firm.

How do you find the right broker? Start with asking your own circle of family and friends if they can recommend someone. If you don't feel comfortable doing that, or if your family and friends don't have any recommendations to offer, use the Internet to find out about brokers in your area. The Financial Industry Regulatory Authority (FINRA; www.finra.org) offers a BrokerCheck service on its Web site where you can look up the professional background of a specific broker or firm. The database covers some 660,000 individual brokers and more than 5,000 securities firms that are currently registered with the Securities and Exchange Commission (SEC).

You can also check out brokers and brokerage firms on the SEC's Web site (www.sec.gov), through your state licensing agency, or through the Better Business Bureau (www.bbb.org).

Your broker should thoroughly understand your current financial status and your goals, and any investments she recommends should fit in with both. If you feel a broker is pushing you in a direction you don't want to go, find a new one or do your investing yourself.

How margins work

When you have a cash account with your brokerage firm, either online or at a bricks-and-mortar operation, you pay the full cost of your stock purchases. With a margin account, you pay part of the cost of those purchases, and the brokerage loans you the rest. You have to pay for at least half of the stock purchase, which gives you a 50 percent equity in the stock. If the stock price goes up, you get all the profit (minus the interest on the money you borrowed from the brokerage). But if the stock price goes down, you take all of the hit (and you still pay the interest). And if the price sinks far enough to drop your equity, you have to give the brokerage enough money to get back to your original equity level.

Say you buy $10,000 of stock on margin. You put in $5,000 and borrow the other $5,000 from the brokerage. The stock goes up to $11,000 — no problem. You've got $6,000 in equity, because you claim all the gains. But if the stock drops to $9,000, you have a problem. Why? Because you also absorb all the losses. So that $1,000 drop in the price means a $1,000 drop in your equity, to $4,000, and you have to give the brokerage another $500 to get back to your 50 percent minimum equity (50 percent of $9,000 = $4,500). Now imagine this happening over and over again, and you can see why investing on margin is an extremely risky strategy.

When your broker recommends an investment, that's your cue to go home and do your own research. There's no need to make a decision immediately, so take your time, and, before you buy, make sure you understand how the recommended stock or fund fits in with your own goals.

Doing it yourself

Back in the 1940s, when Charles Merrill embarked on his campaign to "bring Wall Street to Main Street" by attracting small investors, you had no choice but to select a broker if you wanted to dabble in the stock market. In the Information Age, though, you can make your own investments online at any time and for much less than a bricks-and-mortar brokerage firm will cost you.

A traditional brokerage house typically charges you $45 per transaction. Online brokerages usually charge between $6 and $10 per transaction — a huge savings that means you keep more of your returns.

Technically, online trading is still done through brokers, because all transactions on the stock market have to be made through registered agents. But when you go through a Web site like E*TRADE (www.etrade.com) or TD AMERITRADE (www.tdameritrade.com), you don't have the traditional relationship with an individual broker. You pay a fee for each transaction, usually $10 or less; that's how the brokerage makes its money. These transaction fees are much lower than traditional broker fees because the overhead for these online firms is much lower.

To open an account with an online broker, you have to submit a signed application. Some firms accept electronic signatures, which can be completed online; others require you to mail or fax a hard copy. After your account is activated, you can buy virtually any investment online that a bricks-and-mortar broker could offer — stocks, index funds, mutual funds, and bonds.

Online trading is no different from going through a traditional broker. The risks of the market are the same. However, sometimes there are issues with investing online that you need to be aware of:

- ✔ **High traffic to the site can delay your buy/sell orders or even make it difficult to access your account at all.**

- ✔ **Especially when the markets are experiencing a lot of up-and-down movement, the price of an investment may change drastically between the time you submit your buy/sell order and when the order is actually executed.** That means you may have to pay more than you anticipated for the investment, or the proceeds from a sale may be much lower than you expect.

- ✔ **The ease of trading online makes it tempting to over-trade, and buying and selling too much can put serious dents in your returns.** It also can have unwelcome implications at tax time because of the way short-term capital gains are treated. (See Chapter 17 for more on capital-gains rules.)

Online trading isn't the same as day trading. When you invest online, you still should take the long view about your investments (see "Cultivating Patience," earlier in this chapter). Day trading is a highly risky technique for timing small movements in the market over a short period — buying and selling a given stock in the same day or within a few days.

Just because you can easily buy and sell investments online doesn't mean you should. Do your research, choose your investments, and then let them do what they're supposed to do over the long haul. Remember Warren Buffett's philosophy on investments: "Our favorite holding period is forever."

Avoiding Big Mistakes

If you're new to investing, and even if you're not, you're bound to see times when a certain investment doesn't perform as well as expected or comes with fees you didn't fully understand when you signed up. Don't get your trousers in a bunch when this happens; it happens to everybody. Remember that the longer you're in the market, the better the odds that you'll recover from mistakes and end up ahead.

Instead of worrying about every little detail, keep your eye on the big things that can really hurt your returns: hidden fees, misrepresentations, high-pressure sales tactics, and ceding control to your broker.

Hidden fees

You may have heard or read the term *loaded fund* in discussion of mutual funds. *Loads* are commissions and fees charged to the investor (you). Some funds are *front-loaded*, meaning the commission is taken off the top of your initial investment. Some are *back-loaded*, meaning you pay the commission when you sell your shares. Some funds have *contingent deferred sales loads*, which means the commission goes down — usually one percentage point a year — the longer you hold the investment and eventually zeros out.

There are no-load mutual funds, but *no-load* doesn't mean "no fees." Fund families aren't in business to lose money, and, like any other business, they pass many of their administrative costs onto their customers, the shareholders. Brokers and financial planners should tell you upfront the fee structure for any investment. But it's always wise to check out the expenses yourself.

Always read the expenses section of a prospectus for any investment. This is where you'll find annual fees, surrender or exit fees, commissions, and anything else that may affect your returns.

Fund families can charge lots of fees aside from loads. There may be a *purchase fee* or *redemption fee,* due when you buy or sell your shares and payable to the fund itself to cover the costs of the transaction. *Account fees* cover the costs of maintaining your account; these are often charged only if your account balance dips below a preset minimum. *Exchange fees* may be charged if you trade one class of shares for another class in the same fund. You also may run across *management fees, shareholder service fees, administrative fees,* and that vague-but-useful category *other expenses.*

You can avoid some other-expense charges by signing up for electronic statements. Some funds now charge a hefty fee for mailing out paper statements.

No-load funds can charge many of these other types of fees and still be considered no-load. FINRA rules allow funds to pay their annual operating expenses and a category of fees called 12b-1 fees (usually used for marketing and advertising) and still call themselves no-load, as long as their 12b-1 and shareholder service fees amount to no more than 0.25 percent of the fund's average annual net assets.

The higher the fees and loads, the better a fund has to perform to earn you the same return as one with lower expenses. Even small differences in the expenses can add up to huge differences over time. If you invest $10,000 in a fund with fees of 0.5 percent, you'll have nearly $61,000 in 20 years. But that same $10,000 in a fund with fees of 1.5 percent will be worth only about $50,000 in 20 years.

Use an online mutual-fund expense calculator to see how the fees you're charged will affect your returns. FINRA's Web site has an expense calculator that lets you compare up to three mutual funds or share classes in the same fund (`http://apps.finra.org/Investor_Information/EA/1/mfetf.aspx`).

Misrepresentations

If you're dealing with a broker or financial planner, he has to disclose the fees and other charges associated with the investment as well as other *material facts.* Those other material facts can include bond ratings or other analyses of the investment, how much risk the investment carries, and the financial information of the company you're investing in.

Unfortunately, not all brokers and planners follow these disclosure rules. And, if you don't know what to look for, you may be persuaded to invest even when it's not in your best interest.

Here are some signs that your broker or planner may not be telling you everything you need to know:

- ✔ **She says you don't have to read the prospectus.** A prospectus contains vital information about the company issuing the stock or mutual fund and expenses associated with the investment. If your broker or planner doesn't want you to read the prospectus, ask yourself why.

- ✔ **He gives you a firm prediction of the investment's future gains.** As the fine print on every prospectus says, past performance is no guarantee of future returns. If your broker or planner "guarantees" that the price of an investment will go up, a red flag should go up for you.

- ✔ **What she tells you doesn't square with your own research.** If the prospectus or other research — like SEC filings or analytical reports from reputable sources like Hoover's (`www.hoovers.com`), Moody's (`www.moodys.com`), or Standard & Poor's (`www.standardandpoors.com`) — is significantly different from what your broker or planner has told you, she may be trying to steer you into an investment that will earn her a big commission but do little good for your bottom line.

Take notes every time you talk to your broker or planner, and ask him to put everything in writing for you. And, before you buy, do your own research on the products he recommends.

Trust is everything in seeking the help of a financial adviser. If you run into anything that makes you uncomfortable with a broker or planner, dump that one and find another, or ditch the financial services sector entirely and do it yourself.

High-pressure sales tactics

Scrupulous brokers and financial planners want to make sure you have all the information and time you need to make a decision about any given investment. Unscrupulous ones want you to make a decision right now, even if you have nothing in writing and have never heard of the investment or the firm that's calling you. They prey on your fear that you'll "miss out on something good" and may claim to have "inside information" that isn't public knowledge.

Phrases like *get in on the ground floor, once-in-a-lifetime opportunity,* and *must act now* usually mean the seller is hawking a highly risky investment. These are your cue to say, "No, thank you," and hang up the phone or shut the door.

If you're on the National Do Not Call Registry, you shouldn't receive phone calls from any firm you haven't done business with before (charities and certain other groups aren't limited by the Do Not Call Registry). If you aren't on the registry, go to www.donotcall.gov and register your home and cellphone numbers.

Ceding control to your broker

If you've read much of this book, you know that we are absolutely opposed to giving anyone else the authority to decide when and how you invest your money. But even if you don't actually sign such an authorization with your broker or financial planner, you still have to keep an eye on your statements to make sure they aren't moving your money around without your permission. (No, it isn't legal for them to do it. Unfortunately, not everyone follows the law.)

Even if your broker or planner thinks a different investment is in your best interest, he can't just make the change without your authorization. And he can't try to get your consent after the fact.

Brokers and commission-based financial planners get commissions by making purchases and sales. Moving a client's money around is an easy way to boost the month's commission without having to do much work — and it can be tempting to do it, even without the client's permission.

The best way to detect and resolve any suspicious activity in your investment accounts is to do your due diligence. Read your statements promptly and carefully, and if there's any activity you don't understand, contact your broker or planner immediately.

If that doesn't resolve your question, contact the branch manager, and send a registered or certified letter to the firm's compliance department, saying you refuse the transfer in question. In addition to the letter, call the compliance department, and tell them you didn't authorize and don't accept the transfer.

Chapter 14

Joining the Landed Gentry

*F*or most Americans, the cornerstone for building net worth is home ownership. Historically, home values tend to rise about 4 percent a year, meaning a home you buy for $100,000 today could well be worth more than $300,000 in 30 years.

Of course, as we write this, the country is still reeling from the effects of a real estate bubble that burst in late 2007, combined with a subprime mortgage mess that may take a few years to shake out completely. Lots of people find themselves upside down on their home mortgages, owing more than the property is worth today because they bought when prices were inflated. Some of those people are facing foreclosure because they can't keep up with their adjustable-rate mortgages; others must sell at a loss because, in today's market, buyers are looking for bargains.

But those who can hang on through this and other downturns most likely will see the investment in their homes pay off handsomely. As the Oneida Indians are fond of saying, the Creator isn't making any more real estate. Over the long haul, values are almost bound to rise again.

There are other ways to invest in real estate, too. Like any other investment, there's a certain amount of risk involved, but the rewards can be great if you know what you're doing and bring the right attitude to it. In this chapter, we start with the basics of home ownership: how to figure out how much house you can afford, how to sift through your mortgage options to find one that's right for you, and how to build and keep equity in your home.

Then we turn our attention to other kinds of real estate investing, including the pros and cons of owning rental and vacation property, steps to help you assess a given property's development potential, and the concept of flipping properties for a quick profit.

Finally, we give you an overview of Real Estate Investment Trusts (REITs), showing you how they may fit into your portfolio and what to look for when considering this type of investment.

We don't have enough space here to cover real estate in detail. Fortunately, the good folks at Wiley have several resources for you, covering a variety of specific topics. Check out these titles, all published by Wiley: *Home Buying For Dummies,* 3rd Edition, by Eric Tyson, MBA, and Ray Brown; *Mortgages For Dummies,* 3rd Edition, by Eric Tyson, MBA, and Ray Brown; *Real Estate Investing For Dummies,* by Eric Tyson and Robert S. Griswold; *Second Homes For Dummies,* by Bridget McCrea and Stephen Spignesi; and *Flipping Houses For Dummies,* by Ralph R. Roberts with Joe Kraynak.

Building Wealth in Your Home

According to the U.S. Census Bureau, almost 70 percent of Americans own their homes, and those homes represent more than 40 percent of the owners' net worth. *Net worth* is the difference between your *assets* (what you own) and your *liabilities* (what you owe). For low- and middle-income people especially, home ownership constitutes a huge chunk of their net worth.

Some financial advisers — notably Robert Kiyosaki of *Rich Dad, Poor Dad* fame — consider home ownership to be a liability because owning a home costs money. It's not just your monthly mortgage payment, either; you'll spend money on maintenance and repairs, renovations, property taxes, and insurance, among other things. Even so, especially when you're in the early stages of building wealth, your home represents your greatest asset. Used properly, it can be a rock-steady foundation for the rest of the fortune you intend to amass.

Knowing what you can afford

One of the reasons so many people got into trouble with the real estate bubble and the subprime mortgage market is that they bought more house than they could afford. How did this happen? Primarily through "creative" lending practices — things like interest-only mortgages, or adjustable-rate mortgages with low "teaser" rates that reset after a couple years to much higher rates and, therefore, much higher payments. In most cases, both lenders and home buyers were at fault: Lenders wanted to increase their business and so looked for ways to get more people qualified for loans, and buyers wanted their dream houses and so looked for lenders who would help them buy.

One good thing about the crash is that lenders are returning to established practices that truly pre-qualify home buyers for mortgages they can afford, and home buyers are becoming more discriminating in both the houses they consider purchasing and the mortgage options available to them.

Figuring out your housing budget

Before you start shopping for a home — even before you meet with lenders to find out their loan terms — you should decide on your own how much house you can afford. We recommend being conservative with your estimate, because there are always unforeseen expenses involved in owning a home. If your estimate is too high, you may find that even your "affordable" house puts you in financial straits.

You can use the same formula conservative lenders use to come up with your estimate. Generally, lenders use the 28 percent/36 percent formula to figure out how big a mortgage you qualify for. The percentages represent your total housing costs and your total monthly debt. Housing costs — principal, interest, taxes, and insurance (PITI) — shouldn't be more than 28 percent of your *gross* (before taxes) monthly income. Your total monthly debt, including your PITI, car payment, personal loans, and credit card payments, shouldn't be more than 36 percent of your gross monthly income.

You may qualify for loan programs that have different income or debt-to-income ratio requirements, such as Veterans Administration (VA) loans or first-time home-buyer programs. Your loan officer can help you figure out which programs you qualify for.

To get your own ballpark range, multiply your gross monthly income by 0.28 and 0.36. For example, if you make $2,500 a month, you probably would qualify for mortgage payments between $700 and $900 a month.

Mortgage qualification is based on your gross income, not your take-home pay. Figure out how much you make each month before taxes and other obligations, like Social Security and Medicare contributions, are taken out of your wages.

When lenders figure out how much of a mortgage you qualify for, some debts carry more weight than others. Generally, if you have eight months or less left to pay on your car, a personal loan, a student loan, or other debt, it won't count against you when it comes time to qualify for a mortgage. On the other hand, child support and alimony payments may lower the amount you can qualify for.

Pre-qualifying for a mortgage gives you a good estimate of how much you can spend on a house, but it doesn't guarantee that you'll get financing. To get that guarantee, you'll need to be pre-approved, which means you'll most likely have to pay an application fee.

Coming up with your down payment

There was a time, during the height of the real estate bubble, when you could buy a house without putting any money down. But with the credit crunch that has taken hold recently, most lenders — even those who didn't require down payments before — are going back to the basics.

This is actually good news for buyers, because there are significant advantages to making a down payment. You borrow less for a home, which means you'll pay less in interest over the life of your mortgage. You also may qualify for a lower interest rate, depending on the size of your down payment. And, if you can put down 20 percent of the purchase price, you can avoid paying mortgage insurance.

You pay the premiums for mortgage insurance, but the insurance is actually for the lender; it reimburses the lender if you default on your mortgage.

Some programs require as little as 3 percent for a down payment, and if you go through the VA or the Federal Housing Administration (FHA), all of your down payment can be a gift from a relative or friend. Virtually no lender will allow you to borrow money for your down payment, however, because that's a debt that has to be repaid. The exception to this rule is borrowing from your 401(k), which you pay back with interest (usually around 5 percent). You also can withdraw funds from your 401(k) to make your down payment, but a straight withdrawal will expose you to penalties and income taxes.

There are several ways to come up with a down payment. Here are some options to consider:

- **Set up an automatic savings program.** Have a set amount deducted from your checking account each week or each pay period, and put the money in an account that's separate from your regular savings.

- **Check out state or federal home-buyer assistance programs.** Some have income limits; others are designed to help distressed neighborhoods rebuild. Go to `http://first-time-home-buyer-s.com` for a state-by-state listing of programs. For federal programs, check out `www.usa.gov/shopping/realestate/mortgages/mortgages.shtml`.

- **Get a gift from a relative or friend.** Gifts don't count as debt, so they don't affect the mortgage amount you qualify for. Some lenders have limits on how much of your down payment can be a gift, so check it out when you're shopping for a mortgage.

- **Earmark tax refunds or bonuses for your down payment.** To make sure you aren't tempted to spend them on something else, we recommend stashing these funds in a separate account.

- **Sell some of your assets.** Getting rid of a little-used boat, RV, or motorcycle can put a good sum of cash in your pocket. You also may want to consider liquidating some investments, but keep in mind that selling stocks or bonds can have tax implications.

The bigger your down payment, the smaller your monthly payments will be. In the old days, you had to have 20 percent of the value of the house for a down payment, but these days you have the option of choosing much lower down payments or even none at all. But if you put only 3 percent down, your monthly payments will be higher, and it'll take you longer to build substantial equity in your home (see "Building equity — and keeping it," later in this chapter).

Understanding your mortgage options

As recently as 2006, you could get pretty much any kind of mortgage you wanted, and there were lots of (often confusing) choices to ponder. These days, though, lenders are more cautious, and the chances of securing a loan without having to provide proof of income and a whole bunch of other documentation are pretty low. Your basic choices today are fixed-rate and adjustable-rate mortgages (ARMs).

Fixed-rate mortgages

With a *fixed-rate mortgage,* the interest rate at closing is the rate you'll pay for the life of the loan, which is typically 15 or 30 years. On 15-year loans, your interest rate usually will be lower, but your monthly payments will be higher; the advantage is that you build equity more quickly because more of each monthly payment is going toward the principal. You also drastically reduce the total amount of interest you pay over the life of the mortgage.

Most home buyers choose the 30-year option because, even with higher interest rates, the monthly payments are more affordable. In the early years of a 30-year mortgage, you'll get a bigger tax deduction on a 30-year mortgage because you're paying more in interest.

Say you borrow $100,000 (on top of any down payment) to buy your home. On a 30-year mortgage at 6.25 percent interest, your monthly payments for principal and interest would be $615.72 (insurance and taxes will be extra). On a 15-year mortgage with a lower interest rate — say, 5.77 percent — your monthly principal and interest payment would be $831.48. Add in insurance and taxes, and you're probably looking at around $900 a month for a 30-year mortgage and between $1,100 and $1,200 for a 15-year. (Actual payments vary because they depend on insurance rates and property taxes in your area.)

Look at your mortgage payment in the context of your big financial picture. If you've got sufficient savings and can still contribute to your retirement, college, and investment funds with a 15-year mortgage, go for it. But if you have little savings, or if a higher mortgage payment wouldn't leave enough to fund your other financial goals, go for the 30-year option.

When you shop for a mortgage, make sure there's no penalty for prepaying. Even if you can't manage an extra payment this year, you want the option to do it when you can, and you don't want to get socked with extra fees when you do it.

The mortgage calculator at `www.bankrate.com` lets you see how different interest rates and terms affect your monthly payments. You can also plug in extra payments to see how they would affect your payoff date and the total interest you pay.

Adjustable-rate mortgages

ARMs got a bad rap in the subprime mortgage crisis because many people were approved for low "teaser" rates but couldn't afford the higher payments when their interest rates reset. Under normal circumstances, those people could've refinanced their mortgages, but, when the real estate bubble exploded, housing values went down, and many people ended up owing more than their houses were worth.

This is — and always has been — the risk with ARMs: Your interest rate may go up. It could go down, too, though, because ARMs are tied to the performance of one of three main indices — maturity yields on one-year Treasury bills, the London Interbank Offered Rate (LIBOR), or the 11th District Cost of Funds Index (COFI). ARM lenders use one of these as the base interest rate and then add a margin (which represents their income from the loan) to come up with the rate you pay.

Most ARMs have caps, which control how much your interest rate can go up. Sometimes the caps are annual; your contract may state that your interest rate can't go up more than 1 percent a year, for example. Sometimes there's a lifetime cap, which means you'll never pay more than, say, 9 percent for your mortgage. Some ARM loans even have payment caps, which limit the dollar amount of your monthly payment.

The most common ARM now is called a 5/1 ARM, which means the interest rate is fixed for the first five years and readjusts once a year for the remainder of the loan (subject to the caps). You also can find three-, seven-, and ten-year versions.

ARMs can make sense if you expect to be earning significantly more money when your rate is due to reset — if you (or your spouse) are finishing your college degree, for example, which will qualify you for a better job. It also can make sense if you're confident that property values in your area will go up during the first few years of your mortgage, giving you the option to refinance before your ARM resets.

If you decide an ARM is right for you, make sure you understand when and how your rate will reset. Also find out how much principal you'll have paid when your loan resets; this could affect your ability to refinance.

Mortgage rates and the economy

Mortgage rates are volatile creatures, rising and falling and rising again like mountain goats leaping from crag to crag. In the few months it takes most home-buyers to research their financing options and find a house they want to buy, mortgage rates can change dramatically.

Though it's virtually impossible to predict or time mortgage rates, it is helpful to know that they tend to be lower when the economy is struggling and higher when the economy is good. The Federal Reserve Board doesn't set mortgage rates, and rates aren't directly tied to the Fed's actions, but when the Fed lowers its interest rates, it's because the economy has already given signs of slowing down. So mortgage rates tend to go down when the Fed lowers its rates.

Many ARMs give you the ability to convert to a fixed-rate loan, although you'll probably have to pay a fee to do this. Also check to see if your ARM is assumable if you sell your home. Assumable mortgages allow the buyer, if qualified, to take over your existing mortgage. That can be a strong selling point if mortgage rates are high when you put your property on the market.

Lenders' advertised rates are usually pretty close to one another, if not exactly the same. That's because competition for mortgage business is fierce, and lenders don't want to charge rates that are significantly higher than the competition.

However, don't assume you'll automatically get the advertised rate. Your interest rate will depend on a number of factors, including your credit history, how much money you put down, the type of mortgage you choose, and several other variables.

Building equity — and keeping it

Equity is how much of your house you actually own. If you purchase a $100,000 home with a $20,000 down payment, you own 20 percent of your home, and your mortgage lender owns the other 80 percent. With every mortgage payment you make, your equity grows a little — very little at first, because most of your payments in the early years of your mortgage go toward interest instead of principal. But the longer you stay in your home, the more of each payment goes toward the principal and the more equity you build.

By making one extra PITI payment a year, you shave 7 years and 3 months off a 30-year mortgage and save tens of thousands of dollars in interest to boot. A $100,000 mortgage at 6.25 percent will cost you $121,658 in interest over 30 years. With one extra payment a year, your total interest bill drops to $87, 756 — a savings of almost $34,000. The savings on a 15-year mortgage aren't nearly as dramatic, but you still can drop two years off your mortgage and save a few thousand dollars in interest by making one extra PITI payment a year.

The easiest way to make an extra payment every year is to have your mortgage payment automatically deducted from your checking account every two weeks. Each payment will be half of your regular monthly payment (plus any fees your lender may charge for this), but you end up making 26 payments — 13 months of payments — every calendar year.

Fees for automatic deductions and 26-payment plans differ, and you'll want to make sure the fees aren't so high that they'll defeat your real purpose, which is to save money on interest payments down the line. Meg has used this option on her mortgage since 2005, and her lender charges $4 for each biweekly payment — a total of $104 a year. But she's already added more than $4,000 to her equity, which she wouldn't have had without the extra payments. And she'll save about $40,000 in interest payments over the life of her mortgage, in exchange for about $2,100 in total fees.

If you opt for a biweekly mortgage payment or make any other kind of extra payment, make sure the extra payments are applied to the principal only. Most lenders do this automatically, but some require you to ask in writing that any extra payments go solely toward the principal, not toward interest, taxes, or insurance.

Tapping into your equity

Equity also provides a way for you to access extra cash when you need it, through either a home equity loan or a home equity line of credit (HELOC):

- ✔ **Home equity loan:** Also known as second mortgages, home equity loans use your ownership in your home as collateral for cash. These are fixed-rate loans with 5- to 15-year terms; as with a fixed-rate mortgage, the interest rate stays the same for the life of the loan, and your monthly payments don't change. You get a lump sum to do what you like with — make improvements to your home, pay off credit cards, buy a car, take a vacation, or whatever else you choose.

- ✔ **Home equity line of credit:** Home equity lines of credit have variable interest rates, and, instead of getting a lump sum at closing, you get either a credit card or a special checkbook to access your credit line. You get pre-approved for a HELOC limit, and the HELOC is time limited (usually, 5 to 15 years), but how and when you use that credit is up to you. Monthly payments depend on how much of your credit line you've borrowed and what the current interest rate is.

Both a home equity loan and a HELOC must be repaid in full when you sell your home.

There are good and bad points about borrowing against the equity in your home. On the plus side:

- ✔ Home equity loans and HELOCs usually have lower interest rates than other kinds of loans, so you can save money when you're buying a car or paying off other debts.

- ✔ You can use the cash for home improvements that add real market value to your property.

Not all home improvements will make your property worth more when it's time to sell. A new roof or a remodeled kitchen or bathroom will make your home more attractive to buyers, but an in-ground swimming pool adds little market value and may even be seen as a minus by buyers.

- ✔ The interest you pay on a home equity loan or HELOC — as long as this type of loan isn't more than $100,000 and the total debt on your home isn't more than the property is worth — is tax deductible, unlike interest payments on credit cars, car loans, and other consumer loans.

There are negatives that balance out the positives, though:

- ✔ Unlike credit card debt, home equity debt puts you at risk of losing your home if you default on the loan.

- ✔ The temptation to "reload" your equity debt — using an equity loan to pay off credit cards, and then running up the credit card balances again and getting a new or larger equity loan to pay off the credit cards, and so on — can lead to serious financial problems, even foreclosure and bankruptcy.

- ✔ Leveraging too much of your equity for cash can lead to owing more than your home is worth, especially during downward real estate cycles.

Never borrow against your equity to cover day-to-day expenses. If you're tempted to do this, it's a good sign that your finances are out of whack, and you should seek help from a not-for-profit credit counseling service or a professional adviser, like an accountant or financial planner.

Keeping your equity

Instead of viewing your home equity as an ATM from which you can withdraw cash whenever you need it, think of it as a last-resort savings account. The savings account part is true: If you avoid incurring additional debt on your home, you're really tucking away money with every mortgage payment.

As for the last-resort part, this is a mindset that can help you fight the temptation to use your home to finance lavish spending that you otherwise wouldn't do. Think about it: Is a vacation, however fantastic, really worth risking your home?

Of course, there are times when it makes sense to tap your equity, and there may be times when you don't have any other good options. But if you can let your equity grow without thinking about how you might be able to use it, it'll be there when you really need it.

Considering Investment Property

Investing in real estate is like getting old: It isn't for sissies. All those get-rich-quick-with-real-estate infomercials notwithstanding, buying property as an investment requires a lot of work, both before you close the deal and after you take over as owner. For those who are willing to put in the labor, it can be richly rewarding, in every sense of the phrase. But for the unsuspecting, real estate can turn into a monetary black hole, sucking up your funds and returning virtually nothing.

Investing in real estate (except with a REIT, discussed later in this chapter) ties up your money in ways other kinds of investing avoid. It isn't always easy to get out of investment property once you're in, because, unlike with the stock market, you can't always sell your property just because you want to. Even when you find a buyer and have an offer pending, it can takes weeks — even months — before the deal closes and you see any money from the sale.

Before you decide whether you really want to take the investment property plunge, first think about your strategy. Do you intend to hold on to the property for several years, or do you want to unload it within a few months? Your strategy will, in large part, dictate the location you want to search for suitable property. You'll also need to consider how much time you can or want to devote to managing your property. And, finally, you'll need to build relationships with professionals who can help you: a real estate agent, an attorney, and the local codes enforcement officer, for starters.

When you've figured out how much time and money you'll need to devote to your investment, double both. If you can still make a profit and still want to do it, go for it.

Figuring out your plan

Many would-be real estate moguls attack investment property from the wrong angle — choosing a property first and then coming up with a plan for it. And, when the plan doesn't work out, the investor gets burned.

The better approach is to design your plan first and then look for properties that fit well with your plan. To do this, you have to decide whether you want to buy and hold property or whether you want to flip it for a quick profit.

Buying and holding

Buying and holding real estate is different from buying and holding stock. For one thing, your expenses are much higher; you're responsible for the mortgage, taxes, insurance, and maintenance. In a perfect world, the rent you collect from leasing the property — whether it's a single-family home, an apartment building, commercial property, or farmland — will cover your expenses. And, as the cost of living increases, you can raise rents to cover inflation.

After the mortgage is paid off, most of the rent can go into your pocket as profit. Chances are good that the value of your property will increase over the life of the mortgage, too, offering another opportunity for profit when you're ready to sell.

On the downside, you may have to deal with tenants who damage your property, or the property may sit vacant for months, during which time you'll still have expenses but no income from rent to cover them. If you don't have a pile of cash set aside to see you through these times, you could easily be cornered into either taking on more debt to ease the cash flow or selling the property, possibly at a loss.

Flipping

The first five years of the 21st century saw massive growth in the practice of *flipping* — snapping up undervalued properties and then selling them for a higher price within a few months. As real estate markets cooled off in 2008, flipping became less widespread, but that doesn't mean it won't make a comeback. In fact, depending on the region and the type of property, flipping can still be a profitable strategy.

The advantage to flipping is that you don't have to take on landlord responsibilities, and you carry the debt for buying properties only for a short time. Ideally, the higher price you get when you sell covers both your mortgage and your expenses and leaves you with a nice profit, which you can then parlay into another flipping opportunity.

The disadvantage is that, if the property doesn't sell, or if you don't get the price you expected to get for it, you could lose a substantial chunk of money.

Some flippers focus their attention on fixer-uppers — properties that need work but will be worth considerably more after repairs or renovations are made. Repairs can add a great deal of expense and delay the resale date for these properties, so it's important to make sure your estimate of how much you can sell the property for is a good one.

Most flippers hunt for properties that don't need any work before resale. Here, the key is finding properties that are selling for less than their true market value. However, caution is needed here, too; if the property is undervalued because the entire area's market is soft, it's probably going to be difficult to resell it quickly and at a profit.

Before you get into real estate, have a plan for getting out. Better yet, have two or three exit strategies in case your first plan fails. If you intend to flip a property, for example, what's your Plan B if you can't sell it? Decide how long you intend to hold the property and then examine your options. If there aren't enough options — if having to hold onto to a flip property would be too expensive for you — wait until you find something better.

Understanding the market

The three most important things in real estate, according to the adage, are location, location, and location. This is especially true for investment properties. You can buy a beautiful piece of real estate for a song, but if you can't rent it or sell it, it makes a lousy investment.

Actually, for our purposes, the most important thing about real estate is its profit potential, and the key to making a profit in real estate (or any other investment) is to not overpay for it in the first place. Do your research before you buy, and approach every potential property with a good deal of skepticism and an eye trained to spot the flaws.

If you plan to rent your property, look for an area with low vacancy rates; the fewer rental properties that are on the market, the better your chances of landing a tenant.

High turnover among your tenants can cost you money. Experts estimate a vacancy costs you two to three months in rental income by the time you pay for any repairs, like repainting an apartment and cleaning the carpets, advertising the property, and screening potential tenants. This is one reason so many landlords require one-year or longer leases.

Even when there isn't much in the way of rentals to choose among, you'll have a harder time getting tenants if no one wants to live or do business in the neighborhood. Before you buy a rental property, check out both the neighborhood and the larger community to make sure the property would be attractive to potential tenants.

If you plan to flip the property, make sure it's truly undervalued or at least is in a hot market. A low price may mean the property has profit potential, but it also could be an indication that there are serious problems with the property or that the area's market as a whole is in bad shape.

Dedicating your time

When you're a landlord, you get to collect money from your tenants, but you also get to field phone calls — and pay for the repairs — when the faucet leaks or the furnace breaks down.

When your property is empty, you'll have to devote some time to finding tenants — first advertising for them and then screening them to make sure they can afford to pay the rent. If they don't pay, you'll have to chase the money, and, if you decide to evict a nonpaying tenant, you'll have to follow legal procedures, including paying someone to serve the eviction notice.

This is the part that flummoxes a lot of people. Sure, you can hire someone to come fix the faucet and the furnace, or maybe even a property-management company to take care of maintenance and tenant issues. But those things cost money, and they can easily turn a profitable property into a money-loser.

If you go the rental-property route, keep part of your rental income in an escrow account to finance repairs and other costs. Otherwise, you may find yourself having to dip into your personal funds for these things.

Although the idea of having a property-management company run your rental units is appealing, remember that most of these firms will charge between 7 percent and 10 percent of your monthly rental income. And if you've got a small property — a single-family home or duplex, for example — you may not be able to get a company to manage it for you; they usually prefer larger properties with greater income potential.

The exception to this is vacation rentals. If you own a home in a vacation hotspot — the Gulf Coast, for example, or Aspen — and you're willing to rent it out by the week, month, or season, you shouldn't have much trouble finding a property-management firm to handle the day-to-day operations for you. And, because vacation rental prices are significantly higher than regular rents, you may still be able to make a nice profit even after you pay the property-management company.

For flippers, the time investment comes in researching potential properties and, if necessary, making repairs or renovations to increase the property's value. You may have to work harder than you planned to find a buyer for your property, or you may have to sell for less than you anticipated. Contractors may be hard to find, or they may not meet your deadlines. And every month that passes without a sale is a month that you have to pony up expenses for the mortgage, taxes, and insurance — thus, cutting into your eventual profit.

Developing your professional network

Whether you take a buy-and-hold or a flip-it philosophy, you'll need to build good relationships with professionals who can help you avoid mistakes and get the most out of your investment.

Start with someone who owns a lot of investment properties your area. Ask for a meeting — even offer to pay this person for her time — and explain that you're thinking of entering the investment property business and would like to pick her brain for advice and guidance. If you feel uncomfortable doing this with a potential competitor, find a real estate agent who works with investors. What these experts share with you can help you much more than any book — including this one — in deciding whether this really is a good fit for you and your financial goals.

If you decide to pursue real estate investment, you'll need the services of a real estate agent who can keep an eye out for potential properties and help you evaluate them for your purposes. Again, an agent or broker who has experience working with investors should be your top choice.

You'll also need a knowledgeable real estate attorney. If you're looking at rental property, your attorney also should be knowledgeable about leases, landlord-tenant laws in your state and community, and federal housing laws. If you're buying commercial property, your attorney should review any existing leases before you buy, and you should check out the backgrounds of commercial tenants with the same diligence you'd use for individual renters.

Get to know the local codes enforcement officer, too. He has the authority to shut down your rental property and lock your tenants out if the building doesn't meet minimum safety standards. He also can help you plan any repairs or renovations by telling you which kind of work requires permits or licensed contractors, for example.

It doesn't hurt to get to know contractors, plumbers, electricians, and other technical experts either. Whether you're renovating a property with the intention of flipping it or acting as landlord, you'll need to be able to make repairs quickly, reliably, and at a reasonable cost.

Exploring Real Estate Investment Groups

Another way to get into real estate is to join an investment group. Typically, a company builds or buys residential or commercial property and then lets investors buy in. Depending on how the company is set up, you can own individual properties or a piece of all the company's holdings. The company manages the property, thus freeing you from the hassles of maintenance, finding and screening tenants, and compliance with building codes and other laws. The company takes a cut of the monthly rental income, and some of your rental income is pooled with a portion of the other investors' rental income to cover your costs in case one or more of your units is vacant. Theoretically, you'd always have enough income from the investment group to cover your expenses.

A real estate investment group is only as good as the company that's offering it. Before you buy in, do your homework about the company's history, key personnel, profitability, and so on. Investment groups can make it easier to get into real estate, but it's still darned difficult to get out, so be sure to choose wisely.

Understanding Real Estate Investment Trusts

If you don't want to buy investment property yourself, you can still get a share of the real estate market by investing in a Real Estate Investment Trust, or REIT (pronounced *reet*). REITs were created in 1960 as a way to give all investors — not just institutions and wealthy individuals — an opportunity to reap some of the rewards of being "in real estate." You invest in REITs much the same way you invest in stocks, and REIT investments — unlike actually owning real estate — are *liquid,* meaning you can cash them in at any time.

When they were first formed, REITs invested in mortgages and mortgage-backed securities, providing financing for residential and commercial properties. Since 1986, REITs have been allowed to both own and manage their properties, and most of the revenue from these equity REITs (as opposed to mortgage REITs) comes from rental contracts on the properties they own. Some REITs specialize in certain real estate sectors, like healthcare or shopping malls or condos. Some are umbrella companies with both residential and commercial properties in their portfolios. Of the publicly traded REITs today, about 90 percent own and manage commercial properties.

To qualify as a REIT, a company has to invest at least 75 percent of its total assets in real estate and has to derive at least that percentage of its income from rents or mortgage interest. REITs don't pay corporate income taxes as long as they distribute at least 90 percent of their taxable income in the form of dividends to their shareholders.

Because the REIT doesn't pay income taxes, your gains from investing in a REIT are fully taxable. The 15 percent capital-gains tax limit that applies when you sell stocks after a year never applies to a REIT; you'll always be taxed on REIT income at your current tax rate.

REITs are particularly useful if you're looking to generate income from your portfolio; they carry more risk than investment-grade bonds, but, in exchange, they provide the opportunity for greater returns. Still, REITs shouldn't constitute more than a quarter of your fixed-income investments. And, as with any other investment, you need to do your homework to determine which REIT fits best with your own financial goals.

Things to look for

Assessing REITs isn't quite like evaluating other investments. Yes, REITs list many of the same data other companies do, like net income. But net income isn't always the best way to gauge a REIT's profitability, because depreciation can skew the results. Under accounting rules, property should be depreciated over 40 years. But real estate, especially if it's maintained well, probably will increase in value; even commercial properties, with proper upkeep, can maintain or increase their values for far longer than four decades.

For investors, a more useful measuring stick is something called *funds from operations* (FFO). Even better is the *adjusted FFO,* which accounts for upkeep expenses and includes only the depreciation that exceeds those expenses. But FFOs are widely reported and are a useful guide. When you're evaluating a REIT, look for a history of growth in the FFO. This means the company has a track record of increasing its income from the properties it owns.

Next, compare the FFO per share with the dividend per share. You want to make sure the FFO is more than ample to cover the dividends. So, for example, a REIT that pays a $3 dividend per share and has $4 in FFO per share is probably more financially stable than one that pays $3.50 per share but has only $3.60 in FFO per share.

Finally, look at the types of property the REIT owns and where those properties are. Office buildings probably will generate more income from rental agreements than stand-alone retail properties, and large apartment complexes probably will be more profitable than mobile-home parks. Geographic diversity is important, too, because real estate markets differ greatly between regions. Remember, too, that, because most REITs specialize in a specific type of property, they could take a significant hit if they're concentrated in, say, Northern California and the economy there — or the real estate market — tanks.

Instead of researching individual REITs, consider investing in REIT mutual funds. Fidelity, Vanguard, and Cohen & Steers offer mutual funds that include REITs, with low expense ratios.

Things to avoid

Not all REITs are created equal. Stay away from REITs that aren't publicly traded. There's no advantage to you as an investor, and, in fact, nontraded REITs often have much higher fees than their publicly traded counterparts.

If a REIT's *leverage* (the ratio of debt to the value of the properties the REIT owns) is higher than 65 percent, look for another one. The industry average used to be around 50 percent, although the disruptions in the real estate market between 2006 and 2008 caused some REITs to have higher leverage ratios. In essence, though, you don't want a REIT that's spending all or nearly all of its own money buying property, because that could indicate the REIT isn't as creditworthy as you'd like.

Also, don't invest in a REIT that's externally managed. Fees may be higher, but the real problem is conflicts of interest that can hurt your returns.

Part IV
Managing Your Wealth

The 5th Wave   By Rich Tennant

"I bought a software program that should help
us monitor and control our spending habits, and
while I was there, I picked up a few new games,
a couple of screensavers, four new mousepads,
this nifty pullout keyboard cradle..."

In this part . . .

How often have you read of lottery winners who have nothing to show for their good fortune after a few years? Of heirs who have nothing left of their inheritance but their family name? Of the famous who are hopelessly in debt? This is the dirty secret of building wealth that no one talks about: It takes nearly as much work to stay in the millionaire class as it does to break into it.

This part covers the aspects of keeping and managing your wealth after you've built it, from selecting the right professionals to helping you plan for your own heirs. We discuss the importance of proper insurance coverage, ways to (legally) minimize your tax burden, and the advantages and disadvantages of investing your wealth for growth or income.

Chapter 15

Going to the Pros

In This Chapter

▶ Discovering how professionals can help you

▶ Understanding what you're paying for

▶ Knowing what to look for — and what to avoid

*N*o matter which tools you use to build your wealth, you'll probably need the service of some professionals, at least occasionally, to help you manage it wisely. All those titles and credentials can be confusing, even intimidating. But if you know what services various professionals provide, you're in a better position to decide whether — and when — you really need their help.

Unfortunately, there are a lot of unscrupulous folks out there who make their livings taking advantage of the confused and intimidated. We don't want you to be one of those hapless victims, so, in this chapter, we cover the services of the professionals most people will need at some point during their wealth-building journeys. We show you what these pros can do for you and what you can expect to pay for their services. We give you tips on how to find the right pro for you, including things to look for and things to avoid.

Because this is a book about building wealth, we devote much of this chapter to the services you're most likely to be curious about first: financial planners and investment brokers. But we also discuss finding an attorney (which you'll probably need if you buy real estate or make a will, among other things), an insurance agent (which you'll need to protect all that wealth you're building), and a tax preparer (which most people prefer to have, because the tax code is so confoundedly befuddling to mere mortals).

The one professional service we don't cover here is accountancy, because, unless you're already wealthy or own your own business, chances are you don't need an accountant — unless you have one prepare your tax returns. For a discussion of accountants and their services, see Chapter 9.

Choosing a Financial Planner

For many people who are just getting their wealth-building goals in order, the first task is to look for a financial planner. A good planner can show you how close you are to meeting your goals and how changes in your strategy can get you closer. He can help you create an investment strategy that balances your goals and risk tolerance, with both low costs and maximum tax efficiency. He also can keep his eye on the long-term goal and help you stick with your plan.

The best financial planners also look at your entire financial situation, not just your investment strategy. They'll help you decide what kind of insurance you should have and how much of it you need — without selling you policies you don't need or want. They can help you with estate planning and work with your attorney to make sure your wishes are clear and covered.

Choosing a financial planner can be tricky, because there are dozens of terms and designations for people who give financial advice, and there are no state or federal regulations dictating who can call himself a financial planner. That's why it's so important to know what to look for and what you're paying for.

What to look for

Because anybody can call herself a financial planner, regardless of training or education, the first thing to look for is some indication that your prospective planner knows what she's talking about. Two designations that indicate a planner has earned genuine credentials in the field are

- ✓ **Certified Financial Planner (CFP):** CFPs have to take college-level courses on investment, tax, estate, and retirement planning, as well as insurance and employee benefits. Then they have to pass a two-day exam on those topics. Since 2007, new CFPs have to have a bachelor's degree and at least three years' experience in financial planning before they can use the CFP designation. Planners who became CFPs before 2007 had to pass the CFP exam and have five years' experience if they didn't have a bachelor's degree.

    You can see why the CFP designation is useful when you're looking for a planner. It shows you that he has knowledge and experience in most aspects of financial planning, and he should be able to look at your overall financial picture and come up with recommendations that make sense for you.

- ✓ **Personal Financial Specialist (PFS):** The American Institute of Certified Public Accountants gives the PFS designation to CPAs who have put in at least 1,400 hours of financial planning over five years before taking — and passing — the PFS exam. The exam covers goal setting; risk management (another term for insurance); and tax, estate, retirement, and investment planning. CPAs who have the PFS credential have to submit client references and reapply every three years to keep the title.

Although they have knowledge and experience in other aspects of financial planning, PFSs tend to emphasize accounting and taxes. This emphasis may be more important to you when you've got a big nest egg than when you're just setting out on your making-millions journey.

People who call themselves financial planners use all kinds of impressive-sounding titles: Certified Retirement Financial Adviser, Certified Retirement Counselor, Certified Financial Consultant, and so on. If you consider doing business with someone who has one of these (or dozens of other) designations, ask about the requirements for earning the certification. In some cases, the planner only has to attend a seminar to earn a certification. You want a planner who has to demonstrate knowledge and experience to earn her credentials.

Credentials are only part of the equation when it comes to selecting a financial planner. If a CFP or PFS isn't willing to put your needs and goals first, the professional designation is worthless to you.

Where to look

If you can't get recommendations from family or friends, or if you're not satisfied with those recommendations, check out the Financial Planning Association's PlannerSearch at www.fpaforfinancialplanning.org or call 800-322-4237 for a list of planners in your area. Limit your options to those planners who have the CFP designation. (There are some 53,000 CFPs in the United States and only about 3,800 PFSs.)

The FPA only lists credentials; it doesn't verify them. To make sure your prospective planner has the credentials he says he does, check him out at www.cfp.net, the Web site for the CFP Board of Standards.

To find a CPA with the PFS credential, go to http://pfp.aicpa.org and click the Find a PFS link at the bottom of the left menu.

CPAs have to be licensed by the state in which they operate, and you can check their backgrounds — including any complaints or disciplinary action — online in most states. Go to the National Association of State Boards of Accountancy (www.nasba.org) to get contact information for the CPA regulatory agency in your state.

CPAs don't necessarily specialize in financial planning, so be sure to look for the PFS designation.

Meeting prospective planners

Ultimately, the best test of whether a financial planner is right for you is a face-to-face interview. In most cases, this initial meeting shouldn't cost you anything except about an hour of your time; in fact, we advise steering clear of any planner who isn't willing to meet with you once for free.

When you do meet with a prospective planner, get some basic information from her. Here are questions you should ask before you make your choice:

- **What do you charge, and how do you get paid?** Some planners charge a flat hourly fee; in that case, ask how many hours the planner estimates it will take to go over your goals and come up with recommendations. Ask if there's a minimum or maximum. If the planner refuses to give you at least a range — two to five hours, for example — keep looking.

  Some planners earn money by commissions; that means they'll be trying to sell you certain products. Ask for a written list of all the fees associated with the products the planner sells, including her commissions, account fees, and so on. (See "Knowing what you're paying for," later in this section, as well as Chapter 13, for more on various investment fees.) If you don't understand the product, even after getting all the information, don't buy it.

- **What are your qualifications?** Ideally, you've already checked out the planner's background and credentials before this meeting. This is when you ask about his experience: how long he's been in the business, the type of clientele he serves, and any particular area of expertise he has — retirement planning, for example, or tax planning.

- **Can I have a list of references?** The planner may be able to give you references from other clients whose situations and needs are similar to yours. Two or more references from people who have worked with the planner for several years can give you an idea of how responsive the planner is and how well he handles specific financial needs.

Understand that a planner probably won't give you references unless he has the clients' permission, and those references he does give you will be handpicked by him — meaning they won't necessarily give you an objective assessment. But you can pick up on subtle clues, such as a lack of enthusiasm, by talking to a planner's clients.

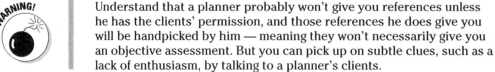

Even if a planner doesn't provide references, you still should interview her. She may not have her clients' permission to share information with you, and that respect for confidentiality is a good sign.

✔ **What services do you provide to your clients?** A full-service planner should be able to look at your complete financial picture and show you how the pieces fit together. So, if she recommends a certain course of action in preparing for retirement, she should also be able to explain the tax implications of that recommendation; likewise, if she recommends changes in your investment portfolio, she should be able to tell you how those changes will help you accomplish your goals.

Some planners emphasize retirement planning and may not offer big-picture advice. If you're just starting out, you want someone who's qualified to assess every aspect of your finances and make both short- and long-term recommendations.

✔ **Do you make specific recommendations for investments, retirement accounts, and so on?** Some planners — usually fee-based ones instead of commission-based ones — will give you general advice, like telling you to invest in mutual funds or start an individual retirement account (IRA), but they don't necessarily recommend specific products or companies. The advantage is that fee-only planners are more likely to recommend no-load funds and other low-cost investments. Depending on how much you want to do on your own, the planner's answer can be a plus or minus for you.

✔ **How often do you meet with your clients?** Most planners meet with their clients at least once a year to review goals, portfolios, and performance. Some may recommend such a review twice a year.

Find out how much these meetings will cost you. If your planner gets commissions only, you shouldn't be charged for annual or semiannual meetings (although the planner may earn more commissions if you make changes to your portfolio). If you go with a fee-based or as-needed planner, you'll have to pay for review meetings, so make sure you know how much you'll be charged for them.

Meg's financial planner, who works on commission, meets with her once a year to go over her investments' performance and see whether they need to be rebalanced. During this meeting, the planner also reviews Meg's 401(k) investments and offers advice on changes to be made there — even though the planner doesn't make any money off Meg's 401(k) plan. Meg's planner also is available on an as-needed basis throughout the year, and, unless Meg orders transfers, deposits money, or withdraws money, the planner doesn't get paid for these sessions.

✔ **What questions do you have for me?** A planner who's interested in your financial picture (instead of just making a sale) should ask you about your situation: whether you have children and are planning to help them with college costs; whether you may have to take care of aging parents; whether there are any health issues you or your spouse are concerned about. He should ask about your goals — whether and when you intend to retire, for example, or whether you want to buy a house or sell the one you have. If a prospective planner doesn't have any questions for you, thank him for his time, and continue your search elsewhere.

Most experts recommend interviewing at least three financial planners before deciding on one.

Credentials and cost are important factors in choosing a financial planner, but even more important is your comfort level. You should feel confident that your planner understands your needs and goals and is motivated to help you meet them.

Knowing what you're paying for

If you understand how your planner makes money, you're in a better position to assess the advice he's giving you. A commission-based planner, for example, gets paid only if he sells a financial product to you. A fee-only planner, who doesn't get commissions, gets paid for her advice regardless of whether you purchase any financial product. And fee-based planners get paid both for their advice and for the products they sell.

Commission-based planners

Commission-based planners usually are affiliated with a specific financial company, which may sell an array of products like mutual funds, bond funds, and insurance. There's nothing wrong with choosing a commission-based planner; just be sure to do your research on the company he represents and the fees and commissions attached to the company's products.

If your commission-based planner pushes you toward a specific product, ask these questions:

✔ How does this fit in with my goals?

✔ How do you get paid if I go with this product?

✔ How do the returns compare with the fees and commissions?

You need the answers to determine whether your planner is recommending something that's better for him than for you. If it also fits in with your goals and doesn't eat up most of your returns through fees and commissions, that's fine. But the time to determine that is *before* you say, "Yes."

Fee-only planners

Some fee-only planners charge a flat fee; some charge by the hour; some charge a percentage of your assets. The main advantage to a fee-only planner is that you don't have to worry about your planner trying to sell you insurance or investments. On the other hand, because fee-only planners earn their living by the consulting fees they generate, you could find yourself pressured to have more review meetings than you think you need. Also, if your planner's fees are based on your assets, she may recommend investing in riskier options than you're comfortable with.

How do these tactics benefit the planner? Flat-fee planners get paid every time they meet with you. Hourly-fee planners get paid not just for meeting with you, but for the time they spend going over your file and coming up with recommendations. Obviously, the more often they persuade you to review your finances, the more they get paid.

Likewise, planners who charge a percentage of your assets have a big incentive to increase your net worth. But, to do that, they may urge you to invest in things that carry more risk, or to use your money to get into the stock market instead of paying off debt or building up your emergency fund.

Costs can vary widely, depending on which type of fee-only planner you choose. According to Forrester Research, people who go with flat-fee planners spend an average of $500 a year for financial advice. The average hourly fee is about $120. Planners who base their fees on your assets usually charge between 1 percent and 2 percent; according to the Forrester Research data, clients of these planners pay an average of $1,600 a year.

The National Association of Personal Financial Advisers represents fee-only planners. You can find an adviser on their Web site (www.napfa.org) or by calling 800-366-2732.

Fee-based planners

Fee-based planners earn money from a combination of fees and commissions. How much of the planner's income comes from each source depends a lot on you — and your understanding of the planner's financial incentive behind the recommendations he gives you.

If you go with a fee-based planner, ask the same questions you would ask of a commission-based planner (earlier in this chapter) whenever he makes a recommendation.

It's your responsibility to figure out how your planner benefits from the advice he gives you. Don't assume your planner will tell you these things. Always ask.

Choosing an Investment Broker

To many people, it seems like stockbrokers' sole reason for existing is to make investors rich. But there's an old saying about stockbrokers: You don't have a broker; your broker has a client. Sure, you're the one paying for the services a broker provides, but that doesn't mean the broker's top priority is making *you* wealthy.

There are times when signing up with a traditional broker — as opposed to going through an online firm, where you make your trades yourself — may make sense for you. If you're just starting out in the investing world, you may be more comfortable having a broker's guidance and expertise, at least until you know the ropes. If you've got a ton of money to manage or lots of different investment accounts (like multiple IRAs, a college savings fund, growth accounts, and income accounts), it may be more convenient to have one broker handle it all. And traditional brokers sometimes have access to deals like high-yield notes, initial public offerings (IPOs), and other special bond or stock issues that you can't get through an online or discount firm.

We're not completely opposed to using stock brokers; after all, brokers are God's creatures, too, and they have to eat. And the best of them do provide valuable services to their clients. However, we do advise caution in selecting a broker, and we recommend keeping a steady eye on your investments, fees, and returns to make sure your money is working for you the way you want it to.

A stockbroker should be able to tell you not just *what* a good investment is, but *why* it's good. She also should be able to explain how a given investment fits with your long-term goals and investment strategy.

What to look for

What you want in a broker or firm depends largely on how much you have to invest and on how much advice and guidance you think you need to get started and stay on track. As your account balance and experience grow, your needs in a broker will evolve, too.

If you don't have much to invest

If you've got $5,000 or less to invest, your highest priority is making sure fees won't eat up your gains or your principal. Some online brokers charge fees for inactivity — that is, you may get socked with a quarterly fee if you don't make a minimum number of trades.

Check out minimum account balance requirements, too. Some brokers won't let you open an account with less than $1,000; some charge you a fee if your account dips below a certain amount.

Here are questions you should ask before opening your small investment account:

- ✔ How much do I need to open an account?
- ✔ Are there different minimums for an IRA account? (Some brokers cut their minimums in half for retirement accounts.)
- ✔ Are there fees associated with opening and maintaining the account?
- ✔ How many trades do I have to make each quarter to avoid a fee?
- ✔ What is the minimum balance required to waive maintenance and inactivity fees?
- ✔ Do you charge *custodial fees* (another term for maintenance fees) for IRA accounts?
- ✔ How much does each trade cost?
- ✔ What, if any, fees are associated with transferring money?
- ✔ What, if any, fees are imposed for closing the account?

Just because you're starting small doesn't mean you'll always be a small investor. You may have a hard time convincing brokers of that, but if you guard against unnecessary fees and make wise investment choices, it won't be too long before you rise up the ranks in "investor class."

If you don't plan to make a lot of trades

Like Warren Buffett, we subscribe to the buy-and-hold philosophy of investing. We like to find good investments; buy the stock; and then let our money do its work for the next 10, 20, or 30 years. We rebalance our portfolios at least once a year, and sometimes we'll kick underperformers out or add new investments, but we don't do more than a handful or so of trades in any given year.

If this is your style, too, you probably won't see a lot of value in paying full-service broker fees. On the other hand, you don't want to spend a lot on account fees, either. Customer service and convenience are important, too: You want a Web site that's easy to navigate and allows you to see how your investments are performing, and a number you can call for help when you need it — ideally toll free, 24/7, and with a live person at the other end.

Find out if you can use the Web or the phone to transfer cash into (and out of) your account and if there are any fees for doing this. Also find out if you have ATM or check-writing access and what fees you may be charged for those conveniences.

If you really have a buy-and-hold philosophy, it doesn't make a lot of sense to have an ATM card linked to your investment account. However, if your emergency savings is parked in a money-market account at the brokerage, ATM and check-writing access are important.

Look for brokerages that let you buy and sell mutual funds without paying a transaction or other fee. Schwab's OneSource Select List is the leader in these no-fee offerings; E*TRADE and Fidelity offer quite a few, too.

Before you sign up with a discount or online brokerage, find out if you can download your portfolio performance numbers to a program like Quicken or Microsoft Money. This can make quarter-to-quarter and year-to-year tracking much easier.

Make sure the brokerage you choose has the investment options you're interested in. A long list of potential investments is worthless if your favorite option isn't on it.

If you need someone to hold your hand

Some people just aren't comfortable navigating the investing maze on their own, and that's okay. First, figure out how much guidance you need (or want). Do you just want someone to go over your portfolio once or twice a year and give you recommendations for changes? If so, check out major discount brokers like E*TRADE, Fidelity, or Schwab; they offer these services for modest fees, often $250 or less.

If you want more comprehensive services — a complete financial plan, stock recommendations, the works — you'll have to find a full-service broker or a financial planner. Ask family and friends for recommendations; your accountant or attorney also may be able to recommend a broker. Consider things like integrity, responsiveness, and fees in weighing your choices.

Use the BrokerCheck feature on the Financial Industry Regulatory Authority Web site (www.finra.org) to check out the professional background of the broker or firm you want to do business with. The SEC's Web site (www.sec.gov) also has information on individual brokers and companies.

A firm's reputation is important, but more important is your comfort level with your specific broker. If you feel that your broker doesn't understand your financial goals or risk tolerance, or that his recommendations seem to benefit him more than you, find another broker.

Full-service brokers reserve their VIP treatment for clients with at least six-figure accounts. You may be better off striking out on your own at first and then exploring additional services when your account balance moves into a higher-rent neighborhood.

Figuring out the fees

Fees can take a huge bite out of any gains you make on your investments, so it's important to shop around for the best deals. Over ten years, just 2 percent in annual fees can erase $30,000 of returns on a $100,000 investment (figuring compound interest at 6 percent).

Two simple equations can show you how much it will cost you to buy or sell investments. When you buy, the equation is

(Stock Price × Number of Shares Purchased) + Commissions

When you sell, the equation is

(Stock Price × Number of Shares Sold) − Commissions

Say you want to buy 100 shares of a stock or mutual fund. The stock price is $100 per share, so it will cost you $10,000 (stock price of $100 per share × 100 shares) for the stock. Now you can figure out how the fees will affect your purchase. If you're buying through a discount broker that charges a flat $20 per trade, your total cost for the investment will be $10,020. But if you go through a broker that charges a 2 percent fee, your total cost will be $10,200 (2 percent of $10,000 is $200). If there are other fees associated with the purchase, such as a transaction fee, your costs will be higher.

When it's time to sell shares, you'll pay fees again. Say the price of the stock you bought for $100 a share is now $150 a share, and you want to sell. If you didn't have to pay any fees at all, your initial investment of $10,000 would now be worth $15,000 — a $5,000 profit.

Unfortunately, you can't eliminate all fees. Even with a flat $20-per-trade fee, your profit will be lower — only $4,960 instead of the full $5,000. That's because you paid $20 to buy the stock and another $20 to sell it.

With the 2 percent fee, the cut into your returns is even greater. On $15,000, you'll pay $300 (2 percent of $15,000) to sell your stock. You already paid $200 (2 percent of $10,000) to buy it in the first place, so your total return after fees is only $4,500:

Current Value of Stock – Initial Stock Costs = Stock's Final Value

$15,000 – $10,200 = $4,800

Stock's Final Value – Broker's Fee on Sale = Total Return

$4,800 – ($15,000 × 0.02) = $4,500

And, just like that, a 50 percent return is slashed to 45 percent.

Of course, no one would complain about getting a 45 percent return on any investment these days. But here in the real world, when average returns are in the 6 percent to 8 percent range, a 2 percent fee represents between one-quarter and one-third of your gains.

Even no-load mutual funds may come with a hefty transaction fee if you buy them through a broker — full-service or discount — instead of purchasing them directly from the fund family. Fidelity charges $75 for most no-load funds outside its own family; Schwab charges $49.95. If you're adding to your mutual fund investments regularly, transaction fees can mount quickly.

Always read the expense disclosures before you invest. You can find fee and commission schedules on discount brokers' Web sites; otherwise, check out the expense section of the prospectus.

Morningstar (www.morningstar.com) has a free tool that allows you to compare a variety of funds according to various expense ratios and other factors. Under the Tools tab on the home page, select Fund Screener — look for the free one; the members-only version has *(prem)* next to it — and enter the values you want to search for.

What to stay away from

Naturally, we dislike high fees because they're so bad for your long-term growth. We also dislike brokers who push investments that plump up their bottom lines but don't really serve the investor, and brokers who can't or won't break down investing lingo into plain English.

We strongly recommend using the resources available to you to check out a broker's or firm's background (see "If you need someone to hold your hand," earlier in this chapter). If others had bad experiences and filed complaints, you want to know that before you jump in; you also want to know how any complaints were resolved. If your broker is a newbie, you want to know that, too; in general, we prefer more experienced brokers.

And, because all brokers have to be licensed in the state in which they practice, don't be shy about checking with your state's regulatory authority. You can find contact information at the North American Securities Administrators Association Web site (`www.nasaa.org`) under the Contact Your Regulator tab.

Choosing an Attorney

Everybody hates lawyers . . . until they need one. The average person needs an attorney only a few times: when you're buying a house, for example, or making out your will. If you get divorced, you'll need a lawyer, and you may need one before you get married or remarried if you want a prenuptial agreement.

If you have a business, you'll need an attorney experienced in business law. This lawyer also may be able to handle your other, personal legal needs, although many attorneys these days are just as much specialists as doctors, especially when it comes to corporate law.

General-practitioner lawyers typically are experienced in most common personal legal matters like wills, debt issues, and real-estate transactions.

What to look for

As with your financial advisers, you want a lawyer you feel comfortable with and who is experienced in the types of legal matters you need assistance with. A personal-injury lawyer may not be the best person to advise you about your will, for example, and one who specializes in employment law probably isn't the one you want handling the closing on your dream home.

Look for an attorney who will give you a free initial consultation. During that meeting, not only do you want to get a feel for how well the lawyer communicates and understands your needs, but you should collect some critical information, too:

✔ **How fees are calculated:** Some lawyers charge an hourly rate, and how much you pay will depend on whether the attorney is an associate or a partner; hourly fees vary greatly by region, too, and if you're on either coast, you can expect to pay more than you would in the Midwest. Fixed fees are commonly charged for routine matters, like drafting wills. Contingency fees usually are reserved for things like personal-injury cases, and the lawyer doesn't get paid unless you win an award, either in court or in an out-of-court settlement.

If you consider going with an hourly-fee attorney, ask for an estimate on the total bill. The attorney should be able to give you a range so you can estimate how much his services will cost you.

✔ **Other costs you're responsible for:** You're responsible for certain costs like filing fees. Sometimes lawyers also charge clients for certain overhead costs, like copies, computer research, and long-distance phone charges. Find out which costs are included in the lawyer's fee and which are extra out-of-pocket expenses for you.

When you select your attorney, ask for a written fee agreement that spells out how much you'll pay the attorney and what extra costs you'll be responsible for.

✔ **Availability:** If you want to build a long-term relationship with a lawyer, find out if she has the time — and the interest — to attend to your needs. Ask how messages are handled and whether the attorney has a partner, an assistant, or a paralegal you can talk with when the attorney isn't available.

Where to look

You could just open the Yellow Pages and browse the listings. And, if you don't have a referral from friends or family to guide you, the Yellow Pages is a useful resource. Lawyers are listed according to their area of practice, which helps you narrow down your choices.

Here are some other resources:

✔ The American Bar Association (www.abanet.org) offers referrals but does not recommend specific lawyers.

✔ The Martindale-Hubbell Law Directory (www.martindale.com) allows you to search by name (of an individual or a firm) or by geographic location. Many of those listed are corporate law firms, but you can find personal-law attorneys, too.

✔ Your state or county bar associations, listed in your phone book, may offer a referral service. Sometimes these attorneys are less experienced, but they're also less expensive.

Check with your employer to see if they offer a legal plan. Sometimes you can get free legal advice for certain matters, like simple wills and review of simple legal documents.

What to avoid

Stay away from attorneys who don't seem to listen to you or give other indications that they aren't all that interested in or knowledgeable about your needs. Also, if you're confused about the fees, or if you feel the attorney didn't explain your options clearly, look elsewhere.

Choosing an Insurance Agent

Insurance is a critical element of protecting your wealth (see Chapter 18 for a full discussion of insurance), and getting the right insurance agent is critical in getting the right insurance. A good agent will ensure that you have the coverage you need, that there aren't any gaps in your coverage, and that you aren't paying for stuff you don't need.

Insurance agents are either affiliated with a specific company (in which case they're called *direct writers* or *captive agents*) or *independent agents,* who can write policies from a variety of insurers. Some agents specialize in certain types of insurance; others write all kinds of policies.

Independents versus captive agents

There are pros and cons in choosing either an independent agent or a captive one. An independent agent can shop around to find you the best price on policies, and you have lots of insurance providers to choose among. On the other hand, if you choose your auto coverage from one company and your homeowner's policy from a different one, you lose out on multiple-policy discounts. And, if you have policies from many different companies, it can be harder to identify gaps in your coverage.

A captive agent or direct writer gives you the convenience of one-stop shopping for all or most of your insurance needs. It's also easier to make sure your coverage limits are consistent across your various policies and to identify places where your coverage needs to be upgraded (or can be cut back). Most insurance companies also provide discounts when you have multiple policies with them, and you have to deal with only one agent for any claims.

However, when you choose a captive agent, your policy choices are limited to what the agent's company offers. If you want coverage the company doesn't provide — long-term care or disability insurance, for example — you'll have to go elsewhere for it.

Where to look

If you want to go with a captive agent, check out the Web sites of the insurance company you want; almost all of them allow you to search for an agent in your area. If you prefer an independent agent, or if you haven't identified an insurance company you like, ask friends and relatives for referrals.

Price is important in selecting insurance, but so are your agent's experience, responsiveness, and personality. You want an agent who will listen to you, help you identify your insurance needs, and answer questions quickly and simply.

As with your other financial advisers, we recommend selecting three likely candidates and interviewing each one before you buy any policy. At your first meeting, find out

- ✔ How much experience the agent has, and in what types of policies
- ✔ How he can help you identify your insurance needs
- ✔ How claims are handled
- ✔ Who handles the day-to-day account business
- ✔ Whether the agent reviews clients' insurance plans regularly and, if so, how often

If you're not comfortable with an agent, keep looking. The last thing you need is an overzealous salesperson who keeps trying to push you into policies you don't want or need.

Choosing a Tax Preparer

If your idea of a good time doesn't involve filling out Schedule A for your 1040, you may want to have a professional prepare your tax return. But use caution when selecting a tax preparer: According to the Better Business Bureau (BBB), almost a third of people who hired others to do their taxes complained that the preparer made mistakes that resulted in penalties or fines. The BBB also fields many complaints about tax preparers who don't respond to calls or e-mails from customers, or who don't provide copies of the tax return. And about 20 percent of complaints are about the fees — people who said they weren't told how much their total tax-preparation bill would be.

And, unfortunately, there are some downright dishonest tax preparers out there who can get you in a world of hurt.

The BBB's Web site (www.bbb.org) has a free Reliability Report for tax preparation firms. Enter your zip code on the home page; then click Check Out a Business or Charity. Type **tax prep reliability report** in the search box, and the site will return a list of tax-prep firms in your area, along with their reliability reports.

Shopping for a tax preparer is just as important as looking for any other professional help. ***Remember:*** Even if someone else prepares your return, you're the one who's responsible for the accuracy of your return and any tax due. And if the numbers on the return aren't correct, you're the one who will pay the penalties.

What to look for

The first thing you want in a tax preparer is credentials. CPAs who specialize in tax planning and preparation are usually a good bet. CPAs, attorneys, and Enrolled Agents can represent taxpayers before the Internal Revenue Service (IRS). Other tax preparers can only participate in an audit of the returns they prepared, not those prepared by the taxpayer or another preparer, and they can't represent you in any other actions before the IRS.

You also want a preparer who will be around even when it isn't tax season. Many tax preparers are open only between February and April, and if there's a problem you need their help with, you're out of luck any other month.

Ask who will actually prepare your return. In some large firms, the work may be delegated to an underling with less experience — and perhaps less expertise. If that's the procedure, ask if anyone else reviews the return before you sign it. You should always know the person who's actually responsible for preparing your return.

Ask what documentation you need to provide. Reputable tax preparers will want to see receipts for deductions and will ask you lots of questions to determine whether you're eligible for certain deductions and credits. Beware the tax preparer who says she doesn't need to see your receipts or who doesn't ask *you* questions to find out what breaks you may qualify for.

Make sure you know how the fee is determined. The preparer should be able to give you a rough estimate.

Tax-prep fees should be in proportion to the complexity of your return. A simple return should generate the lowest prep fee; if your return is more complicated or time-consuming than expected, you can expect to pay more.

Avoid any preparer who bases her fees on the size of your refund. This gives the preparer a strong incentive to cheat, and you'll be left holding the bag. Besides, legitimate tax preparers aren't allowed to charge "contingency fees" based on the results of your return.

As with other financial professionals, arrange to meet prospective tax preparers before you sign up with one. Find out if you'll be charged extra if you call with questions, and ask how long it will take to prepare your return. Also ask whether the tax preparer will represent you if you're audited.

What to avoid

There are several tax-prep ploys that should set your internal alarm bells clanging. Stay away from any firm that says it can get you a bigger refund than the competition; this is a pretty good indication that it plays fast and loose with the numbers.

Never, never, *never* sign a blank return. And never sign a return in pencil.

Make sure the tax preparer is doing your return in the United States. If your information is sent to another country, it isn't protected by U.S. privacy laws — and there's nothing you can do about it if your personal information is compromised by an overseas tax-prep operation.

If a tax preparer recommends a tax shelter or other unfamiliar way to lower your tax bill, check it out on the IRS Web site (www.irs.gov). Remember the adage "If it sounds too good to be true, it probably is."

Never give your tax preparer authority to receive refunds on your behalf. If a prospective preparer wants you to sign such an authorization, say, "No thanks," and keep looking.

Chapter 16

Going for Growth versus Going for Income

Your interest in growing your savings or protecting your nest egg depends mainly on your stage of life. If you're in your 20s or 30s, growth should be a higher priority than safety. If you're in your 50s or 60s, though, your focus should be shifting from going after big gains to preserving your cash so it'll see you through retirement.

As a whole, Americans are lousy at planning for retirement. According to the Employee Benefit Research Institute (EBRI; www.ebri.org), more than a third of U.S. workers have less than $10,000 put aside for retirement. Not surprisingly, younger workers — those between the ages of 25 and 34 — constitute most of this group, but 28 percent of workers age 55 or older find themselves with less $10,000 in their retirement accounts. And 77 percent of people 55 or older have less than $250,000 in retirement savings.

This is not your grandparents' retirement. People are living longer, healthier lives, which means that their retirement money has to last longer. Add to this the virtual extinction of traditional pension plans (70 percent of workers participated in company pension plans in 1979, compared with 10 percent in 2005) and ongoing concerns about the solvency of the Social Security Trust Fund, and you can see how easily your "golden years" can become tarnished if you aren't careful.

One reason so many people are off track with their retirement plans is that they don't invest properly for their time of life. Younger workers often are too conservative with their investments, and older workers, perhaps in an effort to make up for lost time, often take on too much risk. In this chapter, we explain the dangers of going too conservative too early and too risky too late. We show you how to determine the appropriate level of risk for your age by assessing what you need now and your goals for the future. We take you through different kinds of investments based on their risk levels. We explain why rebalancing is important both when you're working and after you've retired, and we discuss common mistakes people make when they're approaching or already in retirement.

In this chapter, we have room only to scratch the surface of investing options and strategies for different life phases. Fortunately, the loss to financial literature isn't irreparable; the folks at Wiley Publishing have a comprehensive line of books focusing on various aspects of investing. Here are our recommendations, which you can find at your local bookstore or at www.dummies.com:

- *401(k)s For Dummies,* by Ted Benna and Brenda Watson Newmann

- *Bond Investing For Dummies,* by Russell Wild, MBA

- *Commodities For Dummies,* by Amine Bouchentouf

- *Futures & Options For Dummies,* by Joe Duarte, MD

- *Hedge Funds For Dummies,* by Ann C. Logue, MBA

- *Stock Investing For Dummies,* 2nd Edition, by Paul Mladjenovic

- *Stock Options For Dummies,* by Alan R. Simon

Determining the Right Mix for You

Your portfolio should look a lot different in your 30s than it does in your 50s. From the time you begin your full-time working life to the middle of your career — say, your mid- to late 40s — your investments should be heavy on growth stocks and light on cash. Most financial planners recommend putting 75 percent to 80 percent of your retirement savings in stocks, which offer greater growth potential for the long term than cash, bonds, or cash-equivalent investments.

As you get closer to retirement, though, the balance should shift. You still want the majority of your investments in stocks, because you want to take advantage of the growth opportunities there, but the size of that majority should be smaller later in your working life — 60 percent to 65 percent instead of 75 percent to 80 percent. And when you actually retire, no more than half of your portfolio should be invested in stocks — or, if you're more risk averse, no more than a third.

The reason for this gradual shift away from stocks is that, as you age, you have less time to make up losses you may incur in stocks. If you go through a bear market in your 30s, you've got decades to recoup your losses, and chances are good that you'll come out way ahead in the long run. But a bear market in your 50s or 60s can seriously damage your nest egg and may even derail your retirement plan.

Table 16-1 is a guide to help you determine how to divvy up your portfolio based on your stage in life. This is only a guide; your portfolio may look quite different because of your circumstances, risk tolerance, or other factors.

Table 16-1	Allocating Your Assets throughout Your Life		
Investment Type	**Early/Mid-Career**	**Late Career**	**Retirement**
Blue-chip stocks	37 percent	37 percent	27 percent
Other stocks	40 percent	31 percent	11 percent
REITs*	6 percent	7 percent	8 percent
TIPS*	1 percent	5 percent	14 percent
Other bonds	9 percent	17 percent	30 percent
Cash	1 percent	3 percent	10 percent

*REITs are real estate investment trusts; TIPS are Treasury Inflation-Protected Securities. See Chapter 13 for more information on TIPS and Chapter 14 for more information on REITs.

The percentage of each investment type changes as you get older. Notice, too, that stocks should constitute a healthy chunk of your investments even in retirement. There are two reasons for this:

✔ Because you can expect to live longer in retirement than your grandparents did, you need to have at least some growth in your portfolio to stay ahead of inflation.

✔ Stocks and bonds tend to move in opposite directions, so, even when you're retired, you want to hedge your bets against low bond yields when stocks are setting new record highs.

If you're married and counting on only one retirement plan to see you through your post-work life, you're still putting all your eggs in one basket. Divorce, illness, or death can leave one of you with little or no income. Each of you needs your own retirement plan — a combination of Social Security, 401(k) or IRA, and investment accounts — for financial stability.

Factoring in your risk tolerance

Of course, Table 16-1 is just a guide. Your actual mix will depend on your *risk tolerance* — how much volatility you can stomach when you look at your monthly, quarterly, or annual statements. (See Chapter 13 for more on determining your risk tolerance.) You may decide you'd rather invest more heavily in blue-chip stocks (which have long track records of reliable growth) than take a chance on other stocks that are more sensitive to market fluctuations, for example. On the other hand, if you're in your 20s and are eager to chase the bigger potential gains of less-established stocks, you may divert more of your savings into, say, small-cap or micro-cap stocks (see "Cap stocks," later in this chapter) and hold fewer blue chips.

The important thing is to avoid putting all your nest egg into a single basket. Even if you're in your first youth and retirement is three or four decades away, you still need some cash and bonds in your portfolio to counter the risk you take in stocks. And REITs and TIPS are there to help protect you against the effects of inflation, which can significantly devalue your cash and bonds.

Being too conservative with your investments is as risky to your long-term financial health as being too aggressive. If you take on too much risk, you could lose most or all of your savings. But if you're too conservative, your savings become vulnerable to inflation, and between inflation and taxes, you risk dooming yourself to a lower standard of living in retirement.

Assessing other factors

Your genes can influence your risk tolerance, too. If you come from a long-lived family, for example, your retirement savings probably will have to last longer than the average, and that may warrant a more aggressive mix in your portfolio even after you retire.

If you got a late start on saving for retirement, you may want to push your risk tolerance a little further to make your money grow faster. Be careful, though; you don't want to cross the threshold from investing to speculating if you're already behind schedule on your savings plan.

Your goals for retirement also figure into your investing equation. If you plan a quiet lifestyle in your paid-off home, and you have enough income to meet your needs, there's really no reason to build extra risk into your investment mix. But if you want to travel around the world (or, what with gas prices and airline fares these days, even around the country) in the first five years of your retirement, you'll want your savings to grow as much as possible so you can comfortably live out your dreams.

Understanding Investment Risks

Different investment vehicles carry different levels of risk, and risk is directly proportional to returns. The safer an investment, the lower your returns will be; the riskier it is, the higher the potential gains. Risk is the premium you pay for the possibility of making more money faster.

Low-risk investments are designed to provide a reliable income stream without putting your capital at risk. Moderate-risk investments earn higher yields than fixed-income investments; although there is a chance you could lose your principal, a diversified portfolio minimizes that risk — and also moderates the gains you can expect. High-risk investments can generate fantastic returns, but they can just as easily tank, taking your capital along for the dive.

Social Security benefits are a fixed-income asset; you get the same monthly payment (adjusted annually for inflation) for the rest of your life. If you have a defined-benefit pension plan, that, too, is a fixed-income asset, providing a reliable, fixed payment for you year after year.

If you have a defined-benefit pension plan, don't give it up by choosing to take a lump-sum distribution on retirement. Too often, retirees who do this either spend their pension proceeds more quickly or buy unsuitably risky investments, and they pay dearly for it later on. Most of the time, you're better off keeping your monthly pension and using a small portion of your own savings to explore riskier investment options.

Low-risk investments

Low-risk investments include your cash savings and fixed-income options like government bonds, REITs (see Chapter 14), and TIPS (see Chapter 13). The chances of losing your capital are virtually nil, and, while your returns won't make you rich, you'll earn a little bit of interest year after year.

There are ways to boost your low-risk returns. Traditional savings accounts typically pay only a fraction of 1 percent in interest, and some don't offer any interest unless you keep a fairly large sum in the account at all times. Online-only savings accounts pay three times or more the interest you'll get at your bricks-and-mortar bank, and you can arrange for automatic transfers from your traditional account to your online account.

Certificates of deposit (CDs) offer higher interest rates because you promise not to withdraw your money for a set period, usually ranging from six months to five years. You'll pay a fee or penalty if you withdraw the money before the CD expires; on the other hand, if you don't need the money, you can roll it over into a new CD so it can keep earning the higher interest rate.

Money-market mutual fund accounts also offer higher interest than traditional savings accounts, and they're a good place to park your cash while you decide what to do with it. One caveat: Many of these accounts have minimum balance requirements, and often you can't withdraw less than $250 at a time.

None of these accounts offers any tax advantage; you fund them with after-tax dollars, and you'll pay taxes on the interest you earn every year. But, because the interest rates are usually low, the tax you'll pay on the interest will be low, too.

With the exception of money-market mutual fund accounts, put your cash in institutions that are insured. The Federal Deposit Insurance Corporation (FDIC) insures each depositor for up to $100,000; the National Credit Union Administration (NCUA) does the same for credit-union members. Money-market mutual fund accounts are not insured, but they're still exceptionally safe investments; no one has ever lost principal in a money-market mutual fund.

Moderate-risk investments

Moderate-risk investments are those that balance risk and reward. They go up and down according to myriad market forces, but they don't vary as much as higher-risk investments. Moderate-risk investments include mutual funds, index funds, cap stocks, and even bonds. We explain cap stocks later in this section; for information on mutual and index funds, see Chapter 13.

We include bonds in the moderate-risk category because, although you're unlikely to lose money on an investment-grade bond, inflation and taxes can take a big chunk out of already-low returns. When you're retired or near retirement, inflation and taxes are your wealth's most powerful and insidious enemies.

Keeping fees low is critical for any investment, including mutual funds, index funds, and bonds. High fees can eat up your returns at a fierce rate, and lower actual returns, after fees, can make a big difference in the lifestyle you can sustain.

Investment-grade bonds

Bonds are debt instruments for the company or government that issues them. Investors buy the bonds, and the issuer promises to repay the loan, plus interest, on a specific date — which could be a year from now or 30 years from now. Both government and corporate bonds are rated by independent firms; the ratings are designed to give investors confidence in the issuer's ability to repay the debt.

Standard & Poor's and Moody's are the best-known independent rating firms for municipal and corporate bonds. These two firms, and others like them (though less well known), analyze the bond issuer's financial stability, looking at things like debt load, economic pressures and opportunities, and any other factors that may affect the issuer's ability to repay investors.

Investment-grade bonds are those rated AAA (S&P) or Aaaa (Moody's) to BBB (S&P) or Baa (Moody's). AAA/Aaaa bonds represent the least risk; they're issued by financially secure companies and state and local governments. BBB/Baa bonds usually carry some long-term risk because of uncertainty over the issuer's future financial stability; some factors have made the analysts nervous about the issuer's long-term financial security.

Junk bonds are those rated below BBB/Baa (see "Junk bonds," later in this chapter).

Just like other investments, the yields on bonds are directly proportional to their risk. The highest-rated bonds offer the lowest yields because there's little risk of losing your money. High-yield bonds are, by definition, riskier.

When Standard & Poor's or Moody's rates a bond or changes a bond rating, it issues a brief report explaining the reasoning behind the rating. You can find these reports on the companies' Web sites. For S&P, go to `www.standardandpoors.com` and click the Ratings tab on the left menu. For Moody's, go to `www.moodys.com` and register for free; then you can search the Ratings News section.

Cap stocks

Cap is investing shorthand for *market capitalization,* which is a fancy way of saying how much the market thinks a company is worth. Market capitalization is figured by multiplying the stock price by the number of outstanding shares. Company stock is designated a small-cap or large-cap stock based on (increasingly flexible) categories of market value. *Large-cap companies* have a market capitalization of $10 billion or more. (A relatively new category, *mega caps* are companies worth more than $200 billion.) *Mid caps* range from $2 billion to $9.9 billion. And *small caps* are worth between $300 million and $1.9 billion. There also are *micro caps* (worth between $50 million and $299 million) and *nano caps* (worth less than $50 million).

Different brokerages assign different thresholds to their cap categories; the ones we offer here are approximations.

The theory behind cap investing is that smaller caps are potentially undervalued; they may grow into large caps over time, so the savvy investor may be able to get a heck of a deal if he picks the right small cap and holds on to it. Large caps are seen as less risky, but that perception isn't always true: Enron and Bear Stearns were both large caps before their spectacular crashes.

Large-cap stocks are followed most closely by Wall Street analysts, which means the likelihood of finding a real value stock among these behemoths is slim.

High-risk investments

High-risk investments promise breathtaking returns, but they also represent a clear and present danger to your capital. Plus, they tend to be extremely complicated for the average investor.

If you don't understand how an investment works, it's time to step back and take a deep breath. Complexity is often an indicator of high risk; just look at the mortgage crisis that snaked its tentacles into virtually every sector of the economy beginning in 2007. The subprime mortgage mess hurt more than just the subprime lenders, because those mortgages were sliced and diced into complex securities and sold to a lot of companies that had nothing to do with mortgages themselves. Then, when the value of those securities plummeted as default and foreclosure rates took flight, guess who was left holding worthless paper?

Hedge funds

Hedge funds derive their name from the practice of *hedging bets* — investing on both sides of a particular asset to limit the overall risk. But some hedge funds actually use their investment strategies to *increase* risk, because higher risk means higher potential returns.

Our problem with hedge funds is that you seldom know what your hedge-fund manager is doing. Hedge funds are private and lightly regulated; disclosure requirements are meager because of the proprietary nature of a fund's investment strategies and position in the market. There's not enough information available to make a true assessment of your risk; you may not even know exactly what a given hedge fund is investing in.

Hedge funds also don't have to follow the same rules as mutual funds or index funds. Managers can profit from the money invested in hedge funds, buy or sell any asset that tickles their fancy, and gamble on both rising and falling assets. They can borrow heavily against investor money, which puts your money at even higher risk if the manager misreads the market.

Most hedge funds are open only to *qualified* (read "really rich") investors, and they charge both management fees and performance fees. The potential returns are enormous, but we don't like the pig-in-a-poke feel of hedge funds.

Junk bonds

Junk bonds are the opposite of investment-grade bonds: There is a good chance the issuer will default on the loan, meaning you could lose both the promised interest and your initial investment. Government bonds aren't immune from low ratings; just ask officials in Orange County, California, whose bonds were considered junk in the 1990s.

There are different degrees of junk bonds, just as there are different degrees of investment-grade bonds. The highest junk-bond rating is BB (S&P) or Ba (Moody's). The lowest is C (for both rating firms). A bond rated D by S&P is one that's already in default.

Futures

Futures dominated the news in 2008, when oil prices were hitting new records virtually every day. Basically, a futures contract is a bet that the price of a certain commodity (most commonly oil or gold, but agriculture products, foreign currencies, and even the S&P 500 index also are traded on futures contracts) will change. Futures buyers are betting that the price will go up; futures sellers are betting that the price will go down. If the buyer is right, he makes money, because he can buy the commodity at the contract price and sell it at the higher market price. If the seller is right, she makes money, because she can buy the commodity at the lower market price and sell it to the buyer at the higher contract price.

Let's use oil as an example. Say oil is trading at $100 a barrel (oh, those were the days . . .), and you think the price is going to go up in the next three months. You buy a futures contract that gives you the right to sell your barrel of oil at the market price three months from today. The seller agrees to buy your barrel of oil at the market price on that date.

To keep things simple, we're using one barrel as an example. In the real world, futures contracts involve hundreds or even thousands of units of the commodity being sold.

Now, let's say oil prices hit $150 a barrel before the trading date, or when the contract comes due. You bought the oil at $100 a barrel, and now you sell it, before the contract expires, for $150; you make a $50 profit.

On the other hand, if oil is selling for $75 a barrel (we know, but this is just an example) as your contract expiration approaches, you probably would sell before the price drops further. You lose $25, but you could lose more if the price is dropping and you wait to liquidate your contract.

Futures trading all takes place on paper; you don't take physical delivery of barrels of oil, bushels of corn, or bars of gold. Instead, you get proof that the commodity has been delivered to a warehouse, you get a cash settlement, or you get another futures contract at the current market price. Futures trading gets complicated at warp speed, and it's not for investing novices.

The good thing about futures is that their values are set by analysts and traders who spend their entire day researching all the factors that can impact the price of their particular commodity; they're truly experts, and they generally do a pretty good job of assessing the future value of their given commodity.

The bad thing is that virtually anything can affect a commodity's value, because it's all driven by supply and demand. The 2008 floods in the Midwest sent corn futures rocketing because so much farmland was under water, and there already was high demand for corn as food, livestock feed, and fuel for ethanol. But if the supply turns out to be greater than the markets expected — if Midwest farmers ended up producing roughly the same amount of corn they would have without the floods — futures would go back down.

Historically, commodities don't increase in value as fast as stocks. Over 100 years, gold doubled in value, but stocks today are worth eight times what they were worth a century ago. Bob says the easiest way to make a small fortune in commodities is to start with a large one.

Comparing oil and onions

In 2008, speculators were blamed for record oil prices; the major U.S. airlines even sent a mass e-mail to their miles-program subscribers, asking them to pressure Congress to put limits on the amount of futures trading in oil. "Some market experts estimate that current prices reflect as much as $30 to $60 per barrel in unnecessary speculative costs," the airlines' letter said.

But *Fortune* magazine compared swings in oil and corn prices, which are traded in futures markets, with price changes in onions — the only commodity you can't buy on a futures contract in the United States. (In 1958, at the behest of onion growers who were convinced that speculators were responsible for falling onion prices, a rising political star named Gerald Ford, then a Michigan congressman, got Congress to pass a law banning futures trading for onions; the law is still on the books.) The magazine reported that onion prices rode a dizzying roller coaster of ups and downs. Between October 2006 and April 2007, onion prices went up fourfold. In March 2008, onion prices took a 96 percent nosedive. And in the very next month, they went up 300 percent.

And oil meanwhile? Up 100 percent between 2006 and 2008 — supporting the theory of some market observers that futures trading actually moderates extreme price changes.

Keeping Your Balance

Some people think that, once they retire, they can just coast along, living off their savings, pension, and Social Security benefits. But, because even retirees should have a significant portion of their investments in stocks, you should review your portfolio at least once a year to make sure you've got the right mix of stocks, bonds, and cash equivalents to meet your current and future needs.

It doesn't take much to skew your investment balance, even when you're retired. A buoyant stock market can significantly enlarge that slice of your investment pie and shrink other slices, and the shift in concentration may jeopardize your goals down the road.

If you have a financial adviser you trust, don't fire her when you retire. Plan to meet with her once or twice a year to review your portfolio, and use this opportunity to discuss tax planning and any changes in your circumstances, like health issues.

Reassessing your goals

Just as important as reviewing your portfolio regularly in retirement is reviewing and reassessing your goals. Circumstances can change dramatically, and those changes can have a profound impact on your financial security.

It's not just the obvious things like your own physical health or an uncertain economy, either. You may find yourself in a familial sandwich — helping your kids through college at the same time you assume more caretaking responsibilities for aging parents. Changes in tax laws, Social Security benefits, and retirement-plan rules can occur at any time; when you're already retired, your options for adjusting to such changes may be more limited.

And, if you want to leave something behind for your heirs, you may have to take more risk with your investments than you initially planned for. Researchers at T. Rowe Price predicted the end value of four portfolios worth $500,000 each, with a first-year withdrawal of 4.5 percent and inflation-adjusted withdrawals for the next 29 years. At the end of 30 years, a portfolio with an 80-20 mix of stocks and bonds would be worth $495,000 in today's dollars. But a conservative portfolio — one with 20 percent in stocks, 30 percent in short-term bonds, and 50 percent in other bonds — would be worth a relatively paltry $180,000 after 30 years.

Don't stop thinking about your goals just because you've punched a clock for the last time. Financial security is a holistic discipline, affected by virtually every other area of your life. Part of keeping your balance is recognizing how changing conditions affect what you want out of life and how you go about getting it.

Avoiding common (and expensive) mistakes

Retirement is more complicated than ever. Gone are the days when you could count on getting the same monthly pension for the rest of your life, augmented by inflation-adjusted Social Security benefits. These days, you have to stay on top of your financial plan for life, or you could easily find yourself paying a high price for inattention, procrastination, or ignorance.

Not saving enough

As we mention at the beginning of this chapter, many people neglect their own savings plan, figuring they'll be able to live off Social Security and perhaps a small pension from their employer. (In 2008, the average Social Security retirement benefit was $1,079.) Lots of people who are eligible to participate in 401(k) programs don't bother, and lots of people who do have 401(k)s leave money sitting on the table because they don't contribute enough to get the full employer match.

Here are some facts from the EBRI that may help you understand the consequences of not saving enough:

✔ For people age 65 and older in 2006 (the latest year for which figures were available at this writing), Social Security benefits accounted for nearly 40 percent of their income. Income from earnings — that is, a full- or part-time job — made up almost a quarter of their income. So, if your retirement plans don't include working at least part-time, chances are your Social Security benefits won't be enough to sustain the lifestyle you envision.

✔ For the poorest retirees — those with less than $8,261 a year in income — Social Security represented almost 90 percent of their income. Earnings from a job accounted for less than 2 percent of their annual income.

✔ For the wealthiest retirees, Social Security benefits represented less than 20 percent of their income. Another 20 percent came from assets, and more than 22 percent came from pensions and annuities. More than a third came from earnings from a job.

✔ The median income (half had higher incomes and half had lower incomes) for people aged 65 and over was $16,770. Between 1999 and 2006, the median income rose by a yearly average of only a third of 1 percent, while inflation ranged from 1.6 percent to nearly 3.4 percent.

First, contribute enough to your 401(k) to get the full employer match; the employer match is free money to help fund your retirement. Then open an IRA and make the maximum contribution to get the tax deduction every year. If you're eligible (there are income limits, which you can find at www.irs.gov), open a Roth IRA next and max it out. Then aim to save an additional 5 percent to 10 percent of your income in a well-balanced portfolio of stocks, bonds, and cash accounts.

Traditional IRAs and Roth IRAs have different tax advantages. Traditional IRAs give you a tax break now, but the earnings on those accounts are taxable when you withdraw them. Roth IRA contributions are not tax-deductible, but the earnings are never taxed. For some people, the lower tax bill today may be more important than tax-free earnings later. Consult your financial adviser to be sure you understand your options and make the best decisions for yourself.

Dipping into your 401(k)

Some 401(k) plans allow you to take out a loan, which you pay back at a low interest rate, or a hardship withdrawal, which you don't have to pay back. If you take a loan from your 401(k), you don't have to pay the 10 percent early withdrawal penalty or taxes on the amount of the loan as long as it's paid back within five years. You don't have to pay back hardship withdrawals, but you will pay taxes on the amount you withdraw, and, if you're not yet 59½ years old, you'll have to pay the 10 percent early withdrawal penalty. In addition, you can't make any contributions to your 401(k) for six months after you take a hardship withdrawal.

Here's the problem with taking money out of your 401(k): Even if you take out a loan that you pay back, you likely pay less in interest than your principal would earn. You also have less principal to earn money for you. Say you have $50,000 in your 401(k) earning 8 percent, and you take out a $10,000 loan. Now you have only $40,000 earning 8 percent. It takes you five years to pay back the loan. In that five years, $50,000 would be worth more than $74,000 at 8 percent. But $40,000, earning the same 8 percent, would be worth only about $59,000 five years later. Not only are you $10,000 short on principal, but that shortage costs you an additional $4,000 in lost earnings. Plus, you repay the loan with after-tax money, so if you're in the 25 percent tax bracket, you have to earn $13,333 to pay back the $10,000. And, finally, if you quit or lose your job before the loan is repaid, you have to pay the remaining balance immediately to avoid getting hit with taxes on the outstanding balance and the 10 percent penalty if you're under 59½.

Some 401(k) plans don't let you make any contributions when you have a loan outstanding, which means you lose out on up to five years of retirement savings (and any employer match), as well as the tax benefits of contributing to your 401(k). Depending on your income, that could push you into a higher tax bracket, making that "easy" loan even more expensive.

Unless the circumstances are truly dire, don't touch your 401(k). You're better off tapping your home equity or getting a personal loan to meet big money emergencies or restructure debt.

Making faulty assumptions

Conventional wisdom says that you'll need less than your current income for expenses and that you'll be in a lower tax bracket when you retire. But conventional wisdom, while comfortable, isn't necessarily correct.

Expectations and reality don't always coincide as neatly as we'd like. In 2007, the EBRI released a report comparing what workers expected to spend in the first five years of retirement and what retirees actually reported as their experience. Twenty percent of workers said they'd spend much less, and 20 percent of retirees said that was true for them. But only 34 percent of workers expect to spend about the same after they quit working, while 42 percent of retirees said their spending was about the same.

One of the reasons for the disparity between expectations and experience is that many people assume they'll be in a lower tax bracket when they retire. That may be true, but it's definitely true that taxes will increase during your retirement years. Some people fail to take taxes into account at all: They figure they'll need $60,000 a year to live on, but they forget about the taxes on that $60,000 — or they forget that, when they have to take mandatory minimum distributions from their retirement accounts, those distributions could put them in a higher tax bracket.

Inflation is another commonly overlooked factor in retirement planning. Say you take $10,000 out of your retirement fund in your first year of retirement, and inflation is 3 percent. In your second year of retirement, you'll have to take out $10,300 to maintain the standard of living you had in your first year of retirement. If inflation stays at 3 percent a year, by your fifth year of retirement, you'll have to withdraw nearly $11,600 to have the same purchasing power you had in your first year of retirement. In 20 years, you'll need more than $18,000 to buy what $10,000 bought when you first retired.

Major investment firms like T. Rowe Price and Schwab advise most workers to assume they'll need to replace 80 percent of their income when they retire. But how much you'll really need to live on depends so much on individual circumstances (whether you'll still have a mortgage payment when you retire, for example, or whether you want to indulge in expensive interests like world travel) that it's difficult to issue a blanket must-have figure that suits everyone. A good rule of thumb: Estimate the expenses you'll have in retirement and then add 5 percent to that figure. That way, if you've underestimated taxes or inflation, you'll have a built-in buffer to cover — or at least ease — the extra expense.

Spending too much too soon

Lots of retirees have expensive plans for the first years after they quit working. They may want to travel or remodel the house or buy that classic car they've always wanted. And they often use historical data on their retirement accounts to decide how much they can withdraw every year.

The problem is, when you start spending, historical returns are meaningless. The only number that matters is your annual return on your investments. If your accounts averaged a 10 percent annual return while you were saving, you may think you can take out 7 percent your first year and be in pretty good shape. But suppose you earn only a 5 percent return in your first year of retirement. Or suppose a bear market hits that year, and your investments stay virtually flat. Then what?

Here's where history offers a cautionary tale. Someone who retired in 1972 with $1 million and took a 7 percent withdrawal in the first year, and then took the same 7 percent plus an adjustment for inflation in subsequent years, would have been broke in ten years. Why? Because a nasty bear market took hold in 1973 and 1974 (the S&P 500 dropped a vertigo-inducing 40 percent), and the country experienced double-digit inflation during several of those years.

Most financial experts recommend withdrawing no more than 4 percent in your first year of retirement and then basing future withdrawals on that 4 percent plus inflation. Depending on how your portfolio is allocated, this strategy gives you virtual certainty that your money will last 30 years.

Retirees don't have the same luxury of recovering from bear markets or periods of high inflation that younger workers do. The best way to cushion the blow from the economy's ups and downs is to act as though you're in a perpetual bear market: Keep a reasonable rein on your spending, even when the economy's doing well.

Withdrawing from the wrong accounts

Although lots of people know how they should allocate their savings for maximum gain and minimum risk, there are lots of retirees who don't know that how they withdraw their retirement funds can have a huge impact on their tax liability and even their income.

For most retirees, it makes sense to withdraw money from your taxable accounts first. That way, you get the greatest advantage from your tax-deferred accounts — IRAs and 401(k)s — and their growth potential. Next, spend your short-term investments. Long-term investments tend to be more volatile, and you run the risk of buying high and selling low if you dip into them at the wrong time.

Finally, consider your tax situation. IRAs and 401(k)s require you to take minimum annual distributions beginning at age $70^1/_2$. Depending on your situation, that extra income could push you into a higher tax bracket. But you can avoid that by taking a bigger distribution in the year before you turn $70^1/_2$.

Here's how it works. Say you're in the 25 percent tax bracket at age 69. You can withdraw enough from your IRA or 401(k) to put you at the upper limit of the tax bracket without going over into the 28 percent bracket. That reduces the balance of your retirement fund; the balance is used to determine next year's minimum distribution, so a smaller balance means a smaller required withdrawal. Plus, more of your income from these accounts is taxed at a lower rate.

Tax planning is just as important in retirement as it is during your working year. Review your finances to determine your tax bracket for each year and then decide whether it makes sense to withdraw money from your retirement accounts to lower your future tax liability.

Chapter 17

Minimizing Uncle Sam's Share

· ·

In This Chapter

▶ Keeping more of your own money to begin with

▶ Figuring out your recordkeeping

▶ Understanding the numbers

▶ Avoiding common errors

· ·

*N*o one likes to pay taxes, but, as Benjamin Franklin said, it's one of the two certainties in this world. And, when you consider that Franklin's other certainty is death, paying taxes doesn't seem all that bad.

That doesn't mean you should pay more in taxes than you have to — but lots of Americans do. According to the Internal Revenue Service (IRS), 63 percent of Americans take the standard deduction on their income taxes every year. For some of those people, of course, it makes sense; they don't have enough itemized deductions, like mortgage interest or contributions to charities or property and state taxes, to surpass the standard deduction that the government gives every taxpayer. (The standard deduction changes every year; in 2008, it was $5,450 for singles and married-filing-separately taxpayers, $10,900 for married couples filing jointly.) But in many cases, the failure to itemize is due more to confusion, poor record-keeping, or sheer laziness. And when that's the case, you're just giving away your money — and to the government, of all things. *That* ought to motivate you to take a good look at your own tax return.

Now, before your eyes glaze over and you start looking around for a comforting Agatha Christie to read instead, there is good news: Making sure you aren't paying more than you really owe isn't difficult. It's just a matter of understanding your filing status, keeping good records so you know what deductions you're entitled to, figuring out whether it makes sense for you to file the short form or the long one, and avoiding common errors that can cost you money — either by paying too much in taxes or by setting yourself up for fines and penalties.

Income alone doesn't equal wealth. You have to get the most out of your income so you can create wealth. One way to get more out of your income is to minimize your tax liability by taking all the deductions, credits, and allowances you're entitled to.

In this chapter, we take you through these topics step by step. By the end of it, you may even feel so confident with your new knowledge that you'll decide to fill out your own tax return this year. (Then again, if you itemize, you can deduct the fees your tax preparer charges you.)

State income tax laws vary enormously; a handful of states don't even collect income tax. We don't have room here to cover each state's rules and regulations, but you can find links to information about your state's income tax laws at the Federation of Tax Administrators Web site (`www.taxadmin.org/fta/link/`).

Filling Out Your W-4 Form

People generally run into one of two things at tax time: They either expect a big refund, often thousands of dollars, or they expect to owe money to the IRS, and they sweat it out, waiting until the last possible moment to file their returns. If either of these scenarios fits you, it means you've chosen the wrong filing status. Your employer is either taking out too much money for taxes (in the case of a big refund every year) or too little (in the case of a big tax bill).

Determining your filing status is just the first step. In the following sections, we also look at the allowances and deductions you can claim on your W-4. Making sure you've filled out your W-4 correctly is a key step toward making sure you're not giving Uncle Sam too much money.

Selecting your filing status

There are four filing statuses for income taxes:

- ✔ **Single:** You aren't married, and you don't have any children or qualifying individuals to claim. (For more on qualifying individuals, turn to the "Claiming Allowances" section, later in this chapter.)

- ✔ **Married filing jointly:** You and your spouse are married (even if you got married on December 31 of the tax year) and were still married and living together on December 31 of the tax year.

If your spouse dies, you can still do your tax return for that year under "married filing jointly." You or your tax preparer simply must note on the return that your spouse is deceased, along with the date of death.

- **Married filing separately:** Generally, this filing status means you and your spouse are separated (but not divorced) and did not live in the same residence on December 31 of the tax year. Sometimes married couples choose to file separate returns instead of a joint one, but that often opens them up to a higher total tax bill. (See the sidebar "The pros and cons of separate returns" for more information on this filing status.)
- **Head of household:** You are single, legally separated, divorced, or widowed, and you have a dependent child or other qualifying individual to claim.

Pretty simple, right? Well, it is if you're single or married and living with your spouse. If you're married but not living together, or if you have to figure out whether you have any qualifying individuals to include, selecting your filing status can seem a little tricky. This is why so many people opt for the path of least resistance: They select the "single" filing status and claim no allowances — that way, they're pretty certain to owe nothing more at the end of the year. In fact, they'll probably get a nice fat refund.

But just because filing as a "single" taxpayer is easy doesn't mean it's the best thing to do. In the long run, it's much better for your financial health to make sure you're having the right amount withheld for income taxes. Why? Because you'll never build wealth by loaning your money interest free — to the government or to anyone else. You're better off taking that extra $10, $20, or $50 every paycheck and investing it where it can earn more money for you. But to get those extra dollars in your paycheck, you have to understand your options when it comes to filling out a W-4 form (shown in Figure 17-1) for your employer.

Form **W-4**

Department of the Treasury
Internal Revenue Service

Employee's Withholding Allowance Certificate

► **Whether you are entitled to claim a certain number of allowances or exemption from withholding is subject to review by the IRS. Your employer may be required to send a copy of this form to the IRS.**

OMB NO. 1545-0074

2008

1 Type or print your first name and middle initial. | Last Name | **2** Your social security number

Home address (number and street or rural route) | **3** ☐ Single ☐ Married ☐ Married, but withhold at higher Single rate.
Note: If married, but legally separated, or spouce is a nonresident alien, check the "Single" box.

City or town, state, and ZIP code | **4 If your last name differs from that shown on your social security card, check here. You must call 1-800-772-1213 for a replacement card.** ► ☐

5 Total number of allowances you are claiming (from line **H** above **or** from the applicable worksheet on page 2) **5**
6 Additional amount, if any, you want withheld from each paycheck . . . . **6** $
7 I claim exemption from withholding for 2008, and I certify that I meet **both** of the following conditions for exemption.
• Last year I had a right to a refund of **all** federal income tax withheld because I had no tax liability **and**
• This year I expect a refund of **all** federal income tax withheld because I expect to have **no** tax liability.
If you meet both conditions, write "Exempt" here. ► **7**

Under penalties of perjury, I declare that I have examined this certificate and to the best of my knowledge and belief, it is true, correct and complete.
Employee's signature
(Form is not valid unless you sign it.) ► **Date** ►

8 Employer's name and address (Employer: Complete lines 8 and 10 only if sending to the IRS.) | **9** Office code (optional) | **10** Employer identification number (EIN)

Figure 17-1: A W-4 form.

The pros and cons of separate returns

You and your spouse can file separate returns if you like, even if you're still married and living together. Some couples choose this option anyway because each spouse wants to be responsible only for his or her own tax; when you file a joint return, each of you is liable for the other's tax bill.

The downside of this option is that your total tax bill will almost certainly be higher. That's because there are special rules for married couples who file joint returns. You usually can't take certain credits, like those for earned income, childcare or dependent-care expenses, or adoption expenses. You also

aren't eligible for the deduction on student-loan interest, or the deduction for tuition and related expenses. Your tax bracket will increase at a lower income threshold, and the exemption for figuring the Alternative Minimum Tax is half of what it is when you file jointly. If you receive Social Security benefits, more of those benefits will be taxed than they would be if you filed a joint return.

Ask your tax preparer if there's any advantage for you and your spouse to file separate returns. Unless one of you is making six figures and the other is making only four figures, chances are you'll be better off filing a joint return.

You can change your filing status on your W-4 form at any time; just ask your employer for a new form. You also can download the form, worksheets, and instructions from the IRS Web site (www.irs.gov).

Claiming single/zero

Many people, even those who are married and/or have dependents, choose the single/no allowances option when filling out their W-4s. This ensures that your employer withholds the maximum amount from your paycheck, and, at the end of the year, chances are, you'll be due a refund.

But claiming no allowances makes sense only if you're single and have no dependents or if you have substantial income from other sources, like your own side business, stock dividends, or interest from hefty savings or money-market accounts. In those cases, having the maximum withheld for taxes can protect you from having to write a big check to the IRS on April 15.

However — and this is a big however — if none of those circumstances applies to you, and you claim single/zero on your W-4, you're essentially taking money out of your own pocket to give the government an interest-free loan for 12 months.

Claiming allowances

Even if you're single, you can claim an allowance — which reduces the amount of taxes taken out of your paycheck — for yourself. In fact, you can claim *two* allowances for yourself — one just because, and another one if any of the following apply:

- You're single, and you don't work a second job.

- You're married, but your spouse doesn't work.

- The combined income from your spouse's job and your second job (if you have one) is less than $1,500 a year. (That figure is subject to change, but it's always a relative pittance.)

The W-4 form includes three worksheets to help you figure out how many allowances you should claim so that the optimum amount is withheld for taxes.

Our definition of *optimum* is that the amount withheld from your paycheck over the course of the year is roughly equal to your actual tax obligation. You may end up owing a few bucks or getting a few bucks back, but the difference between what you've paid in and what you actually owe will be small. The goal is to give yourself as much of your pay as possible throughout the year without having to dip into your money to pay a big tax bill when you prepare your return.

The first worksheet on the W-4 form is the Personal Allowances Worksheet, shown in Figure 17-2. Lines A and B cover the allowances for yourself. Line C lets you claim an allowance for your spouse.

Personal Allowances Worksheet (Keep for your records.)

A   Enter "1" for **yourself** is no one else can claim you as a dependent . . . .   **A** _____

B   Enter "1" if:
- You are single and have only one job; or
- You are married, have only one job, and your spouse does not work; or
- Your wages from a second job or your spouse's wages (or the total of both) are $1,500 or less.

. . . .   **B** _____

C   Enter "1" for your **spouse**. But, you may choose to enter "- 0 -" if you are married and have either a working spouse or more than one job. (Entering "- 0 -" may help you avoid having too little tax withheld.) **.** . . . .   **C** _____

D   Enter number of **dependents** (other than your spouse or yourself) you will claim on your tax return · · · · · ·   **D** _____

E   Enter "1" if you will file as **head of household** on your tax return (see conditions under **Head of household** above) · · · · · ·   **E** _____

F   Enter "1" if you have at least $1,500 of **child or dependent care expenses** for which you plan to claim a credit · · · · · · · · ·   **F** _____
(**Note.** Do **not** include child support payments. See Pub. 503, Child and Dependent Care Expenses, for details.)

G   **Child Tax Credit** (including additional child tax credit). See Pub. 972, Child Tax Credit for more information.   **G** _____
- If your total income will be less than $58,000 ($86,000 if married), enter "2" for each eligible child.
- If your total income will be between $58,000 and $84,000 ($86,000 and $119,000 if married), enter "1" for each eligible child plus "1" **additional** if you have 4 or more eligible children.

H   Add lines A through G and enter total here. (**Note.** This may be different from the number of exemptions you claim on your tax return.) ► **H** _____

For accuracy, complete all worksheets that apply.
- If you plan to **itemize or claim adjustments to income** and want to reduce your withholding, see the **Deductions and Adjustments Worksheet** on page 2.
- If you have **more than one job** or are **married and you and your spouse both work** and the combined earnings from all jobs exceed $40,000 ($25,000 if married), see the **Two-Earners/Multiple Jobs Worksheet** on page 2 to avoid having too little tax withheld.
- If **neither** of the above situations applies, **stop here** and enter the number from line H on line 5 of Form W-4 below.

Figure 17-2:
The Personal Allowances Worksheet on the W-4 form.

Even the IRS doesn't necessarily recommend that you claim an allowance for your spouse. Right on Line C of the worksheet, the IRS notes that claiming zero here can help you avoid a big tax bill in April, especially if your spouse is working and earning more than $1,500 a year.

Line D is where you claim allowances for your dependents. These are your children or other qualifying individuals. So what the heck is a "qualifying individual"? The IRS takes 51 pages to cover all the possible incarnations of qualifying children, relatives, and members of your household. We won't torture you with that. (If you're having trouble falling asleep at night, you'll be pleased to know that you can find the entire thing, Publication 501: Exemptions, Standard Deduction, and Filing Information, online at www.irs.gov.)

Here are the basic conditions that have to be met:

- **A qualifying individual cannot also be your qualifying child.** That is, if you're claiming a child as a dependent, you can't also claim that same child as a qualifying individual.

- **A qualifying individual has to be** *either* **a member of your household (in which case you don't necessarily have to be related)** *or* **a relative (who doesn't necessarily have to live with you in order to qualify).**

- **A qualifying individual cannot have more than $3,500 (as of 2008) in earned income.** (The earned income limit is tied to the personal exemption, which changes every year.)

- **You must provide** *more than half* **of the individual's support throughout the year.** So, if the individual doesn't live with you, you must provide more than half of the individual's living expenses, such as rent, groceries, medical care, and transportation, throughout the year.

All four of the conditions listed have to be met in order to claim an allowance on your W-4 and a deduction on your income tax return. If the individual meets only three of the four conditions, you can't claim her as a qualifying individual.

Lines E through G on the Personal Allowances Worksheet give you the option of claiming additional allowances if you're going to file as head of household, if you plan to claim the child tax credit, and so on. Many people don't bother to claim these allowances for withholding purposes; they simply wait until tax time to figure out whether they qualify for these things.

Keep in mind that the goal is to keep as much of your own money in your own pocket as possible. If you think you'll qualify for these deductions at tax time, go ahead and claim the allowances for them on your W-4.

Figuring deductions and adjustments

Most people ignore the two worksheets on the second page of the W-4, and for good reason: They're too much like filling out your actual tax return. In the following sections, we fill you in on why these forms matter.

Gazing into a crystal ball: The Deductions and Adjustments Worksheet

The Deductions and Adjustments Worksheet (shown in Figure 17-3) requires you to look into the future and predict what your next tax return will look like. Will you itemize? How much will your itemized deductions come to? Will you have extra income to declare or deductions for student-loan interest? What credits will you claim? Small wonder many people glance at the worksheet and say to themselves, "Pooh. I'll wait until April to figure all this out."

There is an advantage to filling out this worksheet, though: It forces you to think about your income and deductions, and weigh your options. If you're accustomed to getting a big refund each year, this worksheet can help you figure out how to take home more money, and you can put those extra dollars every pay period to work for you all year long.

Deductions and Adjustments Worksheet

Note. Use this worksheet *only* if you plan to itemize deductions, claim certain credits, or claim adjustments to income on your 2008 tax return.

1 Enter an estimate of your 2008 itemized deductions. These include qualifying home mortgage interest, charitable contributions, state, and local taxes, medical expenses in excess of 7.5% of your income, and miscellaneous deductions. (For 2008, you may have to reduce your itemized deductions if your income is over $159,950 ($79,975 if married filing separately). See *Worksheet 2* in Pub. 919 for details.) **1**

2 Enter : $\begin{cases} \$10,900 \text{ if married filing jointly or qualifying widow(er)} \\ \$8,000 \text{ if head of household} \\ \$5,450 \text{ if single or married filing separately} \end{cases}$ **2**

3 **Subtract** line 2 from line 1. If zero or less, enter " - 0 -" **3**

4 Enter an estimate of your 2008 adjustments to income, including alimony, deductible IRA contributions, and student loan interest . . **4**

5 **Add** lines 3 and 3 and enter the total. (Include any amount for credits from *Worksheet 8* in Pub. 919) **5**

6 Enter an estimate of your 2008 nonwage income (such as dividends or interest) **6**

7 **Subtract** line 6 from line 5. If zero or less, enter " - 0 -" **7**

8 **Divide** the amount on line 7 by $3,500 and enter the result here. Drop any fraction **8**

9 Enter the number from the **Personal Allowances Worksheet**, line H, page 1 . . . . **9**

10 **Add** lines 8 and 9 and enter the total here. If you plan to use the **Two-Earners/Multiple Jobs Worksheet,** also enter this total on line 1 below. Otherwise, **stop here** and enter this total on Form W-4, line 5, page 1 . . . . **10**

Figure 17-3: The Deductions and Adjustments Worksheet of the W-4 form.

Sidestepping a huge tax bill: The Two-Earners/Multiple Jobs Worksheet

The Two-Earners/Multiple Jobs Worksheet (shown in Figure 17-4) offers a way for you to have additional taxes withheld from your paycheck throughout the year so you don't end up owing the IRS money on April 15. If you and your spouse both have high-paying jobs, or if you have a second job that gives you substantial income, this worksheet can help you figure out whether you're having enough tax withheld. And that can help you avoid a nasty surprise come tax time.

Two-Earners/Multiple Jobs Worksheet (See *Two earners or multiple jobs* on page 1.)

Note. Use this worksheet *only* if the instructions under line H on page 1 direct you here.

1 Enter the number from line H, page 1 (or from line 10 above if you used the **Deductions and Adjustments Worksheet**)	1.
2 Find the number in **Table 1** below that applies to the **LOWEST** paying job and enter it here. However, if you are married filing jointly and wages from the highest paying job are $50,000 or less, do not enter more than "3."	2.
3 If line 1 is **more than or equal to** line 2, subtract line 2 from line 1. Enter the result here (if zero, enter "- 0 -") and on Form W-4, line 5, page 1. **Do not** use the rest of this worksheet	3.

Note. If line 1 is *less* than line 2, enter "- 0 -" on Form W-4, line 5, page 1. Complete lines 4-9 below to calculate the additional withholding amount necessary to avoid a year-end tax bill.

4 Enter the number form line 2 of this worksheet	4.
5 Enter the number form line 1 of this worksheet	5.
6 **Subtract** line 5 from line 4	6.
7 Find the amount in **Table 2** below that applies to the **HIGHEST** paying job and enter it here	7 $
8 **Multiply** line 7 by line 6 and enter the result here. This is the additional withholding needed	8 $
9 Divide line 8 by the number of pay periods remaining in 2008. For example, divide by 26 if you are paid every two weeks and you complete this form in December 2007. Enter the result here and on Form W-4, line 6, page 1. This is the additional amount to be withheld from each paycheck	9 $

Table 1				Table 2			
Married Filing Jointly		**All Others**		**Married Filing Jointly**		**All Others**	
If wages from **LOWEST** paying job are –	Enter on line 2 above	If wages from **LOWEST** paying job are –	Enter on line 2 above	If wages from **HIGHEST** paying job are –	Enter on line 7 above	If wages from **HIGHEST** paying job are –	Enter on line 7 above
$0 - $4,500	0	$0 - $6,500	0	$0 - $65,000	$530	$0 - $35,000	$530
4,501 - 10,000	1	6,501 - 12,000	1	65,001 - 120,000	880	35,001 - 80,000	880
10,001 - 18,000	2	12,001 - 20,000	2	120,001 - 180,000	980	80,001 - 150,000	980
18,001 - 22,000	3	20,001 - 27,000	3	180,001 - 310,000	1,160	150,001 - 340,000	1,160
22,001 - 27,000	4	27,001 - 35,000	4	310,001 and over	1,230	340,001 and over	1,230
27,001 - 33,000	5	35,001 - 50,000	5				
33,001 - 40,000	6	50,001 - 65,000	6				
40,001 - 50,000	7	65,001 - 80,000	7				
50,001 - 55,000	8	80,001 - 95,000	8				
55,001 - 60,000	9	95,001 - 120,000	9				
60,001 - 65,000	10	120,000 and over	10				
65,001 - 75,000	11						
75,001 - 100,000	12						
100,001 - 110,000	13						
110,001 - 120,000	14						
120,001 and over	15						

Figure 17-4:
The Two-Earners/ Multiple Jobs Worksheet of the W-4 form.

Keeping Records

The only sure way to know that you're not paying more tax than you should is to keep records of your income and expenses. You can simply toss every receipt and pay stub into a folder or a shoebox and spend your New Year's Day sorting through it to figure out what might be deductible and what might not be. But, especially these days, there are much easier and more effective ways to keep good records.

Knowing what's deductible

The key to maintaining good records is understanding which of your expenses throughout the year are deductible and which aren't. There's no point in clogging up your tax filing system with receipts for things that aren't deductible, like your weekly groceries. On the other hand, if you don't keep the receipt for the canned goods you donated to the local food pantry, you miss an opportunity to lower your tax bill.

We go into detail about deductions that are commonly missed in the "Avoiding Common Mistakes" section, later in this chapter. For now, here's a quick list of things to be aware of as you set up your recordkeeping system:

- ✔ **Keep track of the miles you drive.** You can't deduct the miles you drive to and from work every day, but you may be able to deduct mileage for trips to the doctor. You can even deduct miles you drive to do volunteer work.

- ✔ **Find out if there are tax breaks for your profession.** Teachers and truck drivers are allowed to claim certain deductions that others can't, for example. Check with your accountant or tax preparer, or go to www.irs.gov to find out if there are any work-related deductions you can claim.

- ✔ **Make notes on checks and receipts.** You can't deduct an expense if you don't know what you spent the money on. Use the memo line on your checks to note what the expense is for, and write specific information on your receipts before you file them away.

Investing in accounting software

If you have a computer at home, consider investing in a good home bookkeeping or accounting software program like Quicken or MoneyCounts (both available at major retailers and office supply stores, as well as online). These programs put your expenses in categories, so you can see at a glance where your money goes and keep a running tally of deductible expenses.

Tracking your expenses is a good way to determine where you can change your budget to find more money for your financial goals. Many people don't realize how much they spend on things like eating out, for example, until they've tracked their expenses for a month or two. When you see what you spend and where, you can decide whether you'd rather spend $100 on a night out or put it in your investment account.

Creating your own spreadsheet

If you don't want to invest in special financial software, you can create your own worksheet with any spreadsheet program, like Microsoft Excel. (Depending on the kind of computer you have, it may have a preloaded spreadsheet program, so you don't even have to buy Excel separately.) You can make these as simple or as elaborate as you like; the calculation functions on these programs can do everything from totaling up your bills to figuring out your cash flow every pay period.

Whether you use a software program or create your own spreadsheet, the information you get out of it is only as good as the information you put in. You still have to identify what you're spending your money on; a broad category like "credit card payments" won't help you (or your tax preparer) decide whether any portion of those payments is deductible at tax time.

When you set up your recordkeeping system, include lines for specific expenses, like "church contribution," "uniforms," "business travel," "business meals," and so on. The more specific you are in your notations now, the easier your life (and your tax preparer's life) will be later on.

Update your records at least once a month. If you put it off, you increase the odds of going off your budget and forgetting to register expenses that may be deductible.

Keep your tax records for at least three years. If you get tagged for an audit, the auditor may want to look at your three most recent tax returns, but most audits don't go farther back than that. (The exception is when fraud is suspected, and then there's no limit on how far back the IRS will look.)

Crunching the Numbers

Now we come to the part of tax preparation that really gives people the heebie-jeebies: Figuring out whether it makes sense to file the short form or the long form, and worrying about that dreadful Alternative Minimum Tax (AMT) you keep hearing about in the news. The trick is figuring out which way you'll be better off — that is, how you can legally pay the lowest possible income tax?

Are you better off itemizing?

To itemize or not to itemize? That is the question — and the answer depends on whether your itemized deductions would be greater than the standard deduction the IRS gives every taxpayer. As we mention earlier, the standard deduction changes every year; in 2008, it was $5,450 for single taxpayers and $10,900 for married-filing-jointly filers.

The IRS also gives each taxpayer a *personal exemption*. On the 1040EZ , the standard deduction and personal exemption are combined; the totals in 2008 were $8,950 for single filers and $17,900 for married filing jointly. On the 1040A (the so-called "short form"), your standard deduction and exemptions are on separate lines, and on the 1040 (the "long form"), the personal exemption ($3,500 in 2008) is separate from your itemized deductions.

So, if your itemized deductions would total more than the standard deduction for your filing status, it makes sense to itemize.

Itemizing is your best choice if any of these applies to you:

- ✔ You have a mortgage.
- ✔ You have large medical expenses.
- ✔ You make large charitable donations.
- ✔ You have your own business, either as a sideline or as your main source of income.

Itemizing means keeping good records (see the "Keeping Records" section, earlier in this chapter) and remembering which kinds of expenses are deductible, but that effort is well worth your time and energy when it helps you lower your tax bill.

Will you run up against the Alternative Minimum Tax?

The AMT is the bogeyman of the federal tax code, and, following in the steps of the best horror fiction, it keeps claiming more victims every year. Back in 1969, when it was enacted, it was aimed at 155 — yes, you read that number right — taxpayers who had enormous incomes but managed to pay exactly zero in income tax, thanks to a variety of tax rules in place at the time. But the AMT isn't tied to inflation, so more and more taxpayers fall into its gaping maw every April. In 1970, fewer than 20,000 Americans had to pay the AMT. In 2007, millions paid it.

Why is this a problem? Because the AMT disallows or decreases many of the deductions that taxpayers typically list, such as mortgage interest. And, if you're subject to the AMT, your effective tax rate can shoot up from 25 percent or 28 percent to 32 percent or 35 percent.

The AMT is complicated, cumbersome, and confusing, and very few people understand it. Even the IRS National Taxpayer Advocate's office doesn't like it. That's the bad news. The good news is that you don't have to let it take you by surprise. The IRS has developed a relatively simple way for taxpayers to find out online whether they'll be subject to the AMT, called the Alternative Minimum Tax Assistant for Individuals (go to www.irs.gov and search for *AMT Assistant*). You fill out a simple form based on your 1040, and the program either says you don't owe the AMT or directs you to a more in-depth form. You don't have to worry about privacy, either. None of the information you enter is saved; it gets erased as soon as you exit the program.

The software that tax preparers use automatically calculates whether you're subject to the AMT. Home-based tax preparation software, like TurboTax or TaxWise, also performs these calculations.

Because the AMT is so complicated, it's hard to make general statements about whether you'll have to pay it. The people who are most likely to get stuck in the AMT trap are those with incomes over $75,000 who have lots of large deductions, like big interest payments on second mortgages, high property taxes, or stock options.

For the past couple of years, Congress has passed AMT "patches" to change the income levels it applies to, so be sure to check with your tax preparer or the IRS Web site to get the latest thresholds.

If you're supposed to pay the AMT and don't, you'll be charged interest and penalties on top of the extra tax you were supposed to pay.

How can you offset capital gains?

Capital gains come into play when you sell stocks or real estate. The gain is the net difference, after expenses, between how much you paid for the stock or real estate and how much you sell it for. Of course, it's possible to have capital losses, too, if you sell for less than you paid.

If you sell your home, you don't have to worry about capital gains unless the difference between what you paid for it and what you sold it for is more than $250,000 if you're single or $500,000 if you're married.

Even moving investment funds from one account to another — from a growth account, for example, to an IRA — can expose you to capital gains. If you sell stocks that you've owned for less than a year, any gains are taxed at whatever your current tax rate is. Those are called *short-term gains. Long-term gains* — for stocks or real estate you've owned for more than a year — are taxed at a flat 15 percent, no matter what your current tax bracket is. So, the longer you hold onto your investments, the better — as long as they're making money for you.

The different tax rules on short- and long-term capital gains is just one reason why keeping good records is so important. A difference of even a day or two in selling can have a big impact on your tax bill.

The only way to offset capital gains is with capital losses. There are two important things to remember about offsetting:

- **Losses and gains have to match.** You can't use short-term losses to offset long-term gains, or vice versa.

- **You can carry losses forward into future tax years.** You can write off only $3,000 of capital losses against regular income. But, if you lost $20,000 last year and used the $3,000 write-off, you can use the remaining $17,000 to offset some or all of your gains this year.

When you carry capital losses forward, the losses cannot exceed your gains. So, if you lost $20,000 last year and gained $12,000 this year, you can use only $12,000 of last year's losses against this year's gains.

Tax software like TurboTax and TaxWise will automatically calculate short- and long-term gains (and losses) and apply the correct tax to each. You just have to enter the dates when you purchased and sold the stocks or real estate, and the prices for each transaction. This information is on your broker statements; if you've lost or destroyed your own records, your broker or planner can look up the information for you. Also, this information should be included on end-of-year statements from your broker, planner, or mutual fund company.

Avoiding Common Mistakes

According to the IRS, the most common mistake taxpayers make is forgetting to sign their tax return. For our purposes, though, the most common mistakes involve giving the government more of your money than you have to.

Don't ignore the tax savings your employer can offer you. From 401(k)s to health savings accounts, there are lots of ways your job can help you minimize your taxes (see Chapter 8 for details).

Missing deductions you're entitled to

As we mention at the beginning of this chapter, the majority of Americans don't itemize deductions, even though they may well end up paying less income tax if they did. But even people who itemize sometimes miss deductions they're entitled to. Here are some typically overlooked deductions:

- ✔ **Out-of-pocket medical expenses:** If your health insurance premiums aren't deducted from your paycheck before taxes are figured, you can deduct those premiums. (Pretax premiums are not deductible, because they lower your taxable income on the front end.) Depending on your income level, you also can deduct co-pays for office visits, prescriptions, lab tests, and hospital stays, as well as your mileage to and from medical appointments. If you have long-term care insurance, you can deduct all or part of those premiums, too, depending on your age.

- ✔ **State income or sales tax:** If your state collects income tax, you can deduct your state taxes on your federal return. Or, if you choose, you can instead deduct the amount you've paid throughout the year in state sales taxes. You should choose whichever option gives you the biggest deduction. Check the tables in the instruction booklet for your 1040 to see which makes sense for you.

If you keep good records, you can deduct the actual sales tax you've paid over the year instead of relying on the IRS tables. This especially makes sense in years when you make major purchases that are subject to sales tax, like a car or RV.

- ✔ **Personal property taxes and fees:** You can deduct the registration fees for personal vehicles.

- ✔ **Home improvements:** If you buy a new shower head, you can't deduct its cost. But if you borrowed the money to buy the shower head, you can deduct the interest you paid on that loan.

Even if you borrow home-improvement money from an individual — a relative, say — rather than a bank, and you're paying interest to that individual, you can deduct the interest. However, the lender has to claim the interest as income in order for you to claim it as a deduction.

- ✔ **Charitable deductions:** Recent changes to IRS rules allow you to claim up to $250 without documentation, but if you're going to declare more than that, make sure you have the paperwork to back it up. For big-ticket items like cars, you have to have it appraised and attach a copy of the appraisal to your return. Some organizations like Goodwill assign a set value to donations — so much for a pair of jeans, so much for a coat, and so on — so be sure to get a receipt when you drop off your old clothes or household goods.

✔ **Mileage to and from volunteer work:** We're not talking about your mileage to and from church or temple every weekend — that's not deductible. But if you volunteer at the fire department's monthly pancake breakfast, you can deduct the miles you drive there and back home.

✔ **Work-related moving expenses:** If your company transfers you to another city and picks up the entire tab, you don't have anything to deduct. But if the company pays only a portion of your expenses (or none), you can claim your out-of-pocket expenses as a deduction. This includes such things as hiring a moving company and even the mileage you racked up driving your car to your new location.

✔ **Tax preparation fees:** If you pay someone to prepare your tax return, or if you purchase tax-prep software like TurboTax, you can deduct those expenses under "miscellaneous expenses."

Tax deductions are not the same as tax credits. Credits reduce your tax bill dollar for dollar. Deductions reduce the amount of income on which your tax bill is based.

Setting yourself up for penalties

The easiest way to get yourself bogged down in penalties is to not pay the tax you owe or not to file a return at all. You can get a six-month extension to file your return, but you still have to pay your taxes by April 15, even if you don't know for sure what your tax bill will be.

There are all kinds of reasons you may not be able to file your return on time. You may not get all the records and statements you need in a timely manner (real estate investment trusts are notorious for not sending out year-end statement on time). Medical issues may keep you from getting your records together. Or your tax preparer may be busy and unable to finish your return by the deadline.

Still, the IRS wants its money, and if it doesn't get it, you'll get socked with penalties and interest on the tax you should have paid but didn't. The solution: Send in a payment for what you estimate your tax will be, but make it a good estimate. If you're off by too much, again, the IRS will levy a penalty.

If you're self-employed or, for whatever reason, you don't have taxes withheld from your paycheck, you'll need to make estimated tax payments in April, June, September, and January to avoid a penalty. The easiest way to figure your estimated quarterly payment is to divide your previous year's tax by four. You may end up owing more tax at the end of the year if your income is higher than it was last year, but you won't get hit with a penalty if you pay as much in estimated payments as you owed the year before. (To find out more about estimated taxes, go to www.irs.gov and search for *estimated taxes.*)

Doing It Yourself or Hiring a Pro

Deciding whether to go to a professional tax preparer or take a stab at it yourself is really a matter of personal preference. The tax-prep software available today makes it quite easy to do your own taxes at home, as long as you don't have a complicated return. TurboTax (www.turbotax.com) and TaxWise (www.taxwise.com) are both easy to use. If you have a home-based business or even a small business outside your home, you can use the Turbo Tax Home & Business Edition. If you itemize, you can deduct the cost of the software under "miscellaneous expenses."

However, if your return is more complicated than average, or if your business is incorporated in any way, we recommend hiring a professional accountant or tax preparer. These folks are up on the latest changes to the tax code, and they can help you find deductions that you may miss on your own. And, remember, if you itemize, you can deduct the fee you pay to have your taxes done professionally.

Chapter 18

Covering Your Assets

- -

In This Chapter

▶ Understanding the purpose of insurance

▶ Balancing coverage, premiums, and deductibles

▶ Considering what insurance you need

▶ Knowing what insurance you may not need

- -

*T*he old saying has it that the best offense is a good defense, and insurance is your best defense against many of the things that can go wrong in life. The right insurance coverage is a key component in any financial plan. It helps protect everything you've worked so hard to build against all the things you can't control: the weather, the actions of others, accidents, illness, injury, and death.

Of course, insurance can be confusing. How do you know if you have enough coverage or the right kind of insurance? How can you make sure you're not getting ripped off?

In this chapter, we look at various kinds of insurance, starting with the basics: understanding what insurance actually does, getting familiar with what's covered and what's not, the relationship between premiums and deductibles, and how to investigate an insurance company before you buy a policy.

Then we take you through different kinds of policies that protect your property, your life, and your income. We also discuss the pros and cons of long-term-care insurance, and we tell you about three kinds of insurance most people don't need.

Insurance Basics

The purpose of insurance is to protect those things you can't afford to replace on your own against things over which you have no control.

Insurance covers *pure loss.* That means that whatever triggers an insurance payment isn't something that gives you an opportunity to gain, only to lose. This is why speculating in the stock market isn't insurable; there's certainly an opportunity to lose money, but there's also an opportunity to gain.

Generally, insurance covers three things: people, property, and liability. Life insurance, worker's compensation, disability insurance, and health insurance cover people. Homeowner's and auto insurance cover property. And liability insurance covers legal claims against you for harm to people and property.

When you buy a policy, your insurance company takes on the risk that you or your property will suffer a loss. That risk is combined with all the policyholders like you — homeowners, for example, or construction workers — and the insurance company figures out the probability of a specific event happening to any given policyholder, and then bases its premiums, in part, on the level of risk. This is why younger male drivers pay higher car insurance premiums than younger female drivers — statistics show that young male drivers are more likely to be in an accident than young female drivers, so their premiums reflect the higher risk.

Understanding coverage and limitations

One of the reasons insurance is so confusing is that the policies are written in dense legalese, and it's hard to figure out exactly what you are and aren't covered for. For example, after Hurricane Katrina, many Gulf Coast homeowners didn't know they weren't covered for flood damage; they assumed their homeowner's insurance covered them against all kinds of loss. The truth is, they would have been better off if their homes had burned down, because then their losses likely would have been covered by insurance.

Most policies exclude coverage for specific events or circumstances. For example, health insurance policies typically have a preexisting-condition exclusion, which means they won't cover expenses for, say, asthma until certain conditions are met (often a waiting period of up to a year with no treatment). Virtually no policy will cover any losses that result from your deliberate action; you won't get paid for the loss of your home in a fire if you set the blaze yourself. And if a firefighter gets hurt putting out the fire you started, your liability insurance won't cover you if the firefighter brings a legal claim against you.

The time to know what your policies cover is before you need them — ideally, before you buy them. Make sure you understand what is and isn't covered by any policy you're considering.

The cheapest insurance isn't always the best deal, no matter what you're insuring. Be sure to understand what's covered and what's not, and get the policy that best matches your needs and your budget.

Weighing deductibles and premiums

The higher your deductible, the lower your premium will be. This is true for any insurance that carries a *deductible* (a set amount that you're responsible for before your policy kicks in), such as homeowner's, auto, and renter's insurance. Life insurance policies don't have deductibles, but health and disability policies often have the equivalent of a deductible, such as co-pays or waiting periods during which you're responsible for your own expenses.

Deductibles and premiums have this inverse relationship because the risk of your filing a claim that exceeds your deductible is smaller than the overall risk of your filing any claim at all. If you have a $0 deductible on your homeowner's insurance, you're more likely to file an insurance claim for a broken window or the fence that got knocked over in last night's storm. If you have a $500 or $1,000 deductible, though, you won't file a claim for these minor things, so the odds of the insurance company having to pay out are lower.

The general rule of thumb is to match your deductible with what you can afford to pay out of your own pocket in the event of a claim. If you've got $5,000 in your emergency fund, for example, your deductible should be between $500 and $1,000 — maybe even as high as $2,500.

If you don't have enough money stashed away to cover a high deductible, go with the largest deductible you can manage for now, and raise the deductible when you have more money in your emergency fund. (And use the savings you'll have on premiums to help fund your investment or retirement account.)

Evaluating insurance companies

No matter what kind of insurance you're in the market for, it's important to know the company you're buying your coverage from. There's no point in buying insurance from a financially unstable company, and the longer the term of your policy, the more important the company's financial soundness is. Fortunately, several firms provide independent ratings of insurance companies, and you can access all the information you need for free on the Internet. Here are the main sites to check:

✔ **A. M. Best (www.ambest.com):** You have to pay for detailed reports on individual companies, but the ratings are free.

✔ **Insure.com (www.insure.com):** Here, you can find S&P ratings, as well as free reports on specific insurance companies.

✔ **TheStreet.com (www.thestreet.com):** This site offers a free list of the nation's strongest and weakest insurance companies.

The companies that are most financially stable have AAA ratings. Don't do business with any insurer rated below at least A; it's entirely possible this company won't be around to pay on your policy when you need it. And, because ratings can change, be sure to look at the most recent ratings — if possible, no more than six months old — before you buy.

We don't have enough space here to go into all the ins and outs of all the different kinds of insurance you can get. For more information, we recommend *Insurance For Dummies,* by Jack Hungelmann (Wiley), as well as the following Web sites:

✔ **The Insurance Information Institute** (www.iii.org) has free personal finance and household inventory software, as well as information about various kinds of insurance, ranging from auto to long-term-care and specialty insurance. The site also has a Life Stages tool (www.iii.org/static/site/tools/life_stages_frset.htm) that helps you calculate your insurance needs based on your circumstances.

✔ **Insure.com** (www.insure.com) has a bevy of tools, including a life-insurance-needs estimator (scroll down the page and look for the Insurance Tools menu on the left side) and a glossary, among other things. You also can use the site to compare quotes from various companies on most common types of insurance.

✔ **The National Association of Insurance Commissioners** (www.naic.org) has a Consumer Information Source (www.naic.org/cis), where you can research insurance companies or file complaints.

Homeowner's Insurance

If you've got a mortgage, you've probably got homeowner's insurance; most mortgage companies require you to provide proof of insurance when you close on the loan. But just because you have a policy doesn't mean you have the right coverage. Here are some things to consider when you look over your policy:

✔ **Replacement value:** Never mind what you paid for your house; what you want is protection in case you have to rebuild that same house at today's construction costs. If you don't have replacement value coverage, your insurance company may well depreciate every piece of your home's structure, right down to the sections of drywall and the nails used to secure them.

✔ **Loss-of-use coverage:** If a fire damages your home and you have to stay in a motel until the damage is fixed, loss-of-use coverage should help you with those extra expenses, even if it doesn't cover all of them. If you don't have loss-of-use coverage, those expenses will come out of your pocket.

✔ **Personal-property coverage:** This is another area where you want replacement value, because depreciation will knock a heck of a lot off the value of your clothing, furniture, appliances, and electronics.

✔ **Riders for high-value items:** If you have expensive jewelry, art, or other high-value items, you may want to attach a rider to your policy to make sure they're covered at their full replacement value.

✔ **Liability coverage:** Anytime someone steps onto your property, whether she's a worker or a guest, you could be liable for accidents or injuries. Make sure your liability coverage is enough to protect you. If you have high-value assets, investigate an umbrella policy that will kick in after your normal liability coverage is exhausted. Umbrella policies typically have face values of $1 million to $5 million or more.

In general, if you rent, your landlord is responsible for insuring the building, but you should have renter's insurance to cover your personal property against theft and damage or loss to fire or other causes. Some leases require you to carry liability insurance for your own unit, but the landlord should be responsible for any common areas like lobbies, hallways, stairways, and so on.

Most homeowner's policies don't cover damage caused by flooding; you have to get a separate policy for that. Even if you don't live in a flood plain, you may want to investigate flood insurance if your area is subject to lots of storms. As Hurricane Katrina taught us, it isn't always easy to draw the line between damage caused by wind and rain and damage caused by flooding. You can get more information on flood insurance at www.floodsmart.gov.

Auto Insurance

Just as your mortgage company insists that you have homeowner's insurance, your auto-finance company insists that you have full insurance coverage on your car, at least as long as you owe any money on it. After your car is paid off, though, many of your insurance options are strictly your decision.

The exception is liability insurance. Even states with *no-fault insurance* (where insurance companies pay claims without requiring a determination of each driver's relative responsibility for the accident) require car owners to carry liability insurance. The minimums vary from state to state, but usually they're so low that most experts recommend carrying significantly higher liability coverage, especially in light of rapidly rising healthcare costs.

There are three basic components of auto insurance: collision, comprehensive, and liability.

Collision

Collision insurance covers damage to your car and any other vehicle involved in an accident. (Damage to buildings, mailboxes, or what have you is covered under the liability portion of your policy.) Generally, the newer the car, the higher the collision premiums will be, because repairs typically will be more expensive. Most collision policies protect you whether you're driving your own car or someone else's (but see the "Car-rental insurance" section later in this chapter).

Collision coverage usually isn't required unless the vehicle is collateral for a loan — either a regular auto loan or a personal loan. Some experts say you should drop collision coverage as soon as the value of your car drops below ten times your annual premium. So, if you're paying $500 a year for collision coverage, you may want to consider eliminating it when your car's value drops below $5,000. You can check out your car's trade-in, retail, and private-sale value for free through the Kelley Blue Book site (www.kbb.com).

Before you drop collision coverage, consider whether you have enough savings for a down payment on a different car and whether your budget can handle a car payment.

Comprehensive

Comprehensive coverage protects you against theft, damage from hail, rocks chipping your windshield, and so on — basically anything that's beyond your control. Some insurance companies also categorize collisions with animals, like deer, as comprehensive claims. Many policies have a deductible for comprehensive claims but waive the deductible for glass repairs.

Liability

Liability coverage protects you against legal claims for property damage and personal injury, whether the claim comes from a passenger in your vehicle or someone outside your vehicle — the driver or passenger of another car, or a pedestrian. Generally, if you're at fault in an accident, your liability insurance will pay for medical bills and property damage, subject to certain limits.

In the states with no-fault insurance laws — Florida, Hawaii, Kansas, Kentucky, Massachusetts, Michigan, Minnesota, New Jersey, New York, North Dakota, Pennsylvania, and Utah — each insurance company pays the claims for its own policyholders, so your insurance would pay for your claims even if the other driver were at fault in an accident.

Liability limits are usually set for each individual and each incident. So, for example, a policy with $25,000/$50,000 limits would pay up to $25,000 in medical bills for each person involved and a maximum of $50,000 in medical bills that are related to the same accident. If you have three passengers in your car and all of them are injured, coverage of their medical bills would stop when the combined total reached $50,000.

State law sets the minimum liability insurance coverage each car owner has to have, but that doesn't mean you're fully protected if you have only the minimum coverage. If medical bills or damage claims exceed your liability coverage, you could be sued for additional damages, in which case all your other assets could be at risk. Make sure you have a reasonable amount of coverage to shelter you from this possibility.

Many states also require you to carry uninsured/underinsured motorist coverage. This kicks in if you have an accident with a driver who either doesn't have any insurance or doesn't have enough to cover your losses. It also covers you in the event of a hit-and-run accident. Your insurance agent can tell you whether this coverage is mandatory where you live. But even if it isn't required, it's a valuable — and usually very affordable — addition to your overall auto coverage.

Insuring against the Inevitable

The mortality rate for human beings is 100 percent. So how is it that 68 million American adults have no life insurance? According to an Ipsos survey, most Americans think they need life insurance, but one in four of the people who say they need it doesn't have it. And more than eight in ten people would rather go bungee jumping or have a performance review at work than talk to an insurance agent. Add to that the general confusion over various types of life insurance policies, and it's small wonder that so many people adopt a Scarlett O'Hara "I'll think about it tomorrow" attitude toward life insurance.

Life insurance is a key component of your overall financial plan if you want to do any of these things:

 ✔ Cover funeral expenses so your family doesn't have to pay for them

 ✔ Settle any debts you may leave behind, like your mortgage, credit cards, or other bills

 ✔ Provide cash for your children's education

 ✔ Fund a trust, a charitable donation, or other specific bequest

 ✔ Provide your spouse or partner with a financial cushion after your death

The two aspects of life insurance that baffle most consumers, though, are figuring out how much you need and figuring out which kind of policy makes sense for you.

How much life insurance you need

Regardless of what an agent may tell you, there is no single "right" answer for how much life insurance you need, because your needs depend entirely on your situation. As your situation changes — when you get married, have children, even buy a house — your life insurance needs will change, too.

Say you're single with no children and no debt to speak of. If you have enough money in savings, investments, or a 401(k) or IRA, you may not need life insurance at all right now — assuming those assets are enough to cover funeral expenses and any miscellaneous expenses your family may encounter in settling your estate.

On the other hand, if you're single with no children and have substantial debt, like a mortgage, big credit card balances, student loans, or a car loan, and you don't have enough savings to cover those debts if you die, you should have enough life insurance to make up the difference between your debts and your savings.

If you're married, have children, or own a business, your life insurance needs will be greater. What you want to provide for your family after your death also is a factor in deciding how much life insurance you should have.

Insurance companies offer this simple calculation to figure out how much life insurance you need:

Current Debts or Expenses and Future Expenses – Savings, Investments, and Currently Owned Life Insurance = How Much (Additional) Life Insurance You Should Have

State Farm has a free life insurance calculator (`https://online.state-farm.com/apps/linc/lincstandalone.asp`) that asks you a few questions about your finances now and what you want to provide for your heirs. We like this calculator because you don't have to enter any identifying information, so you won't be harassed by someone trying to sell you life insurance.

But there are several factors that can change the figures here. Although current debts are pretty easy to tally, future expenses can be far more fluid. And, although your heirs can use your savings and investments to pay off those debts and expenses, you may decide it would be better if they could leave that money where it is. Finally, your spouse and children may get other benefits, like Social Security survivor payments, that will offset some of those future expenses.

The Social Security Administration's Web site (`www.ssa.gov`) has a host of benefit calculators that can help you estimate how much your spouse and children may receive in survivor benefits if you die. There's also lots of information about how benefits may be affected in various circumstances.

Current debts and future expenses

Current debts and expenses include everything you spend now — rent or mortgage; auto, student, and personal loans; monthly living expenses (groceries, gas, utilities, and so on); and any additional expenses like clothing, healthcare, and entertainment.

Future expenses include funeral costs, which average $8,000 or more. Even if you don't want a traditional funeral, your family will have some expenses for things like cremation, burial plot or grave opening, and headstone or other monument. Even the obituary in the local newspaper is likely to cost money; most newspapers these days list only the most basic information for free and charge for everything else.

But there may be other future expenses you want to plan for, too. If you have children, you may want to set aside some money for their college fund. If you've been taking care of aging parents, you may want to ensure there's money to continue that care if you die before they do. If your spouse or partner has a lower-paying job or no job at all, you may want to boost your life insurance coverage to make sure there's enough to maintain the standard of living you've built together.

Credit card companies, auto and personal loan issuers, and even mortgage brokers may try to sell you insurance policies that repay that specific debt if you die (or become disabled and unable to work — we cover disability insurance later in this chapter). We don't recommend buying these policies, because the premiums are usually much higher than what you'd pay for a straight life insurance policy. You and your heirs are better off making sure you have enough coverage to take care of these debts if you die.

Savings, investments, and current life insurance

Once you've come up with a total for your debts and current and future expenses, tally the assets you have that could be applied against those debts and expenses. Say you've got $100,000 in debts and expenses. Your savings account has $10,000, and you've got another $10,000 in an investment account. Your employer pays for $25,000 of life insurance for you, and you have another $20,000 in your 401(k). So you've got a total of $65,000 that could be used to offset your debts and expenses. At first glance, then, it looks like you need an additional $35,000 in life insurance.

But suppose your spouse doesn't have a 401(k) plan at work, and you haven't gotten around to setting up IRAs yet. Maybe you'd rather have your spouse roll your 401(k) money into an IRA. And maybe you'd prefer that your spouse keep the investment account for greater long-term gains. That cuts $30,000 from the amount you want your survivors to use to settle your debts and adds $30,000 to the amount of additional life insurance you should have.

There are other formulas you can use to determine how much life insurance you should have. Some financial advisers recommend figuring out what you expect to earn between now and your target retirement age. Say you're 30, you make $40,000 a year, and you expect to retire at age 67. If your salary stays the same for the next 37 years, you'd need a total of $1,480,000 in life insurance to replace your salary (37 × $40,000 = $1,480,000). Chances are, though, that you'll earn more as your career progresses, which means you'd need more life insurance coverage.

Although replacing all of your income for your spouse is a nice thought, it may be both costly and unnecessary. Discuss how each of you would fare financially if the other died, and the options you would have and would like each other to have, and use that information to help you arrive at a life insurance figure that makes sense for you.

Term life versus whole life

One reason life insurance is so flummoxing to the average millionaire-in-the-making is that the jargon is weird. How do you know whether you should get a term or whole life policy? And what the heck is a universal whole life policy? Here's a (very) brief primer on what all these things mean.

Term life insurance

If you have life insurance through your employer, it's most likely a term policy; *term* refers to the time the policy is in force. In the case of employer-provided insurance, the term is in effect as long as you're employed at your current job, and when you leave the job, you no longer have that life insurance coverage. (Some employers allow you to take your life insurance policy with you as long as you pay the full premium, but this is fairly rare.)

You can get individual term policies through virtually every life insurance company out there, too. Terms usually range from 1 to 30 years. You pay the premium every month or every year, and if you die before the term expires, your beneficiaries receive a lump sum from the insurer.

Most life insurance policies have some kind of exclusions, especially in the early months or years of the policy. For example, most policies won't pay benefits if the insured commits suicide within the first two years; some pay reduced benefits if you die from any other cause within the first two years.

Not all term policies are the same. Some are *level term,* which means the value of the policy stays the same throughout the term; that is, if you buy a $50,000 policy, it will always be worth $50,000 throughout the term. With *decreasing term* policies, though, the face value of the policy goes down as you get older. So a $50,000 policy today may be worth only $30,000 20 years from now.

Then there's *renewable term* insurance. That means you have the option of renewing your policy at the end of the term, at a new premium. Say you buy a 20-year policy, and you pay $50 a month for it. At the end of 20 years, you can renew the policy, but your premium will be higher because you're older. Depending on your age, you may not be able to get another 20-year policy; you may be limited to shorter terms.

Term insurance is the cheapest kind of life insurance, and it's particularly useful in planning for specific future needs — like your kids' college funding, for example. You can buy a term policy that will be in effect until your children are out of college, and then you can decide whether it makes sense for you to purchase another term policy.

The longer your term, the less you'll pay in premiums over the long run. If you get a 30-year term policy when you're 25, you'll be paying those lower premiums until you're 55. But if you get a 20-year policy and renew it when you're 45, your premiums will be higher for an extra ten years. The older you get, the more true this is, because, after age 50, premiums begin a long and fairly steep climb for even modest coverage amounts.

The older you get, the fewer options you have for life insurance coverage. Once you pass your 65th birthday, you may not be able to get a term policy; whole life may be your only choice.

Whole life insurance

Whole life is so called because it doesn't expire until you do. As long as you keep paying the premiums, the policy stays in effect. Unlike term policies, though, your premiums on a whole life policy may increase at regular intervals. Some companies raise your premiums every year. Some have age ranges for their premiums, so your premium doesn't go up until you move into the next age bracket.

The problem we have with whole life is also the main talking point life insurance agents use to sell it: the fact that it builds cash value over time, which you can then borrow against. Whole life policies build cash value by investing part of your premium in stocks, bonds, or mutual funds. Salespeople like to paint this as a valuable perk of whole life, but the truth is that it's almost impossible to know what kind of return you might actually see. Even worse, much of any return is gobbled up by commissions and fees. The salesperson's commission alone may equal the entire first year's worth of premiums.

As for the argument that you can borrow against the cash value of a whole life policy, that's true, but it's a rotten option. In the first place, most policies don't accumulate significant cash value for 12 years or more. In the second place, the combination of high fees and ridiculously low monthly repayments mean even a small loan will cost you thousands over the long run. An example: In the late 1990s, Meg's husband took out a $3,500 loan against his whole life policy to pay for his grandfather's funeral. By the time Meg's husband died in 2005, the balance on that loan was more than $16,000 because the $10 monthly loan payment wasn't even enough to cover the interest, let alone the principal. So, when Meg's husband died, the value of his policy was reduced by the outstanding loan balance.

In our opinion, whole life is appropriate only if you have special circumstances that might make term insurance inadequate — for example, you have a disabled spouse or child and want to make sure you don't outlive your policy, or you're using a whole life policy as part of your estate planning (see Chapter 19) to cover taxes. And, as we mention earlier, if you're 65 or older, you may not have any other choice.

Universal and *variable* life insurance are versions of whole life policies. They usually offer extended investment options, but they're still more expensive than term insurance and still carry high fees that eat up a big chunk of any returns. The face values of these kinds of policies also rise and fall according to the performance of the investments.

Disability Insurance

Nothing can make your financial plans go kerplooey like an injury or illness that prevents you from working. The Council for Disability Awareness has a sobering collection of statistics at its Web site (www.disabilitycan happen.org/chances_disability/disability_stats.asp). Here are some of the more alarming facts:

- ✔ For every ten people who begin working today, three will be disabled before they reach retirement age.

- ✔ One in five workers will miss at least a year of work at some point in their careers because of an injury or illness.

- ✔ One in seven workers will be disabled for five years or more before they reach retirement age.

- ✔ Fewer than four in ten people who apply for Social Security disability benefits are approved, and the time between the disability event and approval of Social Security benefits can be three years or longer.

- ✔ Among those who do receive Social Security disability benefits, the average monthly payment is less than $1,000.

- ✔ The financial hardship from disability is blamed for 350,000 personal bankruptcies each year and almost half of all mortgage foreclosures.

- ✔ As many as seven in ten workers have no long-term disability insurance.

Disability can come in many forms, and most of them have nothing to do with your job, which means you can't count on worker's compensation to help you out. You could be seriously injured in a car accident, or you could develop a life-threatening disease like cancer, for example. Disability insurance covers virtually any event that prevents you from working and earning an income — including pregnancy.

Short-term disability insurance plans limit your benefits to no more than two years; more commonly, these short-term plans provide benefits for only 6 to 12 months. Some long-term disability plans will pay benefits for life or until you reach retirement age, but those kinds of plans are expensive. More typically, long-term plans provide three to five years of coverage, the idea being that, if you're disabled that long, you'll apply for Social Security disability benefits.

There are three main ways to replace at least some of your income if you suffer a disabling injury or become too ill to work. You can rely on your employer's disability insurance plan; you can purchase a private disability insurance plan; or you can plan to collect Social Security disability benefits. To adequately protect your assets, you may need a combination of all three.

Your employer's plan

Most states require employers — at least the large employers — to provide some sort of disability insurance, in addition to worker's compensation insurance. Short-term disability coverage is standard. These plans typically have a waiting period before they kick in; they won't cover you if you're out for a week with a cold, for example, but if that cold turns into pneumonia and you're out for three weeks, you'll be covered for any time missed that exceeds the waiting period. Some plans have no waiting period, but the most common waiting period is between 7 and 14 days.

Many employers require you to use any paid vacation or sick time you have before you put in a disability claim. The good thing about this is that it protects you from losing income while you're waiting for the disability insurance to kick in. The bad thing, of course, is that you may use up all your paid time off for the year in a single throw.

The time to find out how your employer's plan works is before you need it. Find out what the waiting period is (and whether it's working days or calendar days), how long you're covered, the policy on using paid time off, and whether any vacation or sick time you use counts toward the waiting period.

If you pay any part of the premium for disability insurance, even a tiny fraction, your benefits aren't subject to income taxes. In New York State, for example, workers pay 60¢ a week for standard short-term disability insurance, and that minute contribution to the premium protects short-term disability benefits from both federal and state income taxation.

If you don't pay any of the premium for either short- or long-term disability, any benefits you receive from those plans are taxable. So it's possible you could get short-term disability benefits tax free and then be hit with income taxes on long-term disability if you don't contribute to the premium for the long-term insurance. Check with your human resources or benefits department to find out how your employer's plan works.

Disability insurance only replaces a certain percentage of your gross income, usually between 50 percent and 60 percent. If your benefits aren't taxable, a 60 percent benefit may be pretty close to your regular take-home pay, depending on what kinds of payroll deductions you have. However, even with the tax break, most people need substantial emergency savings to augment their disability benefits.

Private disability insurance

You can buy your own disability insurance policy from a variety of companies. Check with your homeowner's or auto insurance agent to see if that company offers disability policies; you may get a discount for having multiple policies with the same company.

Premiums are based on a number of factors, including your age, gender, and occupation. If you work a desk job, your premiums probably will be significantly lower than if you're a long-distance trucker or a construction worker, for example. High-risk professions like law enforcement and firefighting carry higher premiums.

Your general health will affect your ability to get disability insurance, too. If you've had cancer, for example, you probably won't be eligible for affordable disability insurance. Some companies won't even offer policies to people who take blood pressure medication or who meet the medical definition of obesity. All the major insurers require a physical exam, a medical history, or both before they'll write a disability policy.

Assuming you're in good health, here's a checklist of things to look for when you're shopping for disability insurance:

✔ **How *disability* is defined:** Some policies consider you disabled if you can't work in your usual job, and some consider you disabled only if you can't work in any job that matches your educational and experience qualifications. There are also combination policies, which use your own occupation as the benchmark for the first couple years of benefits and then expand the definition to any job.

✔ **Coverage for both accident and illness:** Accident-only policies won't cover you if you can't work because of a heart attack or other illness. Although accident-only policies are cheaper, you're better off with one that covers both accidents and illness.

✔ **How long you can collect benefits:** The longer the benefit term, the more expensive the premium will be. If cost is a factor (and if you've read much of this book, you know that cost is *always* a factor), you may want to consider a benefit term that will bridge the gap between your work-based disability coverage and the time you can reasonably expect to collect Social Security disability benefits. Some policies offer benefit terms that last until you reach your full retirement age, and some even offer lifetime benefits, but these will be more expensive.

- ✔ **Cost-of-living increases in benefits:** You may be able to live pretty comfortably on 60 percent of your gross income today, but if you're disabled for years, inflation will reduce your purchasing power and lower your standard of living.

- ✔ **Renewability:** You can get either a renewable policy or a noncancelable one. Renewable policies guarantee your benefits, but your premiums can go up. Noncancelable policies guarantee both benefits and premiums, and the insurance company can cancel your policy only if you fail to pay the premiums.

- ✔ **Residual benefits for part-time work:** If you can go back to work part-time, you want a policy that will give you partial disability benefits so you don't have a drastic reduction in income. Some policies allow for partial disability payments even if you never are totally disabled.

- ✔ **The waiting period before benefits are paid:** The shorter the waiting period, the higher your premiums will be. Find out how long your work-based disability coverage will provide benefits, and look for a private policy that will pick up when your employer's benefits are exhausted.

- ✔ **Premium waiver or refund:** Look for a policy that waives the premiums after you've been disabled for a certain time; the most common waiver clause calls for 90 days of continuous disability. Some policies also refund part of your premium if you don't have any claims within a certain period.

Any benefits from a disability insurance policy are affected by other disability benefits you receive. Your policy should include a target figure or anticipated total benefits, and your policy will pay only the difference between any other benefits you receive and the target figure. Say your target figure is $1,000 per month. If you receive $800 per month in Social Security disability benefits, your private policy will pay you only $200 per month.

Don't waste your money on the so-called "disability protection" offered by credit cards, auto finance companies, or mortgage brokers. Credit card policies often cover only your minimum monthly payment but charge a premium based on your card balance. The rates charged for disability insurance on car and home loans usually are much higher than straight disability insurance. You're better off getting a good private disability policy that will provide adequate replacement income to meet your expenses.

You can find more information about disability insurance on the Internet. If you or your spouse served in the military, check out the Department of Veteran Affairs (www.va.gov). You also can access more information at the Life and Health Insurance Foundation for Education (www.lifehappens.org).

Social Security disability

If your disability lasts (or is reasonably expected to last) at least 12 months (or could result in death) and prevents you from working at all, you may want to consider applying for Social Security disability benefits. It's not an easy process, and as many as seven in ten initial applications are denied, forcing the claimant to go through an appeals process with the goal of eventually having the case heard by an administrative law judge.

We don't have the space here to delve into the mysteries of filing and winning Social Security disability claims. Suffice it to say that getting approved for Social Security disability benefits is by no means a sure thing, even if your doctor believes you're too disabled to work and even if you're collecting disability benefits from the Veterans Administration or an insurance policy. Remember, too, that, unlike worker's compensation, Social Security doesn't pay partial disability benefits.

People who pursue Social Security disability benefits on their own often find themselves hopelessly bewildered by the process. You don't need an attorney or representative to file an initial claim, but if your claim is denied, we recommend getting help for the appeals process. And do it quickly: Social Security requires that appeals be filed within 60 days of the denial of the initial claim.

The Social Security Administration Web site (www.ssa.gov) has information on the filing process. For more information about how the process works, check out www.disabilitysecrets.com, which explains what Social Security looks for in determining disability and discusses some common misperceptions about getting benefits.

Long-Term-Care Insurance

Long-term-care insurance is something of a misnomer, because not everyone who needs the services these policies cover needs them for a long time. Sometimes people need home-based or nursing-home care to recover from an illness or injury, and, after they've recovered, they don't need the services anymore.

Long-term care insurance has come into vogue in recent years as parents of the Baby Boom generation have aged. Medicare pays only for medical care, not for so-called "custodial care" for help with daily-living tasks. Private health insurance rarely pays for any kind of long-term care. So special policies were designed to fill in this gap in insurance coverage.

The thing is, long-term-care insurance doesn't make sense if you're either very poor or very well off. If you don't expect to have much in the way of cash or assets in your old age, when you're most likely to need long-term care, Medicaid will pick up the cost of your care. On the other hand, if your net worth (not including the value of your home) is more than $1.5 million, you're better off planning to pay for any long-term-care expenses yourself and setting aside money so you can do this.

If you fall somewhere in between, though, long-term-care insurance may seem like a good idea. It can help protect the assets you do have, and it provides a certain degree of peace of mind.

In general, we recommend taking a pass on long-term-care insurance. Our philosophy is that, if you can afford to pay premiums for 20 or 30 (or more) years, you can afford to put that money to work for you in much more efficient ways — thus, putting yourself above the threshold where having long-term-care insurance makes some sense.

If you decide to investigate your options for long-term-care insurance, here are some things to keep in mind:

- **Your age:** Most experts recommend getting your policy before your 60th birthday because, as you age, your premiums likely will go up and your chances of being approved for coverage likely will go down.

- **Where care is covered:** Some policies kick in only if you're admitted to a qualified nursing home; some will pay for a nurse or home health aide to provide care in your home.

- **Length of benefits:** Some policies offer lifetime benefits; some limit benefits to two years. Some policies will renew your benefits under certain conditions — for example, if you're in a nursing home for 6 months, then discharged and don't have any claims for the following 12 months, the policy benefits will revert to their original structure.

- **Inflation protection:** Like healthcare costs in general, long-term-care costs are rising much faster than the rate of inflation, so you want to make sure any policy you have provides at least some protection against rising costs.

- **Elimination or waiting period:** The longer the waiting period, the lower your premiums will be, so it's a good idea to buy the longest waiting period you can afford. If you don't have enough money now to cover 90 days of long-term-care expenses, make saving that money a priority.

If you decide to purchase long-term-care insurance, look for premiums that are no more than 7 percent of your expected monthly retirement income. *Remember:* You'll probably be paying most of the premiums on this policy after you leave the workforce.

Insurance You May Not Need

You can get insurance for practically anything, and various sectors are always looking for ways to promote specialized — and highly profitable — insurance policies. In many cases, though, you don't need these special policies, especially if you've built a solid insurance program for yourself.

Car-rental insurance

When you rent a car for pleasure (not business), the car-rental representative will ask whether you want the additional insurance — and sometimes they'll use high-pressure tactics to get you to agree to the extra charge right before they hand you the keys to your rental. You are *not* required to buy this insurance. And, if you have adequate coverage on your own car, you may not need the rental company's policy.

The key, though, is "adequate coverage on your own car." Some people who drive older cars drop collision and comprehensive (theft, fire, vandalism, and glass damage) and just carry liability insurance. If that's the case, you should pay for the car-rental insurance; otherwise, you could be facing an enormous bill if something happens to the rental car while you've got it.

Even if your personal auto insurance covers collision and comprehensive damage to a rental car, you could end up paying out of pocket for something called "loss of use." This is what the car-rental company charges you for the revenue it loses while the car is in the shop. It may also charge storage fees while the car is being repaired, and some companies even charge "diminution of value," which is the depreciation on a car that's been damaged and repaired. These things are covered by the rental company's collision damage waiver/loss damage waiver (CDW/LDW), which is the basic insurance the company asks you to accept or decline when you pick up your rental.

Except where state law requires them to, most auto insurance companies won't cover loss of use damages for rental cars. If you live in Alaska, Connecticut, Louisiana, Minnesota, New York, North Dakota, Rhode Island, or Texas, your personal auto insurance covers rental loss of use — as long as you have collision and comprehensive coverage on your own car. If you live in another state, paying for the CDW/LDW may be worthwhile for your peace of mind.

Check your own auto insurance coverage before you rent a car. If you aren't sure whether you're covered in a rental car, call your agent or insurance company and ask. Find out if there are any exclusions, like luxury cars or loss of use, too.

You also may be covered by your credit card's insurance if you use it to pay for the car rental. Again, check this out before you rent a car so you know what coverage you do — or don't — have. Keep in mind, though, that there may be exclusions in your credit card coverage. Some cards (or their issuing banks) won't cover rentals outside the United States, for example, and some won't cover certain types of rental vehicles, like SUVs, motor homes, or sports cars. If you do have coverage through your credit card, it kicks in only if you use the same card to pay for the rental.

If you're renting a car for business purposes, you're probably covered by your company's insurance. Check with the department that handles travel arrangements to find out if you're covered and if there are any exclusions.

Travel insurance

Travel insurance can be a good investment under certain circumstances and not such a good idea under others. Much depends on how much you're willing to lose if a trip you planned doesn't turn out the way you expect.

You can get travel insurance that will cover nonrefundable tickets in certain situations, like illness, a death in the family, or extreme weather conditions that force cancellation of the trip. You also can get supplemental medical coverage, which may be a good idea if your health insurance is restricted to a certain geographic area or charges hefty out-of-network co-pays and deductibles. You can insure against lost luggage, trip delays, and medical evacuation to a hospital or back home.

If you're traveling overseas, your health insurance probably won't come with you, so supplemental medical insurance may be a good idea. Even if your regular health insurance covers some costs, you may have to pay for any foreign medical bills first and then ask your health insurer for reimbursement when you get home.

The one thing you can't insure against is changing your mind. Even if you buy trip cancellation insurance, you have to meet one of the covered reasons before you're eligible to be reimbursed, and "I don't think I want to go the Bahamas after all" isn't a covered reason.

If you're looking at a high-priced trip, travel insurance may be worthwhile, especially if you have health issues that might interfere with your travel plans or if you have a family member whose health is unpredictable. For less expensive trips, insurance may not be worth it.

If your airline cancels your flight because of weather, mechanical problems, or staffing issues, you probably can get a refund for even your "nonrefundable" ticket. Ask a ticket agent at the airport how you go about claiming a refund. They'll probably give you a toll-free number to call. Even if you booked your ticket through an online service like Expedia or Travelocity, you'll probably get the price of your ticket refunded. (You won't get a refund of the booking fee charged by the online service, because you did actually use the service to book your flight.)

Life insurance for your kids

There are a couple schools of thought on whether life insurance for children makes sense. Some believe it's just silly to spend the money, because life insurance is meant to replace a wage earner's income, and children — unless they're models or actors — don't earn income. Others view it as a way to guarantee the child's future insurability — protection against an accident or illness that may make the child ineligible for insurance later in life. And some people like getting whole-life policies for children because of the cash value it will have when the child grows up.

We don't think you need to get life insurance for your child unless:

✔ Your child has a disability that may shorten her life or make her ineligible for life insurance when she's an adult. (Most life insurance policies for children don't require medical exams because the coverage limits are low, so you don't have to worry about your child qualifying.)

✔ There's a genetic disease in your family that could affect your child's ability to get life insurance later on.

✔ You just can't sleep at night worrying about whether your child will be able to get life insurance when he grows up.

As for the building-cash-value argument, life insurance is a lousy investment vehicle; you and your child will be better off if you open a high-yield online savings account — or, even better, a 529 college fund — with the money you would otherwise have spent on her life insurance premiums.

If you're worried about covering funeral expenses if something should happen to your child, check with your employer to see if you can add a modest level of coverage for your child to your own work-based life insurance. Some companies even pay the premiums for these small policies, which typically top out at $5,000.

Chapter 19

Planning for Your Heirs

In This Chapter

▶ Understanding why a will matters and what it does

▶ Exploring trust options

▶ Getting help with your estate planning

▶ Making sure your heirs can find your documents

*W*hen Howard Hughes died, he left a $6 billion estate and no will. It took the courts ten years to sort through all the (spurious) claims from supposed spouses and children (Hughes had been divorced for years before he died and, as far as is known, never had any children).

Even if you don't have a Hughes-mongous estate (maybe one of these days we'll write *Making Billions For Dummies*), you sure don't want people clogging the courts claiming to be your spouse or love child just to get a slice of what you leave behind. In this chapter, we discuss estate planning and give you an overview of some of the many tools you can use to make sure your money and property go to the right people at the right time. We also discuss a major concern for many millionaires: how to keep the Internal Revenue Service (IRS) from decimating your estate.

The more successful you are at building wealth, the more complex estate planning can become. We've picked the brain of Aaron Larson, author of *Wills & Trusts Kit For Dummies* (Wiley), for this brief overview. For a much more thorough grounding in all the issues surrounding estate planning, pick up a copy of Larson's book.

Putting Your Wishes in Writing

In our opinion, there are very few people who don't need a will, but it's even more important for people with significant assets. If you die *intestate* (without a will), the distribution of your assets will be determined by the laws of the state where you live, and those laws don't care what your wishes are.

A will covers everything that isn't covered somewhere else. For example, insurance policies and some accounts — like individual retirement accounts (IRAs) and 401(k)s — require you to list a beneficiary, and your will doesn't affect who gets those assets. Likewise, if you've established a living trust, the assets owned by the trust aren't affected by your will. But you can spell out how you want the rest of your estate distributed in your will.

You also choose who administers your estate; who gets what of your personal property and other assets; and, if you have a business, who succeeds you or inherits your shares in the business.

If you have minor children, your will should name a guardian for them. Larson also recommends naming a custodian for your children's assets; this may be the same person as the guardian or someone else. In both cases, though, choose someone you trust to take good care of your children and their inheritance.

Figuring out what you have to leave

Before you can allocate your estate among your various heirs, you have to figure out exactly what you have to bequeath. Take an inventory of your assets — all of them. Your assets could include

- ✔ Cash accounts, including savings and checking accounts
- ✔ Investment accounts
- ✔ Retirement accounts (see the nearby "Inherited IRAs" sidebar)
- ✔ Real estate, including your home and any other real property, like vacation homes or investment property
- ✔ Personal property, including clothes, furniture, electronics, and even things like hunting gear and tools
- ✔ Artwork, antiques, and collections
- ✔ Jewelry
- ✔ Vehicles, including cars, boats, ATVs, and RVs
- ✔ Business interests, whether you have a sole proprietorship, a partnership, or shares in a business (see the "Minding your business" sidebar, later in this chapter)
- ✔ Intellectual property, like royalties from inventions

Inherited IRAs

If you plan to bequeath an IRA to someone other than your spouse, be sure that someone knows the best way to use it, taxwise. Lots of people who inherit IRAs from parents, grandparents, aunts, or uncles cash them out immediately, triggering huge tax bills. Your heir (if it isn't your spouse, for whom there are different and much more lenient rules) has three basic choices in handling an inherited IRA:

- ✔ **She can cash it out right away,** in which case all of the money in the IRA will be considered taxable income for that year.

- ✔ **She can deplete the IRA over five years,** and each year's withdrawals will count as taxable income.

- ✔ **She can elect to stretch withdrawals out over her expected lifespan** (determined by an IRS table), thus allowing the bulk of the IRA to continue earning tax-deferred returns.

From a wealth-building standpoint, the correct choice is easy: Stretch the payments out over your life expectancy. Why? Because, over the course of three or four decades, even a modest IRA can amount to big money (depending on the rate of return, of course). Suppose you inherit a $50,000 IRA when you're in your 40s. By stretching your withdrawals out over the next 30 or 40 years, and assuming an average 8 percent return, that $50,000 could deliver more than $300,000 for you before the IRA is depleted. On the other hand, if you cash out an inherited IRA immediately, or even over five years, you lose the tax-deferred returns *and* you pay taxes on the withdrawals at your current tax rate (and the extra "income" from the inherited IRA may even push you into a higher tax bracket).

Consult your financial adviser before you make any decisions about what to do with an inherited IRA. And if you're planning to leave an IRA to someone other than your spouse, make sure you explain to the beneficiary the advantages of hanging onto it.

Your estate inventory can change over time, so the list you make now you should review and update periodically. You don't want your heirs searching frantically for a painting you sold years ago. Neither do you want them fighting over the antique settee you inherited from your great-aunt Matilda last month or the Lexus you bought last week.

Choosing an executor

Your will names an *executor,* or personal representative, who's responsible for distributing your assets to your heirs according to your wishes. Your executor can be a beneficiary of your will (such as a spouse, sibling, or adult child), or he can be someone else (like your lawyer or accountant). You also can name more than one personal representative, if you like, but Larson warns that, if you do this, you also should

✔ Spell out the specific responsibilities of each co-executor

✔ Provide directions for resolving disagreements between the co-executors

✔ Make sure each co-executor is willing and able to take on the responsibilities of managing your final affairs

Too many co-executors isn't a good idea. "At a certain point, too many cooks spoil the broth," Larson says. "Don't unnecessarily complicate the administration of your will by appointing a whole panel of co-executors."

Your executor will have expenses associated with carrying out your wishes, so consider how you want this person to be paid — and how much. The more complex your estate, the higher the executor's fee will be.

Your executor will be responsible for taking an inventory of your estate, including any debts you leave behind. The executor then pays the debts and distributes the remainder of your estate according to the instructions you left in your will. If the instructions aren't clear, or if there's a dispute between the executor and your heirs, the issue may be settled by a court, through an arbitration process, or through another mechanism that you specify in your will.

You can lay out any kind of dispute-resolution structure you want. You can give your executor final authority. You can direct that the parties go through arbitration. You can even decide that disputes will be resolved by flipping a coin or playing one hand of poker, if you like. Whatever you decide, it's a good idea to put some kind of instructions for handling disagreements in your will. That way, everybody knows what to do when disputes arise.

After you've made your first choice for executor, name a successor in case your first choice isn't able to perform the duties. There may be all kinds of reasons why your first choice isn't available — sickness or death, lack of time, or even lack of interest. It isn't unheard of for executors to resign, and if you haven't named a successor, the courts will appoint someone who may or may not follow your wishes.

Make sure both the executor and the successor are willing to and capable of taking on the responsibilities of handling your estate. There's a lot of number-crunching and administrative work involved, so you want someone who has the time and the inclination to take on these duties.

Divvying up your estate

When Warren Buffett announced he was turning the bulk of his fortune over to the philanthropic Bill and Melinda Gates Foundation and four other charities, many people expressed shock that he would "disinherit" his children.

In fact, Buffett had already given his adult children substantial money gifts, and part of his fortune will go to the charitable foundations his children operate.

Buffett explained his thinking in *Fortune* magazine in 2006: "I still believe in the philosophy . . . that a very rich person should leave his kids enough to do anything but not enough to do nothing. . . . I would argue that when your kids have all the advantages anyway, in terms of how they grow up and the opportunities they have for education, including what they learn at home — I would say it's neither right nor rational to be flooding them with money."

There are lots of things to consider when you're figuring out how to divide your estate among your heirs. As always, the best place to start is with your goals: What do you want to accomplish with your bequests? Some things to think about:

- ✔ **What do you want to provide for your spouse or partner?** Maybe you want to make sure he can afford to live in the house for the rest of his life or be able to indulge a hobby. Maybe you want to provide a steady income rather than an outright inheritance so she can rely on that income for years.

  Many states don't give survivors of domestic partnerships any rights to inherit, so it's even more important to have a will in this situation. Otherwise, your partner could end up with nothing if you die.

- ✔ **What do you want to provide for your children?** If you have young children, you may want to set aside money for their education or for other needs, in addition to providing for their general care until they reach adulthood. If your children are grown, your goals for them will be different.

  In this era of divorce, remarriage, and blended families, one challenge is figuring out whether you'll treat any stepchildren the same way you treat your own. Some remarried couples arrange their estates so that each spouse provides for his or her own children only. In that case, you have to be careful to structure your estate so your children get what you want them to have.

  If you die without an estate plan, your children may not have any legal standing to inherit from your second spouse. Meg's husband had a son from a previous marriage, for example, and after her husband died, Meg learned that her stepson would not be able to inherit anything from her in the absence of a will (which she had drawn up immediately). It's also possible that your second spouse will choose not to leave anything to your children from your first marriage — even the assets he inherited from you.

✔ **What else do you want to accomplish with your estate?** Perhaps you want to leave some memento to your best friend, or give to charity, or provide for the care of a cherished pet.

If you have trouble figuring out what you want your will to say, think about it this way: Your will is a set of directions for what you want done when you're not around to do it yourself. And, because you won't be available to answer questions, you want to make your instructions as clear as possible.

Anytime your family circumstances change — birth, death, marriage, divorce, adoption, remarriage, disability, or any other change — you need to review your will and determine any changes that need to be made. This is also a good time to check the beneficiaries on your life insurance policies and retirement accounts to make sure they reflect your current needs.

Paying final expenses

Your estate likely will have more than just funeral expenses to pay when you die. Your executor will be responsible for using your estate's assets to pay any debts you have, and if there isn't enough cash in the estate to satisfy those debts, the executor will have to sell other assets (thus, lowering the amount that actually gets passed onto your heirs). Your debts may include things like medical bills, as well as mortgages, loans, insurance premiums, and so on. Your executor also may be responsible for paying utility bills, property taxes, and insurance on your home until the distribution of your estate is complete.

On top of all this, there will be administrative costs. Probate courts charge a filing fee for filing a will; this usually runs a few hundred dollars. If there are legal challenges to your will, there will be other court costs involved there, too.

If your executor isn't a lawyer, she may hire one to help her through the probate process. Fees for these services vary, but they often amount to between 2 percent and 5 percent of the value of your estate.

Your executor is entitled to compensation for the work he does on your estate, too. If you don't spell out a fee in your will, the court will likely award "reasonable" fees — again, usually between 2 percent and 5 percent of the value of the estate.

If you do spell out your executor's compensation in your will, be sure to talk it over with your executor. You don't want her to resign because she feels she's being underpaid for the amount of work involved.

Minding your business

If you have a business, you have to decide what will happen to it if you die. Some people expect their businesses to be closed upon their death, and the assets distributed among their heirs along with the rest of their estate. But if you want your business to continue after your death, you need to create a succession plan. A *succession plan* addresses such issues as who will own your interest in your business after your death, who will take over management of the business, who has the right to buy shares in the business, and what rights and responsibilities go with buying those shares.

Succession planning is a complicated process and usually takes several years to implement fully; in other words, you'll likely need a professional to help you set up your plan the way you want it. The Free Management Library (`www.managementhelp.org`) has several perspectives on business succession; click the Staffing link on the home page and look for Succession Planning in the All Aspects of Staffing section. Other resources include Business.com, which has a directory of succession planning services and software, and `www.successionplanning101.com`, which has articles, white papers, downloadable Webinars, and a glossary.

If you've set up trusts outside your will, your trustee also is entitled to fees and may have expenses for the services of a lawyer or accountant. As with your will, you can establish your trustee's compensation when you set up the trust. If you don't, the trustee can charge "reasonable" fees, which may be determined on an hourly basis or as a percentage of the trust's value. Larson says professional trust services usually charge an annual fee of between 0.75 percent and 1.25 percent of the trust's value.

Fees for administering wills and trusts can be much higher than you anticipate. When you discuss compensation arrangements with your executor or trustee, make sure you know what services are included in that base compensation and what services would generate additional fees (which will be charged to your estate). Your executor also can negotiate fees with your attorney, but she should get any agreed-upon fee in writing.

Using Trusts in Estate Planning

Trusts have become increasingly popular estate planning tools, and they can be effective ways to provide for special circumstances, like the needs of a disabled adult or the burning-a-hole-in-your-pocket spending habits of an heir. But trusts aren't necessarily right for everybody, and, as Larson notes, they don't replace a will. "You may or may not need trusts," he says, "but you definitely need a will."

That said, trusts that are properly set up can achieve goals that your will may not be able to achieve, or at least not entirely.

In this section, we're talking about trusts created as separate legal entities, not affected by your will. You can also create *testamentary trusts* in your will by instructing that certain assets be held in trust for the beneficiary. If you don't specify a separate trustee for your testamentary trust, your executor will act as trustee.

Trusts are useful when you want to keep control of your assets but provide for a trustee to take charge if you become incapacitated through illness or injury. They also can limit expenses for your estate. For example, if you own real estate in several states, putting your out-of-state property under the control of a trust simplifies the probate process; without such a trust arrangement, your executor has to go through probate in every state where you own property.

Defining trusts

A *trust* is a mechanism for ensuring that certain assets are available for specific purposes. When you set up a trust, you also set up its terms — that is, how the trust's assets are to be managed, who will act as trustee and what powers the trustee has, who the trust's beneficiaries are, how and when your beneficiaries receive proceeds from the trust, and how long the trust will last. When you put assets into a trust, the trust is the owner, and the trustee — which could be you, depending on the type of trust — is charged with managing those assets according to your instructions.

Revocable trusts allow you to move assets in and out during your lifetime, or even to dissolve the trust altogether. *Irrevocable trusts* are permanent; you can't dissolve it, and once you put assets into an irrevocable trust, you can't take them back out.

Trusts can be simple or incredibly complex, and they have to be set up properly to achieve their intended goals. For example, you may want to use a trust to avoid certain taxes, but if it isn't set up correctly, your estate may end up paying those taxes anyway.

Recognizing the advantages of trusts

Trusts have several advantages over wills:

- ✔ They're flexible.
- ✔ They can be set up to serve specific needs.

>   ✔ They often reduce costs and complications in probate court because any assets that you put into trusts aren't distributed as part of the probate estate.
>
>   ✔ Unlike wills, which become public record through the probate process, trusts enable you to keep much information about your estate private.
>
>   ✔ They can be used to minimize taxes for your heirs.

We cover serving specific needs and minimizing taxes in the following sections.

Preparing for specific needs

Suppose you have an heir who tends to spend money recklessly. You may worry that, faced with a huge inheritance, your heir may run through the money at lightning speed, undercutting your intentions to provide a basis of financial security.

In this case, a *spendthrift trust* may seem like the ideal solution. This kind of trust sets up obstacles between the trust's assets and the beneficiary. It also can protect the assets from the beneficiary's creditors and even from the beneficiary's spouse in a divorce case. This kind of trust also can be useful for young heirs and for heirs who may face financial hardship for reasons beyond their control, like medical issues.

You can set up *charitable trusts* that either give you an income from the assets while you're alive and transfer the assets to the charity upon your death, or vice versa — that is, the charity gets the income from the trust during your lifetime, and the trust's assets are distributed to your estate when you die.

You can even set up trusts for people who receive government assistance like Medicaid or Social Security disability. In most cases, government assistance programs place income and asset limits on participants, so a hefty outright inheritance might disqualify your heir from the program. But with a *special needs trust* or *supplemental needs trust,* you can provide your heir with extra resources to supplement the governmental support she already receives.

Many of these trusts are highly complex and technical, and there are pitfalls that can sideline your best intentions. If you decide to set up any trust, make sure you enlist the help of an attorney who's experienced in the kind of trust you want to establish.

Minimizing taxes

When you've made your millions, you have to start thinking about estate taxes. Congress changed the federal estate tax a few years ago, but, as is often the way with Congress and taxes, the change isn't permanent. It raised the exemption gradually from a relatively paltry $625,000 to $2 million in

2008. In 2009, the exemption rises to $3.5 million, and it disappears altogether in 2010. However, it comes back in 2011, and, unless Congress acts, the exemption in 2011 reverts to $1 million — meaning any portion of your estate that exceeds $1 million could be taxed at an appalling 45 percent.

Larson doesn't expect Congress to let the $1 million exemption stand, but he doesn't expect them to permanently repeal the estate tax either. He predicts that the exemption will be somewhere between $1.5 million and $4 million. So, if you think your estate will be worth more than $1.5 million (and because you're reading this book, *we* think you should expect to have a larger estate), you'll want to look into ways to minimize your estate's tax liability. Trusts can offer a way to do this.

We're talking about only federal taxes here. Each state has its own laws about estate and inheritance taxes, so check with your lawyer or accountant to find out what the law is where you live.

Many people think trusts help you avoid estate taxes. That's not exactly true. You can set up certain kinds of trusts that take advantage of tax breaks or minimize the overall tax burden on your estate, but the IRS has strict rules for allowing these kinds of tax advantages. If the rules and requirements aren't met, the IRS will treat your trust as part of your taxable estate.

For example, if you act as trustee or keep control over the assets in some trusts, the IRS will disallow the tax break associated with that kind of trust. For other trusts, they have to be established for a certain number of years before you die; if you die before the trust matures, its assets are included in your taxable estate.

There are all kinds of tax-minimizing trusts to benefit all kinds of heirs. You can set up something called a *dynasty trust* or *generation-skipping trust,* for example. These trusts provide for multiple generations and, when properly set up, don't generate any tax liability for your heirs. You don't save on taxes when you set it up, but (again, if it's properly structured) neither your estate nor your heirs incur any federal estate or gift taxes on distributions that are made during your lifetime; upon your death; or upon the end of the trust, when its remaining assets are distributed. To maximize the tax breaks, Larson recommends funding dynasty trusts with *irrevocable life insurance trusts* — trusts that allow you to avoid estate taxes on life insurance proceeds.

Then there are trusts that postpone estate taxes and trusts that allow you to maximize the lifetime gift exemptions — gifts that aren't subject to the federal gift tax — for both you and your spouse.

The larger your estate, the more important tax planning becomes. At current tax rates, Larson warns, "If you don't plan and implement an effective tax avoidance strategy, the IRS is going to take almost half of what you leave" above the exemption threshold.

Getting Professional Help

With all the do-it-yourself kits for wills, healthcare proxies, and powers of attorney out there, you may be thinking there's no big trick to handling your estate planning yourself. And, in a sense, you're right: There's no *big* trick. The problem lies in all the *little* tricks that can derail virtually everything you want your estate plan to accomplish.

That's why we (and Larson, by the way) recommend getting professional help with your estate planning. The larger your estate, the more critical getting good help is, because there are more things that can go wrong as the value and complexity of your estate increase.

Starting early

Death may be certain, but when it comes is anything but. Bob's first wife died in her 30s; Meg's husband was 47 when he died. That's why we recommend starting your estate planning as soon as you have any assets to distribute. Even if you're single and have no children, you may want to make specific provisions for your parents, siblings, nieces and nephews, charities, or even friends. If you die without a will, your estate will be distributed according to the laws of the state where you live, and those laws may not coincide with what you really want.

The fewer assets and beneficiaries you have, the simpler your estate planning will be. When you're just starting out, you probably don't need to set up trusts or other intricate mechanisms for distributing your assets; a simple will can suffice. In fact, Larson recommends that young people — those under age 60 or so — and people whose estates are worth $100,000 or less avoid trusts in most cases, because it costs money to revise them.

As your wealth and family grow, your estate planning will get more involved. But if you start out with a basic plan, amending it when you need to won't seem so intimidating.

Getting the right kind of help

Any general-practice lawyer can draw up a simple will for you. But if you need more specialized advice, you'll want to find an attorney who is experienced and expert in estate planning. You also may want to enlist the services of an accountant who's knowledgeable about estate planning.

Your estate planning professionals should be knowledgeable in these areas:

- Wills and trusts
- Tax law (federal and state)
- Business law (if you have a business or a share in one)
- Real estate law
- Personal-property law
- Medicare and Medicaid law (and how it will affect your estate)
- Retirement plans and related inheritance laws
- Insurance products (and their tax treatment)
- Asset valuation

Attorneys and accountants with these areas of expertise can help you devise the most effective ways to accomplish the goals you've set for your estate plan. They can help avoid or minimize taxes during your life and after your death; they can identify potential problems and recommend fixes; and they can explain your options so you can choose the ones that make sense for you.

When you're looking for a lawyer, Larson recommends seeking out one with at least ten years of experience in estate planning and whose practice is largely or solely focused on estate planning and probate. Also look for one who has experience handling estates that are similar to yours — not just in size but also in circumstances (such as business ownership or minor children, for example).

If you have an accountant you trust, ask if she can recommend a good estate planning attorney. You also can check out the directory of the American College of Trust and Estate Counsel (ACTEC), available online at www. actec.org.

Knowing what it'll cost

How much it will cost to devise your estate plan depends largely on how complex your plan is and how your attorney determines his fees. Some lawyers charge a flat fee for simple wills and other documents like durable powers of attorney and healthcare proxies; you may pay extra for customization. Some firms offer a complete customized plan for a flat rate, and some charge an hourly rate — depending on where you live, usually between $175 and $300 per hour — and your final bill depends on how time-consuming creating your estate plan is.

 Some law firms base their fees on the size of the estate, but this can cause problems. For one thing, it gives the law firm an incentive to overvalue your assets, which can lead to disagreements between you and the lawyer. For another, you should pay your lawyer for the legal work she performs, not a commission based on how many assets you have.

 Once your plan is in place, you can expect to pay again when it's time to make revisions. This should keep you from tinkering needlessly with your plan, but don't let it stop you from making necessary changes. What you pay now to ensure that your estate plan is properly structured will save your heirs untold aggravation and expenses later on.

Storing Your Estate-Plan Documents

All the planning in the world won't do your heirs any good if they can't find the paperwork when you're gone. Probate courts require your executor to file an original copy of your will. Copies of your trust documents often are enough to ensure that the trust operates the way you intend, but if copies or the original can't be produced — or if the copy's authenticity is challenged — the assets you transferred to a trust could become part of your probate estate and may be treated as though you died intestate.

Larson describes three common options for storing your will and other estate documents:

- ✔ **A home safe or lockbox,** as long as it's water- and fireproof, and as long as your executor or heirs have access to the combination or key

- ✔ **A safe-deposit box at a bank or credit union** — again, as long as your executor or heirs can access it

> ✔ **With your lawyer,** who has a duty to safeguard them and present them to the appropriate authorities when you die — of course, you need to give your lawyer's contact information to your executor and/or your heirs

In some states, you can register your will and trust documents with the secretary of state or your county clerk's office. Check with your local probate-court clerk to find out what your options are and any fees involved.

Chapter 20

Keeping Your Finances in Good Health

***

In This Chapter

▶ Automating your financial life

▶ Getting rid of what you don't need

▶ Scheduling fiscal physicals

***

*O*nce you've made your millions, you naturally want to enjoy the fruits of your labors. But you also want to make sure your finances stay healthy. After all the work you've put in, the last thing you want to do is start over.

As we mention elsewhere, no one ever gets to a point where she doesn't have to think about money anymore. When you're in the accumulation phase, you have to identify your goals, plan how to handle any debt, and come up with a wealth-building strategy. When you've reached your target, you have to reset your goals and, again, figure out how to get there.

Money that's ignored or neglected loses value to inflation and taxes. You can set up your finances so they don't require an awful lot of oversight, but you can't just forget about them — at least, not if you want to remain in the millionaire class.

Fortunately, it's pretty easy to keep things simple. In this chapter, we show you how to make most of your financial life automatic, how to clear away any financial clutter, and how to manage multiple accounts as if they were one. Then we show you how regular financial checkups can keep you wealthy with minimal exertion.

Keeping It Simple

Getting your finances in order can be time-consuming, but once you're organized, a little light maintenance should keep everything running smoothly. You still need to balance your checkbook and read your statements, but otherwise there isn't a lot of work involved if you keep things simple.

Engaging the autopilot

Direct deposit is one of the greatest inventions of recent memory. It saves time and money, and, with the advent of online banking, it's never been easier to keep track of your monthly income and outgo.

According to the Pew Internet & American Life Project, 53 percent of all adult Internet users do their banking online, and that percentage continues to grow as financial institutions offer more online services — and heightened security — for their customers.

Most banks and credit unions use Secure Sockets Layer (SSL) encryption to protect information in online transactions. SSL prevents a different site from impersonating your bank and verifies that your data hasn't been altered during transmission. If you're not sure how secure your bank's online features are, call or visit and ask to speak to a customer service representative.

You can have virtually all your income deposited automatically into your checking or savings account — paychecks, pension payments, Social Security benefits, retirement savings withdrawals, or whatever. You also can arrange to have your bills — like your mortgage, auto loan, insurance premiums, and utility bills — paid automatically every month, thus ensuring that those payments will never be late.

Online bill-paying services are becoming more common, too, and they're often free.

You can make savings automatic, too. Find out if your bank will arrange automatic transfers from your checking to savings, a certificate of deposit (CD), a savings bond, a money-market mutual fund account, or an individual retirement account (IRA). Such automatic transfers usually are free.

Most banks and credit unions also offer other online services, such as e-statements, transfers, and even loan applications.

Cleaning up the clutter

The more paper and accounts you have, the harder it is to stay on top of your finances. You really don't need your credit card statements from 1988; you don't even need to keep hard copies of cancelled checks or bank statements if you can get them online.

It makes sense to keep some old records, like your mortgage note, home equity loan papers, and insurance policies. But you can get rid of a lot, too. Most income tax audits go back only three years, so you don't have to keep receipts or checks that aren't tax-related for longer than that. If you're not comfortable with three years, trim your records to the most recent five years.

Unfortunately, cleaning up the paper clutter may be the easy part. Making sure your accounts are streamlined can be more challenging. In the following sections, we cover all the bases.

Credit cards

The average American has nearly nine credit cards, according to the U.S. Census Bureau. In our opinion, you don't need more than two. Figure out which of your cards has the lowest interest rates and the best reward or cash-back programs; then begin gradually closing the others.

Closing credit card accounts can ding your credit score (see Chapter 6), so proceed carefully here. In general, it's better to keep older accounts open, because an account that you've had (and managed responsibly) for at least two years boosts your score more than an account that's been open for only a few months. Don't close all your credit card accounts at once. Instead, phase them out — closing one every six months, for example.

You can simplify further by using only cash for daily expenses or by carrying only one credit card in your wallet and keeping the other(s) in a drawer for emergencies.

401(k)s and IRAs

Did you leave your 401(k) with your last employer? If so, consider rolling it over into your IRA. Also, if you have multiple IRA accounts, you may want to consolidate them. Choose the one that has the best investment options for you. This reduces paperwork and makes it easier to see how your retirement savings are performing.

The IRS treats multiple traditional and Roth IRAs as a single account for tax purposes. (SEP IRAs — those for self-employed people — are covered under a separate formula for contributions.) This means that, no matter how many

IRAs you have, you can't get the tax break for contributions that exceed the annual maximum for your age and income. So there really isn't a big advantage in having more than one traditional IRA and one Roth IRA (one each for you and your spouse, if you're married).

Mutual funds

We really like mutual funds, but that doesn't mean you should be invested in every mutual fund out there. The more funds you have, the harder it is to see overlaps or imbalances in your portfolio. If you've got more than 15 mutual funds, consider trimming the list to just your top picks.

According to the Schwab Center for Financial Research, you increase your odds of being overexposed to a single market sector (like healthcare, biotech, and large-cap or international funds) if you own more than three funds in the same asset class. Holding all those funds means you're paying more in fees, too, even if you're in a low-cost fund family.

Keeping it simple applies to what you invest in, too. If you don't understand how an investment works, don't buy it. Derivatives, specialty funds, and other buzzword-laden investment types may (only *may,* mind you) be worth the money, but if they're too complicated or too hard to understand, give 'em a miss.

Taking the universal view

If you're like many people, you're probably juggling several portfolios — and probably even several financial goals — at the same time. If you and your spouse each has a 401(k), a traditional IRA, and a Roth IRA, that's six accounts to manage. And that's just for retirement — it doesn't even count your savings and taxable investment accounts, or 529 accounts for the kids' college.

One way to simplify all these different accounts is to group similar ones together and treat them as a single portfolio. Take those six retirement accounts you and your spouse have: Let's say you've got a total of $100,000 in those accounts, and you want a 65/35 stocks-to-bonds ratio overall. You can achieve this one of two ways: You can fiddle with each account so it reflects that 65/35 mix, or you can look at the $100,000 as a whole and make sure that $65,000 is in stocks and the rest is in bonds.

When you use the second method, you don't have to worry so much about diversifying every single account because, put together, your retirement funds are well balanced. It also allows you to take advantage of the best features of each account. If your 401(k) has a better selection of mutual funds, and your spouse's has better bond options, you can direct the bulk of the money in each account to the better offerings because the other account provides the balance in asset types.

The danger in using one account's asset classes to balance out those in another account is that you may end up holding lots of investments in the same market sector. Be sure you know which investments are in each account, so you can adjust if you have too much money in, say, small caps and not enough in other sectors.

Morningstar.com has an Instant X-Ray tool that identifies overlaps in your portfolio. You enter the ticker symbols and holding values, and the tool shows you how your investments are distributed. Instant X-Ray is under the Tools tab on the Morningstar home page (www.morningstar.com). If you sign up for free membership, you can save your Instant X-Ray portfolio for future analysis.

Letting your money work for you

The simpler your investments are, the less tempted you are to mess around with them much, and that means you leave your money alone and let it do its job, which is to make more money for you.

This is partly why the financial sector came up with *target-date funds.* These are mutual funds that start out with an investment mix that's appropriate for the *time horizon* (the number of years before you want to use those funds for income) and then automatically rebalance every year, gradually getting more conservative as your target retirement date approaches.

Target-date funds are a good option if you're not confident in your investing skills or if you just don't want to take the time to oversee your investments. However, fees on these funds can be high, so be sure to find out what expenses you'll have before you buy.

The advantage to keeping your investments simple is that you can ignore the daily chatter about the markets and keep your eye on your longer-term goals. If you have a target-date fund aimed at retiring in 2030, what happens in the stock market today really isn't relevant to you.

Giving Your Finances Regular Checkups

You wouldn't think of letting your car go without an oil change or a tuneup now and then, and you probably go to the doctor once in a while, even if you're feeling perfectly fit, just to verify that everything's okay. And yet lots of people never look at their financial plan again unless something catastrophic forces them to. Retirees, in particular, seem prone to neglecting the regular review of their finances, perhaps because, when they've left the accumulation phase, they figure they don't need to be as diligent about asset allocation.

Keeping it simple (see the "Keeping It Simple" section, earlier in this chapter) doesn't mean you can ignore it. It's still your money and your financial life, and complacency is just as dangerous after you've made your millions as it was when you were flat broke.

Even if you have a target-date fund that automatically becomes more conservative the closer you get to retirement, it's a good idea to review it at least annually. A lot can change in a year, and you want to make sure your investment strategy changes to match your evolving needs.

Your financial review should include the following:

- **Assessing progress on your goals:** What were your goals for the past year, and how did you fare on realizing them? Are you on track with your debt reduction or retirement savings plans? If you met all your goals, that's great — now it's time to come up with new ones. If you didn't meet all your goals, figure out why you fell short, and move on to the next step in your review.

- **Matching your finances with your goals:** If you haven't reached some of your goals, it may be time to tweak your financial plan so you can achieve them in the coming year. If you're working on new goals, come up with a strategy and timetable for reaching them.

- **Evaluating your disaster plan:** Review your insurance plan, and make sure you have the appropriate coverage for your current situation.

- **Reviewing your estate plan:** Read over your will, and make sure it still reflects your wishes. Check the beneficiaries on insurance policies and retirement accounts, too.

- **Estimating your tax situation:** Withdrawing money from retirement accounts or buying and selling funds within taxable accounts can expose you to income and/or capital-gains taxes. By looking ahead to your next tax return, you give yourself time to adjust for any extra liability you may have.

Plan to do your financial review when you receive your annual Social Security earnings statement. That way, you'll do it at least once a year, and the statement can be your reminder.

Even if you've reached your financial goals, it's important to stay on top of your credit report — both so you know where you stand and so you can spot possible problems. Get reports from each of the three credit bureaus — Equifax, Experian, and TransUnion — at least once a year from www.annualcreditreport.com. The best plan is to sign up to receive one report every four months, because you can monitor any suspicious activity. (See Chapter 6 for more on credit reports.)

Rebalancing your portfolio

In Chapter 16, we discuss different investment strategies for different stages of your life and the importance of matching your portfolio to meet your long-term goals.

But rebalancing your portfolio also is an important tool when you've reached your original goals and have new ones. After you reach that first $1 million, you need to set a new benchmark to reach for. Otherwise, you run the risk of letting your wealth stagnate — and, when that happens, you actually lose value.

Your post–$1 million goals are entirely up to you, of course, but those goals will determine how conservative or risky you want your portfolio to be. If you want to parlay that $1 million into $2 million in five years, you'll have to take on a lot more risk than if you're aiming to add $200,000 to your net worth in that same time frame.

No matter where you are in terms of your working life or your goals, you don't want to get out of growth investments entirely. Fixed-asset investments like bonds and money market mutual funds may not keep up with inflation and taxes, so your money may not last as long as you expect. Even after you've retired and are relying on your investments for income, at least 30 percent of those investments should be in stocks.

The stock market is unpredictable, but you can guard against fickle returns by putting two, three, or four years' worth of expenses in staggered CDs or bonds so you always have some income. For example, you can put a year's expenses in four CDs — one 3-month CD, one 6-month CD, one 9-month CD, and one 12-month CD. That way, you'll have income every quarter.

Stocks and bonds typically move in opposite directions. Bond yields tend to be high during bear markets, when stock returns are low. During bull markets, stocks yield great returns, and bond yields go into the cellar.

Annual rebalancing ensures that gains (or losses) in various types of investments don't put your entire portfolio out of whack — which can sabotage your plans for your newest goals.

Weeding out what you no longer need

Investments and other financial instruments that made sense when you got them may not always make sense. Weeding out what you don't need takes some analysis, but it's well worth the effort: Doing it ensures that your finances are geared toward your current needs and goals.

The weeding process involves looking at the purpose of an investment or insurance policy, evaluating its performance, and determining whether it's still a good fit for you.

Revisiting the reasons each item is in your portfolio

Some investments outlive their usefulness. That fund you bought to help finance the kids' college expenses, for example — after your children have graduated, do you really need that fund? Or would the money be better invested elsewhere?

The same goes for life insurance policies. At some point, it may not make sense to keep paying premiums on a policy with a declining face value or one that was designed to replace income for your family. As your wealth grows, the role of life insurance may change significantly.

We're not saying you don't need any life insurance once you've made your millions — only that the policies you do have deserve another look. If your children are grown, and you have enough other assets to provide for your spouse and anything else you want to do with your estate, maybe it's time to let the life insurance policy go. On the other hand, you may have good reasons for hanging on to it, such as using it to fund an endowment or trust, or to help offset estate taxes.

If you drop a policy and later decide you need or want it after all, it'll cost you. Your premiums will be higher, and you may not be able to get the same kind or level of coverage you had before.

Evaluating an investment's performance

Look at the returns each investment has yielded since your initial purchase, and then ask yourself this: If you were going to buy stock today, would you buy this one? If the answer is no, it's time to get rid of it and invest in something else.

Don't let misguided loyalty get in your way when you're weeding, either. Your parents or grandparents may have done great with U.S. Steel and General Electric, and you may have cleaned up on AOL or Google back in the day. But just because an investment has been good to you in the past doesn't mean it'll always be good to you. Analyze it as though you've never heard of it before and don't have any history with it.

It may help to write a "policy statement" for your investments when you're weeding. Think about what you want to accomplish next, and write out a general plan for getting there. Then build your investment strategy around your plan, tossing anything that no longer fits.

Figuring out whether the investment still fits

If a particular investment hasn't lived up to its potential, or if changing circumstances affect its overall return, it could mean that it's like those old jeans you've been keeping in the bottom of your dresser drawer for years — not a good fit anymore.

Lots of things can make a once-sensible investment less than desirable down the road. Management changes at the fund or company can affect performance or stability; fees can go up, making the net return less attractive. Your risk tolerance can change, turning what was once a thrilling stock holding into a migraine trigger.

When you go through your investments, think about why you originally bought each one. Then decide whether it still fits in with your current circumstances and goals.

Part V
The Part of Tens

The 5th Wave   By Rich Tennant

"...and don't tell me I'm not being frugal enough. I hired a man last week to do nothing but clip coupons!"

In this part . . .

The Part of Tens is a favorite feature of *For Dummies* books because it gives readers useful information in small, easily digestible nuggets — like a snack in between the main courses of earlier chapters. Some readers even like to read this section first, as a kind of appetizer for the four-course meal in the rest of the book.

Want to know how millionaires think? Our list of ten traits of millionaires is here. Wondering how you can squeeze more out of the money you already have? We give you ten ways to find more of your own money. We also offer our ten favorite ways to make your money work harder. And, because many people don't quite know how to gauge whether they've reached their financial goals, we give you ten ways you can tell you're a millionaire.

Chapter 21

Ten Traits of Millionaires

In This Chapter

▶ Understanding how millionaires think

▶ Cultivating these traits in yourself

*W*hat does it take to be a millionaire these days? If you're starting from scratch, as most of today's millionaires have, it takes more than just a desire to be rich. It takes an "I can do this" attitude and a willingness to put in the thought, time, and energy to identify and work toward your goals.

It also takes a sense of independence — wanting financial independence, but also wanting to do it yourself, your way. Millionaires don't let their money control them, and they don't let anyone else control their money. They'll learn as much as they can from others, but, in the end, they're the ones making the decisions, so they're responsible for their own successes and their own mistakes.

Perhaps most important, millionaires never view themselves as victims. They don't take it as a personal insult when others have more than they do; instead, they figure out what they want and then they figure out a way to make it happen. They steer clear of situations where they might be defrauded or taken advantage of, and when one of their money ventures doesn't work out, they figure out what went wrong and how to avoid the same situation again.

If you're thinking there's a theme here, you're right. Today's millionaires are do-it-yourselfers. They don't want a handout, and they don't expect a bag of money to fall at their feet. They figure no one else is going to take responsibility for their financial security, so they'd better do it themselves. Keep reading to learn about ten traits most millionaires have in common.

Seeking Independence

Most millionaires don't like money for its own sake — they like what money represents: choice, freedom, independence. Millionaires don't want to be enslaved by their jobs or their bills. Having money means having that independence — being able to take care of yourself instead of relying on others.

Money also opens the doors to countless possibilities. Millionaires want to be able to do the things that matter to them.

It's natural to want an interesting, fulfilling life. Money is a tool that can make it easier for you to live the life you want. So, wanting wealth is a natural desire, too.

Living Life, Not the Lifestyle

You've heard the stories of lottery winners who blew their windfalls on big houses, fast cars, custom-made clothes, and flashy jewelry — only to declare bankruptcy a few years later. Why does this happen? Because those people get caught up in the popular conception of the millionaire lifestyle, without ever considering the logical consequence of spending all their money.

Most of today's millionaires weren't born into money; they worked their way up, usually from the middle or working class, into the echelons of the wealthy. And they brought with them the values of hard work, comfortable but modest living, and doing it yourself. They may hire a landscaper to redo their yard, but they're just as likely to do the gardening and yard work themselves. They may have a cleaning service come in once a week, but they don't hire servants. And they may splurge on a super-cool sports car, but if it isn't a classic when they buy it, you can almost bet it will be when they sell it.

The millionaires who are most likely to *still* be millionaires ten years from now aren't those who flaunt their wealth to excite admiration or envy. They're the ones who live quietly, well within their means, and go about their business without flash or splash.

The self-made millionaire knows that becoming wealthy is not a matter of sacrifice but of choice. When you choose to become a millionaire, you undoubtedly also choose to forgo a purchase today so you can do something bigger and better tomorrow. Instant gratification holds little power over you; you find delayed gratification much more seductive and satisfying.

Working Hard — And Long

Millionaires don't believe in easy money — at least not in the sense of every get-rich-quick scheme you've ever encountered. They dream big, and they accept the reality that big dreams take time and effort to come true. They take the long view, focusing not just on what they *can* do today but on what they *have* to do today so they can do what they want to do tomorrow or next year or next decade.

They're not shy about putting in the effort it takes to realize their dreams, either. Naturally inclined to be independent, millionaires-in-the-making don't look around for others to give them what they want. Instead, they figure out what needs to be done and then they do it themselves. They scorn shortcuts, because they know these are really detours that will delay their dreams.

Winning the lottery might be nice, but millionaires-in-the-making don't trust their financial security to luck. In fact, the millionaire mindset thinks lottery tickets are a rotten investment; the risk of losing your money is astronomical compared with the odds of getting any return.

Staying Positive

Millionaires and those who become millionaires tend to be optimistic creatures. They've learned to turn negative thoughts and statements into positive ones — changing *I can't* to *How can I . . . ?* and *never* to *when.* They see opportunity even in tough times, because they know that Warren Buffett is right: If the dollar is weak, other currencies are strong.

Millionaires don't think small, but they're willing to start small. They know that even a little pile of money, with the right handling, can grow into a bigger pile. And if the pile shrinks from time to time, they don't panic, because they know that short-term losses can still lead to long-term gains.

Millionaires also tend to avoid pessimists, because negativity is contagious.

You begin where you are, even if you're deep in debt. Your current circumstances are temporary, and you can take action to change your circumstances. Even setbacks are temporary. You can't always control events, but you can always control your response to them.

Overcoming Failure

Millionaires understand that some of the things they do to create money will fail. They don't let the specter of failure keep them from acting, though, and they almost always have a backup plan ready to put in place when they do fail. Planning lets them take the risks they know that they have to take to maximize their returns.

Planning is a fluid term. The most successful millionaires-in-the-making don't rely on a single plan; they always have a backup plan in case their first plan doesn't work out. Sometimes they have three or four backup plans. And, because they do all this planning, they have enormous flexibility to react when conditions change.

Millionaires don't delude themselves into thinking that they have some sort of magical power over their finances. They take a practical, down-to-earth view that gives them the knowledge to assess real risk, the confidence to try something risky, and the ability to learn from their mistakes.

When the markets are up and the economy is rolling along, good. If the markets are down and so is the economy, it's still good — it means there are opportunities to be discovered.

Being Organized

Millionaires are the kind of people you want to do business with. They keep their promises, show up on time for appointments, and share their knowledge. If they didn't do these things, they wouldn't be millionaires — at least not for long.

They also keep tabs on their goals and their money. They get rid of the financial clutter — unwanted credit offers, stale accounts, random receipts, and unreconciled statements. These days, they often use computer programs like Quicken (www.quicken.com) to keep their finances organized; doing so cuts down dramatically on the piles of paper that otherwise can swamp your desk.

Routine can be a great friend when it comes to your finances. It keeps you focused on your goals and allows you to track your progress easily — a key factor in staying motivated. A routine also helps with the drudge work: making sure bills are paid on time, for example.

Building a Network

The term *self-made millionaire* is a little misleading, because it implies that you can do it without help from anyone else. The truth is, millionaires have a strong network of friends, business colleagues, and advisers who help them visualize and attain their goals. Certainly, you're the best judge of what wealth-building steps make sense for you. But that doesn't mean you can't take in information and suggestions from others.

It also doesn't mean you should follow the "experts" blindly. Instead, millionaires-in-the-making educate themselves about how money and specific investments work, so they can decide for themselves whether a specific action represents an opportunity to grow their wealth.

Learn from others worthy of your study, but don't place unquestioning faith in people who call themselves experts. Keep your mind open to possibilities, but use your critical-thinking skills to spot the difference between an opportunity and a waste.

Being the Boss

Not every millionaire got there by starting her own business. But the ones who will be millionaires for the rest of their lives don't delegate responsibility for their finances. Your money is *yours*. Your net worth is *yours*. And growing your money and your net worth is *your* responsibility. This is what we mean by "being the boss."

You make the decisions and handle the transactions. You don't turn your finances over to anyone else, because no one else is as interested or invested in your financial security as you are. Those cautionary tales of accountants and trust managers who run off with their clients' money? They're called cautionary tales for a reason.

Millionaires don't mind paying a fair price for services or advice. But they instinctively mistrust anyone who shows an inclination to climb into their checkbook and take control.

Striking a Balance between Money and Your Life's Work

You've undoubtedly heard some people say, "Do what you love, and the money will follow." And you've undoubtedly heard other people say, "Follow the money." Of course, there are people who choose their careers based more on how well they pay than on how much they enjoy the work. And there are people who, by accident or design, do work they love that also happens to pay well.

We believe both these philosophies miss the point. Your focus shouldn't be on choosing a job or a career for how much you'll get paid. Instead, the emphasis should be on what you do with the money you make, regardless of how much or how little it is.

The path to becoming a millionaire involves lots of decisions, and the choice of a job or career is an important one. The amount you receive is important, but so is your satisfaction with your work. Enjoyment and a sense of accomplishment can be had at all income levels (and, naturally, so can drudgery and a sense of futility). How you handle your income is more critical to your financial goals than the number on your paycheck.

Ideally, of course, you can do what you love and get paid for it — at least well enough to cover your basic expenses and have some left over to devote to your financial goals. But if that isn't possible right now — if you need to stay in a just-okay job because the pay, the schedule, or the benefits (like health insurance) are too critical to your overall well-being to give up for the time being — remember that this, too, is a choice. And if you see it as a stepping stone to a job or career more in tune with what you really enjoy doing, you can feel good about doing what you need to do now to get closer to your goals.

If your passion in life won't provide a living for you, look for something you do well that will earn you enough for today and for your long-term goals. Just remember to balance your financial needs and wants with what you really do love.

Growing, Growing, Growing

Maybe you have a set figure in your head of how much money would be "enough." Maybe you even think that, when you reach that figure, you can cross off every item on your list of goals and just bask in the glow of a job well done.

Millionaires don't think in terms of "enough"; they always think in terms of growth. Why? Because they know that when money doesn't grow, it loses value — through inflation, a downturn in the economy, or a dip in the stock market. If you aren't going forward, millionaires know, you're bound to go backward. The value of money doesn't stand still.

If you want to be a millionaire, obviously your target figure is $1 million or more. But beyond that, there is no "enough." There's only growth — or loss.

Wanting your money to grow, even if you're already worth millions, isn't a function of greed. It's simply a recognition of the fact that the value of money is always in motion. And after you've experienced moving forward, you never want to go back.

Chapter 22

Ten Ways to Find More (Of Your Own) Money

*H*ave you ever wondered why you're so strapped for cash when you're making more money than ever? You're not alone. Lots of people have no idea where their money goes and even fewer clues as to how to go about finding more of the money they already have. This is why so many Americans live paycheck to paycheck and fail to save enough to meet even unexpected emergency expenses, much less build toward their financial goals.

In this chapter, we highlight ten simple areas for you to examine in your search for the money you already have — from figuring out where you spend it (and then making adjustments) to looking for money you may have forgotten about.

Keeping Track of Your Spending

The first step in finding more of your own money is figuring out where your money goes. Most people fritter away much more money than they realize and would be hard-pressed to identify where each of their dollars went in a given day, week, or month. Having a budget helps, but merely keeping track of your regular monthly expenses — mortgage and car payments, utilities and insurance, credit cards and groceries — may not be enough to show you where you're letting your money slip through your fingers.

Try this experiment: For a week, track every bit of your spending, from the check you send to the electric company to the $3.26 you paid for this morning's coffee and doughnut. Get receipts for everything — especially when you pay cash — and write down the spending you didn't get a receipt for. At the end of the week, tally the results. You may be surprised at how much you spend on things that don't really matter much to you.

Doing the same experiment for an entire month will give you an even clearer picture of where your money goes, and that will help you identify where you can redirect your spending toward building wealth.

If the idea of redirecting your spending makes you uncomfortable, start small. Take $5 or $10 a week out of your discretionary spending, and put it aside — in your interest-bearing savings account or even in a separate account. As you get used to saving, you'll enjoy the feeling and want to save more.

Your money should work to make more money, so stashing your extra cash in the cookie jar defeats the real goal of saving that extra $5 or $10 a week. Think of it this way: Every day your money spends in the cookie jar is a day you don't earn interest from it.

Online-only savings accounts often pay two or three times the interest you'll get from your regular bank, and they usually don't have high minimum balance requirements, so you can open them with only a few dollars. You also can set them up so your money (even that $5 or $10 a week) is automatically transferred from your regular account. Go online and check out HSBC (www.hsbc.com) or ING Direct (www.ingdirect.com), or search for *online savings accounts*.

Distinguishing Between "I Need" and "I Want"

Tracking your actual spending also helps you draw the line between things you *need* to spend money on — gas for the car, for example, so you can get back and forth to work — and things you *want*, like a latte to help you over the midafternoon energy slump. Knowing the difference can help you gain control over your spending.

Sometimes, of course, needs and wants overlap. A couple years ago, Meg stood in front of a rack of spring coats at a popular retailer, lusting after a gorgeous lilac raincoat. At first, she was aware only that she wanted it, but the $70 price tag made her pause. She argued with herself for several minutes, trying to decide whether wanting that coat was a good enough reason to spend $70 (see "Assigning Your Own Value to Purchases," later in this chapter). She still hadn't resolved that point when she realized that her London Fog raincoat was (a) 11 years old and (b) disfigured by an ugly blotch where some careless hand had spilled bleach sometime earlier. The serendipitous dovetailing of want and need prompted Meg to buy the $70 raincoat, and the two have lived happily together ever since.

We're not arguing that buying stuff you want but don't need is wrong. Quite the contrary: What's the point of making your millions if you can't do what you want to do with it? But, for many people, giving in mindlessly to the instant-gratification factor does more than just delay the realization of their financial goals — it makes reaching those goals all but impossible.

Here are some questions to ask yourself to figure out the difference between what you need and what you want:

- **What will you use this purchase for?** Will it save you time, energy, or money? Will it help you do something you must do or want to do?

- **When will you use this purchase?** Does it make more sense to spend the money now or wait a while? What are the pros and cons of buying it now versus waiting?

- **What do you give up if you make this purchase now?** Do you have to dip into your savings? Put off your plan to pay down debt? Delay another purchase you were thinking of making?

    The cost of any purchase isn't merely the sum of its price and the sales tax. Whenever you spend money, you may be passing up an opportunity to have that money work for you in a different way.

- **Is "wanting it" a good enough reason for you to spend the money now?** Sometimes the answer to this question is "yes," and that's okay.

Don't go shopping — either in person or online — when you're feeling blue. A 2007 study funded by the National Institutes of Health and the National Science Foundation shows that people spend a lot more money when they're feeling sad and self-absorbed than when they're on a more even emotional keel — and often you're not even aware of why you're spending more. Buying something extravagant may give you a momentary mood boost, but it also can lead to a great deal of buyer's remorse when you emerge from your feeling-down period.

Assigning Your Own Value to Purchases

Ignore the price tag on an item you're interested in. Instead, before you go out to purchase something — a car, a flat-screen TV, even today's lunch — decide how much that something is worth to you. When you set your own price point, you're less likely to overspend on a passing fancy.

The trick is to decide not how much an item is worth, but how much it's worth *to you*. Say you'd like a flat-screen TV. There may be all kinds of benefits to having one: You could get rid of your clunky old entertainment center; you won't have to worry about the switch to digital broadcast; you could finally watch the high-definition cable or satellite channels you're paying for but can't watch now. How much are those benefits worth to you? Five hundred dollars? Eight hundred? Twenty-five hundred? Thinking of purchases in this way lets you step back from the giddy passion of spending and assess what really matters to you.

It also empowers you in your spending choices. When you realize that you're not willing to fork over more than X dollars for something, you'll find that those once-unending yearnings for the trappings of a rich lifestyle fade away. You feel free to walk away if the price doesn't match what the item is worth to you.

Being willing and able to walk away from something you'd like to have because the deal isn't quite right for you puts you in charge of your spending.

It used to be that negotiating the price was done only at garage sales and car dealerships. But, particularly in a sluggish economy, there may be some wiggle room on prices even at big retailers. Don't be shy about asking for discounts or freebies to go along with your purchase. You may be able to get a substantial discount for a demo model, or wangle things like free delivery and installation of appliances or electronics, for example, or discounts on service agreements.

Avoiding Bargains That Really Aren't

People who lived through the Great Depression (or who were reared by people who lived through it) probably are familiar with the saying "I can't afford a bargain." Too often, things that look like good deals at first glance turn out to be black holes that suck up your hard-earned cash.

Here are some indicators of faux bargains:

- ✔ **It's something you won't use.** Books you won't read, software programs you won't install, CDs you won't listen to, DVDs you won't watch, exercise equipment you won't use, and clothes or shoes you won't wear — all these things do is take up space in your life without adding any value to your lifestyle. In fact, spending money on these things instead of investing it in stuff you actually will use ends up threatening your lifestyle.

- ✔ **It's something you'll have to replace early and often.** Poor-quality goods that don't last may be cheaper to begin with, but they can be enormously expensive in the long run. If you really want a buttery leather messenger bag to carry your laptop in, set aside money for the genuine article instead of throwing your money away on a series of cheap and cheaply made ones.

Money you spend on a "bargain" item is money that you can't use to buy a higher-quality version. If you allow yourself to get caught in the bargain trap, that genuine leather messenger bag could cost you twice as much as (or more than) the original price, by the time you add up all the money you spent on not-nearly-as-good substitutes.

- ✔ **You wouldn't be interested in it at full price.** If the main (or only) reason an item catches your eye is that it's cheaper than normal, ask yourself whether you would be willing to buy it at full price. Just asking yourself this question makes you stop to think about the purchase instead of being hypnotized by the prospect of short-term savings.

- ✔ **Your initial thought is that you can always put it in your garage sale later.** If you're thinking about selling something before you even buy it, and if that something isn't a valuable piece of artwork or a similar commodity, it's probably not a wise use of your money. Keep your wallet closed, and continue your search for something you like better.

Spending Now to Save Later

Most people are familiar with the savings that can be gleaned from purchasing food in bulk; the per-pound price of meat, for example, generally is lower when you buy several pounds at once and freeze it for future use. However — and this is a big *however* — if you end up throwing out the meat because it spoils or gets freezer burn before you use it, it's a darned expensive bargain.

Spending now to save later is the opposite of chasing so-called "bargains." The upfront cost often is greater, but it's offset by savings later on. Things that fall under this category include

✔ Insulating your house to conserve heating and cooling energy

✔ Installing energy-efficient appliances to reduce utility costs

✔ Having your car tuned up regularly to cut the odds of major repairs later

✔ Purchasing equipment for your home-based or small business to improve productivity or revenue or cut future costs

Those are some of the more obvious ways you can spend to save. But that theory also is the premise behind your retirement plans, your investment portfolio, and most of your other major financial decisions.

Think about it: You spend money today to fund your 401(k) or individual retirement account (IRA) so you can (presumably) save money on taxes when you retire. By spending money on investments today, you save yourself the (presumably) higher prices those same investments will cost later on.

One of the biggest ways you can save later is by spending more on your mortgage today. If you make the equivalent of one extra payment a year, you'll shave about seven years off a 30-year mortgage and save yourself tens of thousands of dollars in interest.

There are dozens of online calculators that show you how much you can save by making extra mortgage payments. Try DecisionAide Analytics (www.decisionaide.com), BankSITE (www.banksite.com), or Bloomberg.com (www.bloomberg.com) — or go to your favorite search engine and search for *mortgage prepayment calculator.*

Getting Rid of Credit Card Balances

Back in the old days, credit card companies made money even from those customers who paid their balances in full every month by charging annual fees for the privilege of carrying their card in your wallet. Today, annual fees have pretty much disappeared, but the credit card companies are still making plenty of money — from interest, late fees, over-limit fees, and transaction fees. In fact, between 2003 and 2007, the industry's profits rose from $27.4 billion to nearly $41 billion. Most of the industry's revenues come from interest, but a big chunk — almost 40 percent — comes from fees. Even more profitable for the credit card companies: behavior that triggers a fee, like making a payment late or going over your credit limit, because these things often prompt an interest-rate hike, too.

The only way to avoid interest and fees is to pay off your credit card balance every month. If you can't do that, pay as much as you can toward the balance until it is paid off, and don't use it for any other purchases until then.

Some credit card companies are considering establishing fees for customers who pay off their balances every month. Read the fine print on your existing cards and any cards you're thinking of applying for to make sure there's no penalty for using your credit card responsibly.

Minimum payments are structured to yield the highest returns for the credit card company. If you make only the minimum monthly payment on a $2,000 balance at 14 percent interest, you'll pay more than $1,500 in interest over the $14\frac{1}{2}$ years it takes you to pay it off.

If you're carrying a balance on more than one credit card, pay the most on the card with the highest interest rate first. When that's paid off, you can concentrate on eliminating the balance of the card with the next-highest interest rate, and so on until they're all paid off.

To figure out how getting a lower interest rate or making more than the minimum payment can affect your credit card debt, go to www.bankrate.com/ brm/calc/MinPayment.asp. You can figure out how long it will take you to pay off your credit card at the current interest rate and minimum payment, and compare that to lower rates or larger monthly payments.

You may be able to save a lot of money by transferring balances from a high-interest card to a lower- or no-interest offer, but be sure to read the fine print carefully. Most balance transfer offers carry a fee, typically 3 percent or 4 percent of the balance you're transferring. Sometimes there's a cap of $75 or $100, but if there isn't a cap, you could end up paying more.

Eliminating Hidden Fees

Credit card companies aren't the only ones hiding fees in the fine print. Your mortgage company, your bank, your airline, your phone company, your stock broker, and even your trash collector may be collecting fees from you that you aren't aware of. Sometimes these fees are unavoidable; fuel surcharges, for example, have become common among airlines, cruise ships, and trash collectors since gas prices began hovering around the $3-a-gallon mark.

In some cases, though, you may be able to find ways around paying the fee. If your bank charges a fee for your checking or savings account, look around for no-fee accounts. Fees at credit unions are generally lower than at traditional banks, and they often don't have a minimum balance requirement. You probably won't earn interest on your checking account, but interest rates on savings, money-market, and certificate of deposit (CD) accounts are usually comparable to bank rates.

Debit cards sometimes carry fees for using them, like credit cards. It may be only a few cents per transaction, but that can add up quickly if you use your debit card to pay for groceries, gas, and other regular purchases. Select the "credit" option whenever possible, and you'll avoid those niggling fees.

Beware of prepayment fees on anything, from your mortgage to credit cards to auto loans. These fees are set to discourage you from getting rid of debt — thereby saving yourself a ton in interest payments. Always ask whether there's any penalty for paying your balance off early, and if the answer is yes, walk away.

Maximizing Tax Deductions

Don't give Uncle Sam more money than you have to. Keep good records so you can claim deductions you're entitled to at tax time, and make sure you're not having too much withheld from your paycheck.

If you get a big refund every year, it means you're giving the government an interest-free loan.

To get the most out of your pretax and tax-deferred or even tax-free options:

✔ Sign up for your employer's pretax benefits, like health insurance premiums or health savings accounts and 401(k) plans.

✔ Open a traditional IRA to take advantage of tax deductions now and a lower tax rate later.

✔ Open a Roth IRA; you don't get any tax benefit now, but you don't have to pay tax — ever — on the interest you earn.

See Chapter 17 for more information on withholding and tax deductions.

Using Coupons, Rebates, and Rewards Programs

Sometimes coupons, rebates, and rewards programs can give you killer deals on things you would use anyway, but sometimes they can lead you to spend money you otherwise would hold on to. Apply the same critical thinking to these offers that you use for your other purchases.

Here are some questions to ask yourself:

✔ **How does this save me money?** Coupons that offer $1 off the purchase of two items save you 50¢ per item. That's great if you'll use two right away. But if one of the items is going to sit in your cupboard for weeks or months, you may be better off forgoing the 50¢ discount.

✔ **Will I mail in the rebate forms?** An estimated four out of ten rebates are never claimed, which means manufacturers and retailers get to keep the money you thought you would save by getting the rebate. Be honest with yourself when considering rebate offers on potential purchases: Will you really go through all the steps required to claim a $3 rebate on that cordless phone or ink cartridge? If not, don't let the mere offer of a rebate influence your purchase.

✔ **What does it cost me to get the reward?** Some reward programs will sign you up for free; those are the best deals. Other programs charge a membership fee, and for those you'll have to run the numbers. Spending $25 to join a reward program at a store you visit only once or twice a year may not give you any net savings. But if the program saves you 20 percent at a store you visit at least once a month, the membership fee likely will pay for itself within a couple months, and you can still enjoy the savings for the remainder of the year.

Finding Lost Money

Ever wonder if you or your relatives have left money in a bank account or pension fund and forgotten about it? You may even be solicited by companies who offer to find this "lost" money for you — for a fee. But you can do your own search for free. Here are some good places to start:

✔ The National Association of Unclaimed Property Administrators has a Web site (www.missingmoney.com) with links to individual state programs.

- ✔ The U.S. Treasury Department keeps records of unclaimed savings bonds and bonds that have stopped earning interest but haven't been cashed in. Go to `www.treasurydirect.gov/indiv/tools/tools_treasuryhunt.htm` and click the Treasury Hunt button. You can use your Social Security number to find out if any savings bonds have been issued to you.

- ✔ The Pension Benefit Guaranty Corporation's Web site (`http://search.pbgc.gov/mp`) can help you find forgotten pension accounts from previous jobs.

Before you start your search for lost money, plan what you'll do with anything you find. A good generic plan, which works for any amount of "found" money, is to save half and use the other half for something you want.

Chapter 23

Ten Ways to Make Your Money Work Harder

In This Chapter

▷ Making saving a priority

▷ Getting your money to earn more money

▷ Finding free money from others

▷ Staying in it for the long haul

The secret to building wealth lies not in making more money, but in making the money you already have earn more money for you. This basic fact is often the main philosophical difference between millionaires and wannabes: The money you make by your own effort — from your job, your business, or any other source — is paltry compared to what you can make by putting your money to work for you. Here, we share our favorite simple steps for getting your money to make more money.

Paying Yourself First

Benjamin Franklin said it best: "If you would be wealthy, think of saving as well as getting." Add saving into your budget, and pay your savings bill as you do any other bill. If you can (and most banks and credit unions will do this), have your savings automatically deducted from every paycheck. Even better: Put your savings in an account that you can't access with an ATM card. That way, you won't be tempted to spend it needlessly.

Making Your Money Earn Its Keep

Albert Einstein called compound interest "the most powerful force in the universe." We think it's pretty cool, too, because not only does your own money make more money, but the extra money your money makes also makes money for you.

Huh?

Here's how compound interest works. Say you deposit $100 in an account with a 3 percent interest rate. If you were earning only simple interest, you'd have $103 at the end of a year. But with *compound interest* (figured on a quarterly basis), you actually end up with $103.03 at the end of the year, because you earn interest on both your initial deposit *and* the interest your initial deposit generates. If you add $100 every month to that same account, at the end of the year you'll have $1,223.81 — $1,200 that you invested, and $23.81 in compound interest earnings.

Compound interest is why you often see two rates in advertisements for savings accounts, certificates of deposit (CDs), and so on. The annual percentage rate (APR) is the interest rate on the account. The annual percentage yield (APY) is the percentage the account actually earns, thanks to compound interest. The APY usually is a fraction of a percent higher than the APR, and that fraction of a percent depends on whether the interest is compounded monthly, quarterly, or annually.

You can find lots of compound-interest calculators on the Internet. Try moneychimp (www.moneychimp.com/calculator) or Young Money (www.youngmoney.com/calculators). Calculators like these make it easy to determine where you'll get the biggest return on your savings; you just plug in the amount you're saving, the percentage rate, and how often interest is compounded. You can even look forward 5, 10, 20, or more years to see how your savings will grow if you stick with your plan.

Traditional savings accounts don't pay much in interest these days, so shop around for the best deals. An online-only account may pay three or more times the interest offered by your regular bank or credit union; check out ING Direct (www.ingdirect.com) or HSBC (www.hsbc.com) on the Internet, or go to Bankrate.com (www.bankrate.com) and search for interest rates on various kinds of accounts.

When you're just starting out with your savings plan, look for an account that offers reasonable interest with no minimum balance. Some financial institutions require you to maintain a balance of $2,500 or even $5,000 to qualify for higher interest rates. If your balance dips below the threshold for even one day of the month, you may forfeit the more favorable interest for that month.

After you've got a good amount built up in your savings, you can decide whether it makes sense to put your excess savings in a higher-interest savings account or invest it elsewhere.

Your money can't work for you if it's sitting in a coffee can or even in an account that doesn't pay interest. And every day you delay putting money in an interest-bearing account is a day you lose out on the magic of compound interest.

Socking Away Money in CDs and Money-Market Accounts

Certificates of deposit give you a higher interest rate in exchange for a promise that you'll keep the CD for a set period. The terms usually range from six months to five years — the longer the term, the more favorable the interest rate. If you cash out the CD before the term expires, you'll pay a penalty — usually the equivalent of a month's or a quarter's interest. The penalty is higher for longer-term CDs.

CDs are particularly useful if you have trouble thinking of your savings as untouchable. The threat of paying a penalty (which can affect your principal, if you cash out before your money has earned any interest) is a pretty good motivator for leaving your CD alone. On the other hand, because of the penalties for cashing them out early, CDs aren't as liquid as regular savings accounts, so you shouldn't use them as your sole savings vehicles.

If you aren't sure whether you're comfortable with tying up your savings in a long-term CD, try starting small. Some institutions offer six-month CDs for as little as $500, and, if you don't need the money at the end of the six months, you can roll it into another six-month CD.

Most banks and credit unions give you a couple of weeks to decide whether you want to cash out your CD when it matures. If you don't give them other instructions, the full amount of your CD, including the interest you've earned, will be rolled over into a new CD (with the same time restriction, and at the current interest rate, which could be the same as or higher or lower than the rate on the original CD).

Money-market accounts let you earn interest without tying up your cash for a fixed time. You can get them at your bank or credit union for either checking or savings accounts, and they're usually insured just like any other checking or savings accounts. Some institutions require you to keep a minimum balance in the account to earn the advertised interest rate; some also charge a fee for these accounts. Shop around to see what deals are available in your area. If you can't find something you like, search online for money-market accounts that you can link to your regular account.

Money-market *accounts* are not the same as money-market *funds.* Accounts are offered at banks and credit unions, are usually insured by the federal government, and are less risky investments than money-market funds. Money-market funds are usually offered through stockbrokers, may include investments that aren't backed by the federal government, and usually offer a slightly higher rate of return (in recognition of their slightly higher risk) than money-market accounts.

Money-market funds are a mainstay of any fund family, like Vanguard or Fidelity. These fund families want a place where shareholders can park their money between investments. Although money-market funds are not federally insured, fund families in the past have always covered any problems that sent the value below $1 per share. So, although technically money-market funds carry a slightly higher risk than money-market accounts, they are still very safe investments.

Maximizing Matching Funds

If you have a 401(k) plan at work and your employer offers any kind of match, make sure you're contributing enough to take full advantage of the match. If you don't, you're just throwing free money away. And you're not just forgoing the principal your employer is offering — you're losing out on the miracle of compound interest on that principal, too.

Say your employer will contribute 50¢ for every $1 you put in your 401(k), up to 3 percent of your annual pay. And say that your annual pay is $30,000. If you put in the full 3 percent, you contribute $900 a year to your account, and your employer contributes another $450, for a total of $1,350. If your account yields 6 percent in earnings in one year, you've got $1,431 at the end of 12 months.

But if you put in only 2 percent, you contribute $600 and your employer contributes only $300, for a total of $900. At the end of a year, assuming the same 6 percent yield, you've got only $954. Not only did you lose out on $150 of your employer's money, but also, you lost out on the money that extra $150 could have earned for you.

The more principal you have working for you, the more interest you earn, and the more interest you earn, the more money you have working for you to earn more.

Finding Free Money

Your 401(k) plan isn't the only place to find free money. Here are some things to check out:

- ✔ **Banks and credit unions:** Financial institutions are always trying to attract new customers, and sometimes they offer cash rewards for opening accounts or referring friends.

- ✔ **Rewards programs:** Airlines, hotel chains, credit card companies, and even groceries stores offer rewards programs to build loyalty among their customers and attract new ones. If it's something you would use anyway, and if there's no fee for joining, go ahead and sign up. You may end up with unexpected savings on something else — airline programs often team up with florists, for example, for specials on Valentine's Day and Mother's Day — and even if all you earn is a free greeting card, you're a couple of bucks ahead.

- ✔ **Cash discounts:** Gas stations sometimes offer a break on the per-gallon price if you pay cash instead of using your credit or debit card. They can do this because card companies charge the gas station a fee for processing each credit transaction; if you pay cash, there is no processing fee, so the gas station still makes a profit on the sale. Check with other retailers to see if they offer cash discounts, too.

Saving for Major Purchases

If you're going to be in the market for a car, a house, or even a computer or plasma TV in the next two, three, or four years, set up a separate savings account specifically for that purchase. Online accounts and CDs are excellent choices for this kind of targeted saving, because you'll be less tempted to dip into them for other things, and you'll earn a higher interest rate than you would with a regular savings account. Plus, you put the power of compound interest to work, and the earnings can be used to help you buy the thing you're saving for.

Saving for purchases makes better financial sense than using credit cards, especially if you won't be able to pay off your credit card bill all at once. When you save money, your money has a chance to earn more money. When you whip out the credit card, your credit card company has a chance to earn more money.

Funding Traditional IRAs

Individual retirement accounts (IRAs) not only make your money work harder, but they save you money, too. Depending on your income, you can deduct all or part of your annual contribution on your income taxes, which lowers the amount of tax you owe. They also can save you money in retirement if you're in a lower tax bracket then than you are now.

Taking Advantage of Roth IRAs

Roth IRAs don't give you any tax savings today, but because the earnings on them are never taxed, they can save you a ton of money in the long run. Talk about finding free money: Unlike virtually any other savings plan, you never have to declare the interest and dividends from a Roth IRA as income, as long as you wait until you're at least $59^1/_2$ years old before you withdraw anything from your Roth.

Saving for College with 529 Plans

529 plans are named for the section of the federal tax code that deals with state- or college-sponsored savings and tuition prepayment programs. Depending on the plan, you either prebuy credits at the current state-college or university tuition rate (part or all of which can be transferred to a private or out-of-state college when your child reaches college age), or you save whatever amount you like and use the fund to help pay your child's college costs.

You don't get to deduct 529 contributions on your federal taxes, but if the money is, in fact, used for your child's college expenses, you don't have to pay taxes on the interest or dividends your 529 plan earns. Some states do allow you to deduct your contributions; check with your state's tax authority to find out what the rules are where you live.

529 plans are investment vehicles similar to 401(k)s and IRAs. There are penalties for taking the money out early or using it for something other than college costs. Check out the Securities and Exchange Commission's Web site (www.sec.gov/investor/pubs/intro529.htm) for detailed information on the different 529 plans and the rules governing them.

You can earn extra money for your 529 plan by joining Upromise, an organization that offers rewards based on purchases you make with their network of participating companies. You can even have family members and friends sign up so their purchases can add to your college savings plan, too. And joining is free. Check out `www.upromise.com` for full details on this program.

Taking the Long View

Building wealth takes time, even with the power of compound interest. The "rule of 72" can give you a general idea of how long it will take to double your money: Divide 72 by the interest rate you get on your savings. If you're earning 6 percent, it will take about 12 years for your money to double ($72 \div 6 = 12$). If you earn 8 percent, your money will double in about 9 years. Even at 10 percent, it'll take about 7 years for your money to double.

Our point is that, even at generous rates of return, you're not going to be rich tomorrow (unless you're already rich today). If you save $1,000 this month and spend it next month, you're right back where you started. Actually, you're a bit behind where you started, because you can't gain back the time that $1,000 could have been working for you.

To make your money work for you, you have to leave it alone and let it do its job, which is to earn more money.

Chapter 24

Ten Ways You Can Tell You're a Millionaire

In This Chapter

▷ Enjoying your freedom of choice
▷ Following your own good habits
▷ Rising on the stepping stones of growth
▷ Basking in the glow of success

Sure, you can look at your net worth and see at a glance whether you're above or below that seven-figure threshold. But being a millionaire is as much about attitude as it is about the bottom line. Here are some ways you can tell you've really arrived in the millionaire class — attitude and all.

What Got You Here Stays with You

Those good habits you developed during your accumulation phase don't just disappear once you've reached your magic number wealthwise. You still make conscious choices about your spending. You still assign your own value to purchases and pass on them if the asking price is more than the thing is worth to you. You still write down your goals and remind yourself of them regularly. You don't believe in financial shortcuts, and you can smell a fishy financial scheme from 50 miles away.

You Work Because You Want To

When you hear people say they'd quit their jobs in an instant if they won the lottery, you shake your head almost pityingly, because you know better. You know that work gives you a sense of purpose and accomplishment. It provides a challenge, which wards off boredom and depression. It gives you an outlet for your creative energy and buoys your sense of *self*-worth — not just your net worth.

To be sure, some millionaires amass their fortunes doing jobs they don't like. But as soon as they've achieved their financial goals, they typically switch careers to something they really do enjoy; in fact, being able to do the work you love is a major motivator for accumulating wealth in the first place.

And that's a big advantage to having wealth: You don't work because you need the income to make ends meet. You work because you want to — because you've found something that challenges and inspires you and makes you want to get up in the morning.

You Focus on Yourself — Not on What Others Have

Envy, peer pressure, and keeping up with the Joneses are things of the past for you. You have a clear vision of what you want and what your values are, and you aren't tempted to follow the crowd just for the sake of fitting in. Sure, you investigate new opportunities, analyzing them with an open mind. But you aren't swayed by flattery, hyperbole, or pretty arguments; you trust your own judgment.

Because you're focused on yourself, you don't view making and managing money as a competition; after all, you can't compete without an opponent, and if you aren't focused on what other people are doing, you can't see them as opponents. Other people may not understand the choices you make, either financially or in other areas of your life, but that doesn't really concern you, because you've learned to listen to yourself and do what makes sense for you.

You Update Your Goals

Franklin Roosevelt once said, "No one ever got anywhere by standing still." You know that complacence is the antithesis of achievement, and continual goal setting is the trick to avoiding complacence. Some of your goals still are financial — partly because today's other goals may cost more than the ones you set when you were just starting to build wealth, and partly because you know that financial growth is your only insurance against inflation and the subsequent devaluing of what you've already amassed.

You also know that the passage of time and your own personal growth and experience influence both your goals and your priorities. You're flexible enough to recognize and act on these changes, and strong enough to figure out how to meet new challenges.

You Stay Informed and in Control

No one cares about your financial health as much as you do. You seek out and listen to others' advice and opinions, but you don't abdicate your financial authority to anyone else; you have the final say in how your money is managed. This attitude protects you from hucksters and charlatans, and it keeps you from falling for style over substance.

You understand that competently managing your money requires thought and energy. You're happy to invest that thought and energy because you're focused, as no one else can or should be, on what you want for yourself. You enjoy being in charge of your finances because it gives you a sense of independence, confidence, and security.

You Say No

You're comfortable saying no when it's appropriate — not to be mean or hard-hearted, but because whatever's being proposed isn't in either your or the requester's best interests. You know there's a difference between a hand up and a handout, and you know that a hand up does more good in the long run.

Maybe you've been approached by friends or relatives who want you to bail them out of a jam, or invest in their business, or finance their education. Maybe they've tried to play on your sympathy for their circumstances or the guilt they expect you to feel for being in different, better circumstances. Maybe they think that, because you have money, you should always foot the bill for dinners out, parties, and extravagant gifts.

But you recognize these pleas for what they are: a surefire way to sabotage everything you've worked for, with no guarantee that your investment will pay off for you or anyone else. You can say no without feeling guilty, and, because you can do that, you can say yes with genuine enthusiasm.

You See the Benefits of Risk

You may have trouble understanding people who are more risk-averse than you are. You know that the formula for building wealth always boils down to maximizing return while minimizing risk, so you may be puzzled when others make choices that don't really maximize their returns.

You've learned how to manage risk, so it doesn't scare you. In fact, you may even be more leery of something that's too safe, because you know safety limits opportunity. You still weigh risks carefully and do what you can to minimize them, but you're not afraid to take calculated risks. You can see the line between sensible and foolish, and you're rarely, if ever, tempted to cross it.

You're Prepared

You don't take things for granted — not your current situation, nor the future. Sure, you know that if your fortune were wiped out by another stock-market crash, you could always rebuild it. But you're not worried about that happening, because you haven't put all your financial eggs in Wall Street's basket. Your finances are diversified and balanced so you can weather a storm from virtually any direction.

You're also prepared for other contingencies. You've got health insurance to protect you now and in the case of a major illness. You've got good insurance coverage on your home, your car, and your other belongings. You've got enough life insurance to provide for your loved ones. You've figured out how you want your assets distributed among your heirs, and you've put your wishes in writing.

You Enjoy the Abundance in Your Life

You know that wealth and abundance are not the same thing. Having money gives you more choices, but often the things you choose are the things that are available to all: the company of friends, the love of family, the warmth of the sun on your face, the cool of the grass on your feet. Openness and generosity of spirit are second nature, and you applaud others' successes as sincerely as you celebrate your own.

You know that others can do what you've done, because the "secrets" you've employed are really matters of choice, common sense, dedication, and patience. You encourage others to look for opportunities and freely share the knowledge you've gained from your own experience.

You Count Your Blessings

Part of enjoying the abundance in your life is focusing on what you have, not on what you lack. This is the attitude that got you to millionaire status, and this is the attitude that helps keep you there. You understand that you are among the most fortunate of the world's citizens, even if you've made some mistakes or encountered some setbacks.

You have a sense of gratitude and accomplishment but not one of entitlement. You know that you've earned your success, and you don't feel guilty about enjoying it.

You believe in living an examined life — one in which your physical needs are met; your wants are in line with your moral compass; and your mental, emotional, and spiritual health carry their proper weight in decision-making.

Index

• E •

• N •

• O •

BUSINESS, CAREERS & PERSONAL FINANCE

Accounting For Dummies, 4th Edition*
978-0-470-24600-9

Bookkeeping Workbook For Dummies†
978-0-470-16983-4

Commodities For Dummies
978-0-470-04928-0

Doing Business in China For Dummies
978-0-470-04929-7

E-Mail Marketing For Dummies
978-0-470-19087-6

Job Interviews For Dummies, 3rd Edition*†
978-0-470-17748-8

Personal Finance Workbook For Dummies*†
978-0-470-09933-9

Real Estate License Exams For Dummies
978-0-7645-7623-2

Six Sigma For Dummies
978-0-7645-6798-8

Small Business Kit For Dummies, 2nd Edition*†
978-0-7645-5984-6

Telephone Sales For Dummies
978-0-470-16836-3

BUSINESS PRODUCTIVITY & MICROSOFT OFFICE

Access 2007 For Dummies
978-0-470-03649-5

Excel 2007 For Dummies
978-0-470-03737-9

Office 2007 For Dummies
978-0-470-00923-9

Outlook 2007 For Dummies
978-0-470-03830-7

PowerPoint 2007 For Dummies
978-0-470-04059-1

Project 2007 For Dummies
978-0-470-03651-8

QuickBooks 2008 For Dummies
978-0-470-18470-7

Quicken 2008 For Dummies
978-0-470-17473-9

Salesforce.com For Dummies, 2nd Edition
978-0-470-04893-1

Word 2007 For Dummies
978-0-470-03658-7

EDUCATION, HISTORY, REFERENCE & TEST PREPARATION

African American History For Dummies
978-0-7645-5469-8

Algebra For Dummies
978-0-7645-5325-7

Algebra Workbook For Dummies
978-0-7645-8467-1

Art History For Dummies
978-0-470-09910-0

ASVAB For Dummies, 2nd Edition
978-0-470-10671-6

British Military History For Dummies
978-0-470-03213-8

Calculus For Dummies
978-0-7645-2498-1

Canadian History For Dummies, 2nd Edition
978-0-470-83656-9

Geometry Workbook For Dummies
978-0-471-79940-5

The SAT I For Dummies, 6th Edition
978-0-7645-7193-0

Series 7 Exam For Dummies
978-0-470-09932-2

World History For Dummies
978-0-7645-5242-7

FOOD, GARDEN, HOBBIES & HOME

Bridge For Dummies, 2nd Edition
978-0-471-92426-5

Coin Collecting For Dummies, 2nd Edition
978-0-470-22275-1

Cooking Basics For Dummies, 3rd Edition
978-0-7645-7206-7

Drawing For Dummies
978-0-7645-5476-6

Etiquette For Dummies, 2nd Edition
978-0-470-10672-3

Gardening Basics For Dummies*†
978-0-470-03749-2

Knitting Patterns For Dummies
978-0-470-04556-5

Living Gluten-Free For Dummies†
978-0-471-77383-2

Painting Do-It-Yourself For Dummies
978-0-470-17533-0

HEALTH, SELF HELP, PARENTING & PETS

Anger Management For Dummies
978-0-470-03715-7

Anxiety & Depression Workbook For Dummies
978-0-7645-9793-0

Dieting For Dummies, 2nd Edition
978-0-7645-4149-0

Dog Training For Dummies, 2nd Edition
978-0-7645-8418-3

Horseback Riding For Dummies
978-0-470-09719-9

Infertility For Dummies†
978-0-470-11518-3

Meditation For Dummies with CD-ROM, 2nd Edition
978-0-471-77774-8

Post-Traumatic Stress Disorder For Dummies
978-0-470-04922-8

Puppies For Dummies, 2nd Edition
978-0-470-03717-1

Thyroid For Dummies, 2nd Edition†
978-0-471-78755-6

Type 1 Diabetes For Dummies*†
978-0-470-17811-9

* Separate Canadian edition also available
† Separate U.K. edition also available

WILEY

INTERNET & DIGITAL MEDIA

AdWords For Dummies
978-0-470-15252-2

Blogging For Dummies, 2nd Edition
978-0-470-23017-6

**Digital Photography All-in-One
Desk Reference For Dummies, 3rd Edition**
978-0-470-03743-0

Digital Photography For Dummies, 5th Edition
978-0-7645-9802-9

**Digital SLR Cameras & Photography
For Dummies, 2nd Edition**
978-0-470-14927-0

**eBay Business All-in-One Desk Reference
For Dummies**
978-0-7645-8438-1

eBay For Dummies, 5th Edition*
978-0-470-04529-9

eBay Listings That Sell For Dummies
978-0-471-78912-3

Facebook For Dummies
978-0-470-26273-3

The Internet For Dummies, 11th Edition
978-0-470-12174-0

Investing Online For Dummies, 5th Edition
978-0-7645-8456-5

iPod & iTunes For Dummies, 5th Edition
978-0-470-17474-6

MySpace For Dummies
978-0-470-09529-4

Podcasting For Dummies
978-0-471-74898-4

**Search Engine Optimization
For Dummies, 2nd Edition**
978-0-471-97998-2

Second Life For Dummies
978-0-470-18025-9

**Starting an eBay Business For Dummies,
3rd Edition†**
978-0-470-14924-9

GRAPHICS, DESIGN & WEB DEVELOPMENT

**Adobe Creative Suite 3 Design Premium
All-in-One Desk Reference For Dummies**
978-0-470-11724-8

**Adobe Web Suite CS3 All-in-One Desk
Reference For Dummies**
978-0-470-12099-6

AutoCAD 2008 For Dummies
978-0-470-11650-0

**Building a Web Site For Dummies,
3rd Edition**
978-0-470-14928-7

**Creating Web Pages All-in-One Desk
Reference For Dummies, 3rd Edition**
978-0-470-09629-1

**Creating Web Pages For Dummies,
8th Edition**
978-0-470-08030-6

Dreamweaver CS3 For Dummies
978-0-470-11490-2

Flash CS3 For Dummies
978-0-470-12100-9

Google SketchUp For Dummies
978-0-470-13744-4

InDesign CS3 For Dummies
978-0-470-11865-8

**Photoshop CS3 All-in-One
Desk Reference For Dummies**
978-0-470-11195-6

Photoshop CS3 For Dummies
978-0-470-11193-2

Photoshop Elements 5 For Dummies
978-0-470-09810-3

SolidWorks For Dummies
978-0-7645-9555-4

Visio 2007 For Dummies
978-0-470-08983-5

Web Design For Dummies, 2nd Edition
978-0-471-78117-2

Web Sites Do-It-Yourself For Dummies
978-0-470-16903-2

Web Stores Do-It-Yourself For Dummies
978-0-470-17443-2

LANGUAGES, RELIGION & SPIRITUALITY

Arabic For Dummies
978-0-471-77270-5

Chinese For Dummies, Audio Set
978-0-470-12766-7

French For Dummies
978-0-7645-5193-2

German For Dummies
978-0-7645-5195-6

Hebrew For Dummies
978-0-7645-5489-6

Ingles Para Dummies
978-0-7645-5427-8

Italian For Dummies, Audio Set
978-0-470-09586-7

Italian Verbs For Dummies
978-0-471-77389-4

Japanese For Dummies
978-0-7645-5429-2

Latin For Dummies
978-0-7645-5431-5

Portuguese For Dummies
978-0-471-78738-9

Russian For Dummies
978-0-471-78001-4

Spanish Phrases For Dummies
978-0-7645-7204-3

Spanish For Dummies
978-0-7645-5194-9

Spanish For Dummies, Audio Set
978-0-470-09585-0

The Bible For Dummies
978-0-7645-5296-0

Catholicism For Dummies
978-0-7645-5391-2

The Historical Jesus For Dummies
978-0-470-16785-4

Islam For Dummies
978-0-7645-5503-9

**Spirituality For Dummies,
2nd Edition**
978-0-470-19142-2

NETWORKING AND PROGRAMMING

ASP.NET 3.5 For Dummies
978-0-470-19592-5

C# 2008 For Dummies
978-0-470-19109-5

Hacking For Dummies, 2nd Edition
978-0-470-05235-8

Home Networking For Dummies, 4th Edition
978-0-470-11806-1

Java For Dummies, 4th Edition
978-0-470-08716-9

**Microsoft® SQL Server™ 2008 All-in-One
Desk Reference For Dummies**
978-0-470-17954-3

**Networking All-in-One Desk Reference
For Dummies, 2nd Edition**
978-0-7645-9939-2

**Networking For Dummies,
8th Edition**
978-0-470-05620-2

SharePoint 2007 For Dummies
978-0-470-09941-4

**Wireless Home Networking
For Dummies, 2nd Edition**
978-0-471-74940-0

OPERATING SYSTEMS & COMPUTER BASICS

iMac For Dummies, 5th Edition
978-0-7645-8458-9

Laptops For Dummies, 2nd Edition
978-0-470-05432-1

Linux For Dummies, 8th Edition
978-0-470-11649-4

MacBook For Dummies
978-0-470-04859-7

**Mac OS X Leopard All-in-One
Desk Reference For Dummies**
978-0-470-05434-5

Mac OS X Leopard For Dummies
978-0-470-05433-8

Macs For Dummies, 9th Edition
978-0-470-04849-8

PCs For Dummies, 11th Edition
978-0-470-13728-4

Windows® Home Server For Dummies
978-0-470-18592-6

Windows Server 2008 For Dummies
978-0-470-18043-3

**Windows Vista All-in-One
Desk Reference For Dummies**
978-0-471-74941-7

Windows Vista For Dummies
978-0-471-75421-3

Windows Vista Security For Dummies
978-0-470-11805-4

SPORTS, FITNESS & MUSIC

Coaching Hockey For Dummies
978-0-470-83685-9

Coaching Soccer For Dummies
978-0-471-77381-8

Fitness For Dummies, 3rd Edition
978-0-7645-7851-9

Football For Dummies, 3rd Edition
978-0-470-12536-6

GarageBand For Dummies
978-0-7645-7323-1

Golf For Dummies, 3rd Edition
978-0-471-76871-5

Guitar For Dummies, 2nd Edition
978-0-7645-9904-0

**Home Recording For Musicians
For Dummies, 2nd Edition**
978-0-7645-8884-6

**iPod & iTunes For Dummies,
5th Edition**
978-0-470-17474-6

Music Theory For Dummies
978-0-7645-7838-0

Stretching For Dummies
978-0-470-06741-3

Get smart @ dummies.com®

- **Find a full list of Dummies titles**
- **Look into loads of FREE on-site articles**
- **Sign up for FREE eTips e-mailed to you weekly**
- **See what other products carry the Dummies name**
- **Shop directly from the Dummies bookstore**
- **Enter to win new prizes every month!**

* Separate Canadian edition also available

† Separate U.K. edition also available

Available wherever books are sold. For more information or to order direct: U.S. customers visit www.dummies.com or call 1-877-762-2974.
U.K. customers visit www.wileyeurope.com or call (0) 1243 843291. Canadian customers visit www.wiley.ca or call 1-800-567-4797.

Printed and bound by CPI Group (UK) Ltd, Croydon, CR0 4YY

13/04/2025

14656501-0001